DEFENDING ANIMALS

DEFENDING ANIMALS

Finding Hope on the Front Lines of Animal Protection

KENDRA COULTER

The MIT Press
Cambridge, Massachusetts
London, England

This book was written on the traditional territories of the Anishinaabek, Haudenosaunee, Lūnaapéewak, and Chonnonton Nations.

The MIT Press would like to thank the anonymous peer reviewers who provided comments on drafts of this book. The generous work of academic experts is essential for establishing the authority and quality of our publications. We acknowledge with gratitude the contributions of these otherwise uncredited readers.

This book was set in Adobe Garamond Pro by New Best-set Typesetters Ltd. Printed and bound in the United States of America.

Library of Congress Cataloging-in-Publication Data

Names: Coulter, Kendra, 1979– author.
Title: Defending animals : finding hope on the front lines of animal protection / Kendra Coulter.
Description: Cambridge, Massachusetts : The MIT Press, [2023] | Includes bibliographical references and index.
Identifiers: LCCN 2022045235 (print) | LCCN 2022045236 (ebook) | ISBN 9780262048286 (paperback) | ISBN 9780262375634 (epub) | ISBN 9780262375627 (pdf)
Subjects: LCSH: Animal rights. | Animal welfare. | Human-animal relationships. | Well-being—Psychological aspects.
Classification: LCC HV4708 .C685 2023 (print) | LCC HV4708 (ebook) | DDC 179/.3—dc23/eng/20221017
LC record available at https://lccn.loc.gov/2022045235
LC ebook record available at https://lccn.loc.gov/2022045236

10 9 8 7 6 5 4 3 2 1

Contents

Preface *vii*

INTRODUCTION: BEYOND SOUND BITES AND SLOGANS *1*

1 **SMALL VICTORIES** *9*

2 **IN THE FIELD OR THE TRENCHES?** *21*

3 **PARTNERSHIPS AT WORK** *33*

4 **LINKED HARM AND PROTECTION** *55*

5 **SOCIAL HARMS AND PROTECTIONS** *69*

6 **THE SCIENCE AND POLITICS OF INVESTIGATIONS–
AND PROSECUTIONS** *87*

7 **CONSERVING WHAT AND WHO WE LOVE** *117*

8 **THE WILD THINGS AREN'T THINGS** *137*

9 **THE ANIMALS IN BETWEEN** *155*

10 **HORSEPOWER** *179*

11 **THE ELEPHANT IN THE ROOM IS A CHICKEN** *199*

CONCLUSION: THE FUTURE IS HUMANE *223*

Acknowledgments *231*
Notes *233*
Index *245*

Preface

The dog in this photo was beaten and deprived of food and water for the first year of her life. The workers at the boarding kennel where she was housed after being removed from the abusive situation said she was the most terrified dog they had ever seen.

When my husband and I first met her, we brought our dog Buster, who was lovingly named after Buster Bluth from *Arrested Development*. Buster had been abandoned and found roaming in a rural area by a humane society. Initially, he experienced separation anxiety and would damage things when humans weren't home, even though he had another canine family member with him, Ms. Macey. Macey was a German shepherd–Doberman cross with giant ears who had been in and out of animal shelters in a community that was plunged into economic turmoil after the major employer shrunk its workforce from nearly twenty thousand people to nine hundred. Macey was saved from premature death by a tireless woman named Deanna who runs a rescue group. Hilarious but also a regal lady with a mature bearing, Macey had endured a lot of upheaval and gotten a second chance at life. Despite her calming presence, Buster was clearly scared that he would be abandoned again. With time, he finally learned that he was safe. He was a gentle yet protective and majestic gentleman who commanded attention wherever he went, and his devotion to his family was unwavering.

The young female German shepherd in the photo thought us humans were nice, but she, too, was completely enamored with Buster. As we left, she cried like she was in a state of primal terror at the prospect of losing him. Something about him and his energy drew her in. Maybe he made her feel safe. We will never know exactly what was going on in her mind and heart, but she really did not want Buster to leave her.

Needless to say, we adopted her. Her name is Sunny, and she is now sensitive, bold, incredibly loving, fiercely loyal, and most of all, protected. In fact, she is both protective and protected. Sunny has told us so much about what happened to her. Her head was struck. She was not allowed to play with toys. For many years, she drank in a panicked way. When the human members of her family are going through a tough time, she will internalize our stress and stop eating.

In many ways, her body recovered more quickly from the violence than her mind did. Abused animals can learn or decide to trust people again, or at least some people. Yet the psychological scars of the abuse Sunny experienced will never be fully healed, and she will always hate broad-shouldered men with beards. She will never be as carefree and social as many other dogs. But she isn't just a victim, she is also a survivor, and has chosen to trust us. That is a deep expression of love—one we have committed to cherishing and reciprocating every day.

Sunny spent many hours wrapped around my feet as I wrote this book. Her muzzle and even eyelashes are now gray, but her body and spirit remain strong. She could tell when I was writing the more difficult sections, those that interweave intense pain and courage. She would look right into my eyes as if inviting me to stroke her head and remember what's possible, her presence a testament to the power of love that is at the heart of animal protection work.

It was an extraordinary honor writing this book as well as a duty and responsibility I take seriously given the stakes. Whether in the streets of the biggest cities or remote barns and dense forests largely out of view, animal protection is an urgent social issue with life-and-death implications. Animals feel pain. They feel fear. What people condemn and condone has serious implications for animals' bodies and their minds. Human decisions affect billions of animals. That number is utterly staggering. But behind the statistics are thinking, feeling individuals like Sunny. Animals who want to give and receive love.

We cannot cultivate free, caring, and humane societies in soil poisoned by suffering. I have confronted ugly facts, but I have also witnessed and marveled at the inspiring and beautiful. Both of these realities and the messiness in between reflect the truth about animal protection. Pretending that harm isn't part of our reality won't help animals, but unsettling topics and cases are handled with sensitivity—out of respect for those involved, and out of respect for you. Plus, this is a book about animals, and the people and organizations at work defending them. Animal protection is fundamentally about solidarity.

This book is dedicated to the animals we have saved, those we have failed, and those whose fates are still in our hands.

INTRODUCTION: BEYOND SOUND BITES AND SLOGANS

With a list of animals who needed help as our guide, we crawled along in gridlock at a turtle's pace across a major US city. Olivia was driving, and Andrea was in the front passenger seat. A man veered off the sidewalk and walked right toward us. The vehicle was clearly marked with the name of the animal protection nonprofit.

The stories I've been told by animal protection workers who have been sworn at, spit on, or worse immediately came to mind. A little part of my Canadian brain dug up tragic media stories about US gun violence and leaped to the worst-case scenario so for a few seconds I considered ducking.

The man came up to the driver's side, and Olivia rolled down the window.

"Hey, there's a dog running around my neighborhood, and I'm worried she's going to get hit by a car," he said. "She's friendly so I think I could catch her. Can you help with that?"

Olivia explained that a different nonprofit, contracted by the city to manage homeless and abandoned pets, would be the one to contact and recited the number to call that she knew by heart. The exchange was pleasant, and my tension dissipated.

Andrea and Olivia returned to their conversation. Andrea is a veterinarian, and Olivia has multiple degrees in therapy. They were exhausted from an intense animal-hoarding case that involved over seventy large dogs who had taken over an entire house. It had gotten so filthy and dangerous that the human resident had to hide out at a neighbor's home. Olivia and Andrea were clearly affected by what they'd seen just days before, and now we were headed to another suspected hoarding case.

Once you smell animal hoarding, it is forever seared into your nasal memory. I would describe it as vicious—not a word you would normally associate with smell, but appropriate for hoarding. In this case, the smell saturated the entire floor of a low-rise building.

The elderly woman welcomed us into her tiny apartment. Cats were everywhere. A single litter box was overflowing. And I noticed the turtle immediately.

Picture a turtle in a small fish tank half full of water. There was nothing in the tank but water and the turtle. Turtles spend time in water, but they also need to breathe oxygen. This tank didn't have anywhere for the little creature to stop and rest above water. No rock. No perch of any kind. The turtle just had to keep swimming and swimming.

As the vet examined the cats—more than a dozen of them—Olivia spoke to the woman about what services were available to help her. The woman had a number of health issues and clearly needed more support. This situation with the excessive number of cats was not helping anyone. Hoarding is complicated and often a mental health issue, made even more challenging when animals are involved. The vicious smell was likely something the woman did not even notice.

I kept staring at the turtle. I desperately wanted to pick up this little shelled animal to give them a break, a moment of peace, or get them out of there altogether. But I was there to observe. I watched and listened to how the professionals handled the situation. They see cases like this every day. They treated the woman with respect and talked to her about solutions that would help the animals—and get her more assistance. The woman agreed that some of the cats could be taken.

"They won't be put down, right?" she asked. "They can't go if they're going to be put down."

"No, they'll be in our beautiful facility downtown until they're adopted. It's nicer than my apartment," Olivia said.

The woman wouldn't surrender all the cats, but the animal protection wheels were in motion. The organization's mobile veterinary clinic would be brought right outside her building within a few days, and the remaining cats would be spayed and neutered without cost at least. And more conversations would take place.

"What about the turtle?" I asked when we were back inside the vehicle, passing around an industrial-sized jug of antibacterial gel.

"I'll give her a larger tank with proper contents and perches so the turtle can rest. I'll go back with that tomorrow."

Utter relief.

This story reveals a lot about animal protection. I think about that turtle often, and how everyone in this story was, in different ways, trying to keep their head above water.

Two-thirds of US households now include other animals, and people in the United States spent $103 billion to care for them in 2020. In Canada, the proportion is similar. In the United Kingdom, close to half of all homes have pets or companion animals as I'll call them. These numbers keep climbing around the world. Animals are part of our families, neighborhoods, and communities. And every time I do a TV or radio interview about animal protection, the host or producer will reveal that animal abuse coverage generates more audience responses than any other topic.

Choosing to keep a cat indoors is for their own protection from cars and predators—and the safety of songbirds and chipmunks who live nearby. Ensuring that the horses you care for have access to hay or grass throughout the day and night is about protecting their bodies and minds. These individual and interactive choices are critical for animals' well-being. In this book, I focus on coordinated efforts to protect animals, and specifically the organizations and people whose work revolves around protecting animals from harm. Animal protection is an ethical and practical goal. It is also a process, and one that requires workers. Animal protection involves physical, intellectual, and emotional labor. Some of it involves working directly with animals, while many efforts concentrate on the members of a particularly complicated species—our own. In other words, animal protection work includes both care and advocacy. Crucially, the term *animal protection* emphasizes that animals need protecting—from humans.

When animals are being abused or in danger, who will help? What will help involve? Could harm be prevented? These pivotal questions propel this book, and the answers can be found beyond the headlines, sound bites, and slogans.

I have been studying the animal protection landscape in depth since 2015. I lead a team that includes fellow professors, graduate students, and other research assistants who have dug into different parts of this terrain—the laws, policies, finances, and reports. I have examined organizations of all sizes and shapes. I have taken copious notes at conferences and webinars, and watched debates among analysts, practitioners, and advocates play out. I have gathered the perspectives of people directly involved, and when possible, observed their work firsthand. I have consulted, job shadowed, and/or interviewed more than sixty frontline workers and other experts who do this challenging and lifesaving work. They are investigators, veterinarians, lawyers, researchers, care providers, conservationists, entrepreneurs, policy makers, and advocates. Many of them are women, and many of them are white, but people of all backgrounds and identities work to protect animals in different ways. Often sources spoke on the record. Some, and especially cruelty investigators, have been given pseudonyms, and I blur their identity and location given the need for discretion, privacy, and personal security.

There are differences around the world as well as distinctions within countries. Animal protection strategies often reflect and reinforce particular areas' political and cultural trends, but some deliberately challenge the status quo. The approaches are also shaped by the choices of organizational leaders and the results of internal deliberations. Civil society is central, and nonprofits and nongovernmental organizations (NGOs) of all sizes are involved, as are governmental agencies. Two organizations that seem alike on the surface may employ different strategies. Organizations that have a lot in common can have different positions on specific issues. The divisions can also be deeper and the result of divergent assessments of the challenges along with their causes and solutions. People may disagree about which animals need protecting, from whom, and what should be done as a result. Those at work defending animals should not be painted with a single brush, and key sources of unity and division will become clear.

The full landscape of animal protection is too large to map in a single book, and I cannot delve into the level of detail that each sector deserves; every chapter's focus could form the basis for multiple books. Many of this book's examples are from the United States and Canada, but work from countries around the world is included too.[1] Details vary across geographic regions and countries, and I emphasize insights that transcend borders and are really at the heart of animal protection. Crucially, I integrate different views and strive to provide nuance. Animal protection supplies mirrors that reflect, windows that reveal, and microscopes that magnify the best and worst of human behavior. In it, we can see the outline of a humane future and how to make that vision a reality.

The result is a unique journey that begins with a focus on familiar animals, especially dogs and cats, the companion animals around whom a significant amount of protective work is organized. These animals are most likely to be seen and have suspected harms against them investigated. This investigative work introduces a central theme of this book: the interconnectedness of people's and animals' vulnerabilities and well-being.

This pattern appears in three significant and overlapping ways. First, the safety and working conditions of those responsible for frontline animal protection directly impact the well-being of animals. Second, in homes where animals are in danger or are being abused, people are often also at risk. At the same time, shared vulnerability can be more than physical and psychological. People's economic security affects their relationships with animals—and with different animal protection programs.

As our journey reaches into lush tropical rain forests, these dynamics are especially important for people who live and work around wild animals, including highly endangered species like gorillas and elephants. Conservation work near some of the poorest communities in the world, including those with armed conflicts, augments the stakes for people and animals alike.

The significance of money cuts across these terrains, including whether protective work is undertaken by government agencies or nonprofits, and how people who do the work are paid (or not). This is certainly evident among wildlife rehabilitators who work in communities of all sizes trying to protect and care for animal neighbors with little, if any, funding. How money affects animals, for better or worse, is central when we consider how to protect wild animals like tigers and chimpanzees who are sold as pets or performers. The power of money is most influential when we travel to rural areas that are home to both celebrated species like horses and less cherished animals like chickens and cows.

To return to the image of water, this quote circulates online periodically: "There comes a point where we need to stop just pulling people out of the river. We need to go upstream and find out why they're falling in." It has often been attributed to the late clergyman and political activist Desmond Tutu without reference, although it could have roots in South African oral traditions. Versions of this fundamental idea keep reappearing wherever I go within the animal protection landscape: the importance of going upstream to identify and address the causes, not only responding to the effects.

To apply this metaphor and way of thinking, picture animal protection as a landscape. It has both similar and distinct terrains, and different animals are facing varied hazards. There are groups of people at work in each of these areas who have things in common with each other as well as differences. A stream runs through this landscape. People work downstream as they help animals who have been thrown in the water. But people may also move further up the stream, wanting to identify what caused the animals to be harmed in the first place. Sometimes people reach across the stream to try to work with those on the other side. All are trying to repair damage, and develop more humane and compassionate pathways forward. Some think even further downstream to what the landscape could look like if animals' well-being was really taken seriously.

The diversity of people and animals involved is clear, but the foundational interconnectedness of human and animal well-being remains consistent. For these reasons, animal protection involves and requires what I call *humane jobs*—that is, work that benefits both people and animals. To more thoroughly defend animals, we need *more* humane jobs both in number and in quality. Animals benefit, first and foremost, when there are more people working in protection in sheer numbers. Animals also benefit when those jobs are safe, secure, and have good working conditions—when people are best positioned to effectively and thoughtfully do protective work.

At the same time, the promise of humane jobs goes further. Replacing work that causes harm to animals with humane job alternatives is not only an important part of the animal protection story but essential to creating a more humane future too.[2] Animal protection is about morals and ethics. It is about laws and law enforcement. It is also fundamentally about political and economic choices, and the work people do, and whether it hurts or helps others.

The experiences of other animals are crucial when thinking about their protection.[3] They may not speak human languages like English, but they have strong opinions and a lot to say in their own ways. This emphasis challenges a slogan used by some animal defenders who assert that they are "the voice of the voiceless."[4] Animals need people to communicate with other humans, undoubtedly, but it is our species' duty to work to understand, empathize with, and then amplify animals' own perspectives, not to deny that they have things to say, especially about their own lives, deaths, and families.

Animals are commonly referred to with the pronoun *it*. A kangaroo lifts its baby, the photo caption will say, even though it's obvious the kangaroo mother is female. Sometimes this underlying issue manifests in slightly different terms. "Barn fire kills thirteen hundred pigs, no one injured."

I never refer to animals as it. Animals are not phones or cars. They are not objects. But animals are victims of both illegal and legal cruelty, of people's callousness, negligence, desperation, and greed.

People are the problem, and the solutions.

1 SMALL VICTORIES

Most regions and countries have at least one law that defines illegal animal cruelty and neglect. This means both the harmful actions that are prohibited and what basic standards need to be met by people who are responsible for animals' lives. Laws and law enforcement are one major way the idea of animal protection is put into action. Of course, people and organizations need to follow the law for the intended goals to be achieved. That requires professionals whose job it is to enforce the law. Suspected crimes need to be investigated.

Yet when it comes to animals, who exactly is responsible for the initial investigations varies widely and can be pictured as a patchwork. Animal protection laws can be enforced by first responders, but for nonemergencies, even if they seem serious and criminal, depending on the area, the police may or may not be expected to respond. It might be an animal care and control or welfare service. It could be a nonprofit—a local humane society or Society for the Prevention of Cruelty to Animals (SPCA).

Law enforcement is normally a core government responsibility. But when it comes to animal protection laws, in countries like Canada, England, Scotland, Wales, Ireland, Australia, and New Zealand, it is most often an SPCA that has been assigned responsibility for enforcement. The United States is a bit different yet no less confusing. Phil Arkow, coordinator of the National Link Coalition, an organization focused on combating violence against people and animals, dug into the details for the entire country and found that in 46–47 percent of places, police are the first responders for animal cruelty concerns. In another 46 percent of areas, it's the animal care and control services. In the remaining 7 percent, this work has been assigned to a nonprofit. Tribal police or native animal care and control services normally have responsibility on reserves and in other Indigenous communities.

But which kind of organization is responsible and where does not follow a predictable pattern. It can depend on the type of animal, time of day, or day of the week. In some places, organizations do overlapping work. On the other hand, callers trying to report suspected cruelty sometimes get bounced around like a pinball among different agencies that think investigations are someone else's responsibility. Outside of the Netherlands, I know of no countries with dedicated national hotlines for reporting suspected animal abuse . . . yet.

Emergency and other responsive services cannot function without dispatchers. Some regions contract this work out to private companies, but often dispatch is deemed to be a core government responsibility because of its importance. Dispatchers need to have the quick responses of a rabbit, nerves of an Olympic athlete, and patience of a cactus. Dispatchers try to glean as much information as they can from callers reporting legitimate issues and emergencies to get help to the right place as quickly as possible. They may only handle animal-related calls, or may be multitaskers who are responsible for a host of services and agencies.

The importance of dispatchers came up right away when I was in the field with Mike, an animal welfare officer. "By far I prefer it when complaints have come in on the phone," he said as we rolled along the highway. We were headed to the first call of his shift on a warm spring day in the southern United States.

In his area, nonemergency concerns about animals are reported to the city services—the main 311 people call whether they have an issue with garbage collection or think their neighbor is hitting their dog. He is called to respond to welfare concerns and suspected cruelty, and is responsible for collecting strays and barking dog complaints. Moreover, the types of animals he encounters include reptiles, snakes, and other assorted creatures with lethal powers.

In contrast to a historical emphasis on the more "control"-oriented tasks like rounding up strays and animals seen as a risk to people, today a broader combination of responsibilities is more common, as reflected in the name "animal care *and* control" or "animal services." The scope and emphases of these organizations are far from consistent, however. Some animal care and control officers are appointed as peace officers and empowered to enforce laws, while others are not. Animal care and control itself is another patchwork, within the larger animal response patchwork.

Whether having a single agency responsible for "all things animal" is a good strategy or not is a matter of debate. On the one hand, having one organization, and a local one at that, responsible for everything animal related streamlines the reporting process for members of the public, and allows cities and counties to consolidate their services and facilities. But some people working in enforcement think collecting strays is fundamentally different work from investigating suspected cruelty that requires different skills and training. An animal care and control agent is not synonymous with an animal cruelty investigator or animal protection officer. However, some animal care and control officers are indeed responsible for investigations and protective work. In Mike's area, he wears multiple hats as an animal care and control officer who investigates suspected cruelty.

"Everything comes here," he said, pointing to the mounted computer in his van. "I can see how the complaint was submitted, and almost always when there's a problem, like an address that doesn't exist, it's from a web form."

In contrast, when there is a real, live person at dispatch receiving the complaint by phone, they gather as much information as possible and check the address immediately. Incorrect and nonexistent addresses were a frustration for Mike, and he's far from alone. His point was proven twice that very day, when we drove twenty or thirty minutes only to find that an address didn't exist. Meanwhile, we had spent all that time traveling to nowhere useful, and the animal who was the reason for the report was still out there somewhere, experiencing who knows what.

Animal welfare services are chronically underfunded and understaffed almost everywhere. As a result, it's not uncommon for small numbers of investigators to be assigned large geographic areas or have mountain-sized caseloads even if they are only responsible for one part of a city. Some have to drive hours to get to the other side of their territory so if the address is wrong, that's hours wasted, and animals are left in waiting.

Lesson #1: the process for reporting suspected cruelty should be streamlined–and dispatchers answering phones are a priority.

How best to report concerns about animal cruelty may seem like a small operational issue, but as the crucial spark that ignites the investigative engine in most cases, it is a significant matter. Accurate information and prompt response times have a tangible impact on animals' suffering. In areas where different organizations are responsible for initial investigations depending on the day, specific place, and type of animal, it should not be up to concerned members of the public to have to navigate that labyrinth. Centralized hotlines and dispatchers to staff them are worthy investments that will help protect animals.

When investigators arrive at animal calls, a number of things can happen. Assuming someone is home, first comes discussion. The investigator will visually examine and often touch the animals, looking for physical signs of distress like a wound, tender area, or untreated mass. The physical condition and weight of animals are indicative of their welfare, and so is their behavior. Investigators may also ask to see other parts of the property. The initial visit is crucial for establishing if there is an issue or crime.

Sometimes the investigator determines that there isn't that evidence of wrongdoing. The animals might appear fine, or weight loss can be explained by a documented medical diagnosis. Sometimes people report others for animal cruelty maliciously and without basis because of a neighborly dispute, or worse, as payback for breaking off a relationship, refusing romantic advances, or because someone doesn't like "those kinds of people." Dispatchers attempt to rule out these sorts of calls with pointed questioning, but it's difficult, and people exaggerate and lie. Hence investigations.

During the entire process, investigators pay close attention with all of their senses: To what is being said—and betrayed. To people's levels of cooperation, agitation, and hostility. To what the animals reveal with their bodies and behavior. To other objects and people in the home or on the property.

Investigators have different training, operating procedures, and options available, depending on their area and employer. They might opt to provide directives verbally, and this might or might not be accompanied by a warning, an order, an ordinance, a ticket, or some other tool to promote compliance. They might want to involve another law enforcement agency, veterinarian, or social service provider, or be required to hand off the file to another organization because of what and who they found. There might be reason to obtain a warrant for additional evidence gathering. Animals may be voluntarily surrendered or seized depending on the specifics. Criminal charges might be laid, and in a minority of those cases, there will be a trial. The process might take minutes, hours, days, weeks, months, or years.

Sometimes people being investigated are aggressive or intransigent, and what powers investigators have to demand access to the animals varies depending on the area's laws. Investigators are expected to follow the established procedures and protocols.

Mike and I arrived at the first stop of the day in a neighborhood of mostly detached houses, some of which were run-down while others were well maintained. A neighbor had reported that a dog kept escaping from the yard and running onto the road. It sounded more like minor negligence than cruelty, but the dog could still get hurt. People are expected to be responsible for the well-being and containment of their animals, and may need to learn about the minimum standards of animal care and safety while being given the opportunity to improve their behavior, even if they are not purposefully causing harm. Mike still suggested I stay physically behind him. Often seemingly simple issues really are just that, but not always.

A woman answered the door, and Mike asked to see the dog, a little Chihuahua who studied us with his saucer eyes. Every visit is an opportunity to examine an animal and talk to people about good-quality care. Thankfully this little dude seemed to be content and in good health, his risky adventures on the road notwithstanding. Together, Mike and the woman identified precisely where in the fence the dog was escaping, and pulled over a large flower pot to block the gap.

"Hopefully this file can stay in the small victory column," Mike said as we walked back to the van.

A few blocks away, Mike spotted a stray dog—a thin, black mixed breed—running skittishly on the road. He pulled over and got out a short pole with a wire loop that serves as a temporary collar. "You're okay, sweetheart," Mike said calmly.

The dog eyed him nervously and then tore past him. In a futile attempt to help, I spoke to her and she slowed down, studying me. This was clearly a dog who feared men.

"That's a good girl," I said, and Mike gently reached his pole forward toward her head. Then she noticed it and tore off around the corner.

As we drove, I asked Mike about how he feels going up to new doors and whether he gets anxious. "Nah, not really. I'm a big guy," he said with a laugh.

"You don't ever feel unsafe?"

"Well, sure, sometimes, but then I just leave. We have training in evasive tactics, and people know it's a serious offense to assault a government employee." He raised the badge worn around his neck for effect.

Mike seemed more tense, though, as we pulled up to the next, bigger house a few minutes later. "You should stay here for this one," he said. "It's starting to rain." I could tell from the shift in his energy that the rain was more of a useful excuse, but I wasn't going to object.

Vehicles packed the driveway, and in one of trucks, there was a metal dog crate. The curtains to the house were drawn. Mike rang the doorbell and knocked on the front door, twice, and then walked around the side to take a look. There were all of those vehicles, but no one answered the door.

Mike made a quick note in his computer back in the truck, and we sat for a minute. He was watching the property. The curtain moved, just slightly. As we stared at the inhabited yet inhospitable house, an older woman knocked on the driver's side window.

"There are people there," she said.

"Yes, ma'am, but they're not answering the door."

She shrugged and walked off down the street.

"I know the property," he said as we drove off. "It all started with this young couple that bought a puppy, and the dog got sick right away and then died."

But Mike can't break the door down (or even call a locksmith) to see if there are sick mothers or puppies.

"You'll go back?"

"Yep. I'll try again another day."

"Could you get a warrant?"

Mike pulled over, grabbed his pole, and rushed out of the van. A tan dog was peeing on a hedge but had no collar or person nearby. I was not used to seeing so many stray dogs running around.

This dog walked right over to Mike. The van was equipped with pods for transporting animals, and the dog cooperatively jumped in. Mike gave him a pat and closed the door. I glanced at my watch. It was 11:30 a.m. and the southern heat was already intense. Mike noticed.

"The AC is on. He's good in there," he said.

Then we both noticed the thin black dog from earlier eyeing us from around the corner. Mike tried whistling, but she wasn't having it.

We moved on and pulled in front of a small house with a low, stone fence. "This will just take a second," Mike said. He walked up to the edge of the property, looked over the fence, and then turned around. The house had a sign on its door that said, "Trespassers and government will be shot on sight."

"A couple of the others were here last week," Mike said, and I understood that he meant other animal care and control officers. Half a dozen officers work in this area. It's not sufficient for the number of communities and calls in their jurisdiction, in my view, but enough that at least two people were in the field every day.

"The guy was illegally tethering a dog. A real charmer apparently. I'd bet a hundred bucks that he just let the dog loose in the street and that's the black dog we keep seeing. But all I can do right now is confirm that he has complied—he no longer has a tethered dog in the yard."

The law in the area prohibits tethering. Abandoning dogs is not permitted either, but there's no proof that's what the guy did. This wasn't the first time I'd seen the consequences of well-intentioned protection efforts having a less than ideal effect on an animal, although maybe the street was a safer place for that dog, at least temporarily. In any event, there was nothing more Mike could do.

"You asked about a warrant for that dog breeder house," he said as we drove off.

I consistently find that in addition to fine-tuned observational skills, the people on the front lines of enforcement have exceptional memories. This is particularly impressive given the number of animals, people, and places they see. They'll refer to details from years ago, even if they weren't high-profile cases. "Barb the hoarder." "Old man Dumont." "Big Red." "The peanut butter man."

"Could you get a warrant or work with the police to get one?"

"It's technically possible, yes, but honestly, I try not to get my hopes up about the criminal justice piece of things."

He told me in detail about what he thought was going to be a barking dog complaint. Well-intentioned folks report based on what they can tell from the outside, but officers everywhere emphasize that often people over-estimate the severity of some issues and unfortunately underestimate others. This isn't surprising; you can only tell so much from the outside. Sometimes simple-sounding calls expose horrific and dangerous situations.

For instance, across the US-Canadian border outside the city of Calgary, Rod Lazenby, a local peace officer with decades of experience in law enforcement, arrived at a property responding to a barking dog noise complaint. The resident fatally shot Lazenby and was ultimately found not criminally responsible due to mental incapacity. He was known to the Royal Canadian Mounted Police in the area, but not to the local bylaw enforcement agency.[1]

The case Mike described also had noisy dogs, but the victims were canine, not human: Dobermans. Blood was everywhere. Mike put in months of work and collaborated with the police because of the extreme violence. The case only resulted in a few hundred dollar fine.

"Not even a prohibition," Mike said, referring to a court-ordered ban on possessing animals, one of the tools used in animal cruelty cases that make it into the criminal justice system.

"That really broke me," Mike admitted. "I lost a lot of faith." His frustration was understandable, not only because of the amount of time he'd invested, but because of the severity of the abuse. "Now I mostly just do the best I can out here."

Mike's reaction isn't new or uncommon for animal cruelty officers. Sociologist Dr. Arnold Arluke studied SPCA investigators in Massachusetts in the early aughts.[2] He dubbed the pattern of lowering expectations as a result of budget cuts, uninterested prosecutors, and repeat offenders *humane realism*. Officers come to accept what they cannot accomplish and make choices accordingly.

Back at the shelter, Mike unloaded the friendly tan dog we had collected in the morning. I wondered what it had been like for that dog to spend hours in the pod, unable to see anything except the metal walls. A cheerful young animal caretaker greeted us, walked the dog over to a grassy spot for a quick bathroom break, and then they went inside. I followed them to a row of kennels for new intakes. Those already inside barked at us—bouncy little terriers and lab crosses. Some sat stoically, including a large mastiff. A pit bull–type dog with soulful eyes huddled in the back. The smell of feces was strong.

"He's really friendly, got a good chance of finding a home," the shelter staff person said as he closed the kennel. "Don't you, pupper?"

This was a city shelter that had invested heavily in adoptions. It has over a hundred employees, and most of them are women who work behind-the-scenes caring for the animals and trying to get them adopted. Euthanasia rates at this facility are considered low; under 10 percent of the animals admitted do not leave alive. But when you host upward of six hundred animals each week, that's still sixty animals who don't get to lounge in a living room with a family or chase a ball. On the facility tour, I declined the offer to view the euthanasia suite. I didn't even want to see it for a couple of minutes. Imagine the emotional toll of having to walk and carry dozens of animals to their death every week.

The place of euthanasia in animal shelters and animal protection overall has long been controversial. It used to be common, particularly in "pounds" with minimal space and even smaller budgets. There was a stigma surrounding animals who ended up in shelters; they were seen as damaged, dangerous, or unworthy of love, and so had few prospects. "The bad old days" is how this history is often remembered.

Rich Avanzino, who served as president of the San Francisco SPCA for twenty-three years, is widely considered the founding father of the "no-kill" movement. In addition to working to transform policy and practice in San Francisco, his ideas helped inspire a broader movement within the space of companion animal welfare in the 1990s to confront the high death rates that were the norm in both public and nonprofit shelters. This was not a disagreement about which animals were worthy of care but rather about what that care should look like. Some people began referring to conventional animal facilities as *kill shelters*. The term upset those who had to do the difficult work of euthanasia and were hauling around their guilt, particularly when they had no say in the matter.

In 2004, nearly two dozen leaders of animal protection organizations assembled in Peace Grove, California, to engage in dialogue. They developed common definitions for terms like *healthy*, *treatable*, and *untreatable* animals as well as a standardized way of tracking animal shelter statistics—an agreement known as the Asilomar Accords. A cross-section of different animal groups, with varying positions, not only sitting around a table and talking, but coming to some consensus? It's remarkable. Today, some people look back and admit they were upset by the no-kill movement's demonizing language at the time, but now think that it provided the necessary impetus for important transformative change.

The debates have not vanished.[3] Certain organizations will keep animals indefinitely if suitable outside homes cannot be found or the animals are deemed not appropriate for conventional family life. Other organizations oppose the ongoing housing of individuals, especially in kennels, and consider this a life not worth living. Whether these kinds of places are dog and cat "sanctuaries" or "warehouses" depends on your perspective. Even some organizations widely considered ambitious when it comes to animals, like People for the Ethical Treatment of Animals (PETA), argue that no-kill strategies end up leading to more animal suffering and death because the shelters may remain at capacity for longer periods of time, and therefore are not able to admit new animals. Unadmitted animals may reproduce, end up with hoarders, or simply die, slowly and in pain, on the streets.

Ongoing debates notwithstanding, a major transformation has occurred both inside and beyond shelters in how cats and dogs in particular are understood and handled. The strategies included and still involve promoting widespread spaying and neutering to reduce the number of animals needing to enter shelters. Bob Barker used to end every episode of the TV show *The Price Is Right* with a plea for viewers to get their animals spayed and neutered for that reason. New York City–based North Shore Animal League began connecting people with low-cost spay and neuter services. The San Francisco SPCA partnered with Macy's to showcase video footage of adoptable animals in the department store's holiday windows. Prominent spokespeople celebrated pet adoption, the "adopt don't shop" campaign was born, and online tools like PetFinder were created to help people find adoptable animals, as were more rescue groups and foster networks run entirely by volunteers. A cultural makeover for animals in shelters involved many moving parts.

By interweaving strategies focused on both the causes (like expanding spay and neuter services) and symptoms (reshaping how people understood animals in need of adoption), a dramatic change in policy, practice, and culture has taken place in the United States and many other countries around the world. The Netherlands boasts that it has completely eliminated stray dogs, for example—and not by killing them. As cultural ideas about animals changed and Dutch animal advocates pushed for political action, a large-scale campaign was launched complete with an especially noteworthy component: government funding for spay and neuter services.

Across the Atlantic Ocean, today the Shelter Animals Count, an extension of the Asilomar Accords, gathers and tracks detailed figures about shelter "intakes" and "outcomes" for 341 public, nonprofit, and some foster-based organizations of the estimated 14,000 in the United States. Of the shelters that submit data, in 2021, 264,893 animals were admitted, a drop from 346,982 in 2019. Ninety percent of the animals admitted to shelters left alive, usually adopted or returned to their families. Shelter workers also regularly have a network of foster-based rescue contacts, and will try to find backdoor, work-around solutions, with or without the approval of their employers.

Yet the North Shore Animal League, a major no-kill proponent, argues that 2 million homeless animals are still euthanized in the United States each year. The American SPCA (ASPCA) asserts that 6.3 million companion animals are admitted into US animal shelters each year and approximately 920,000 shelter animals are euthanized (390,000 dogs and 530,000 cats). The numbers are far from firm, and the challenge continues, particularly in regions with larger free-roaming animal populations.

Knowing all of this, I gave the dog Mike and I had collected from the street a little rub through the chain-link door, and he looked right into my eyes. "You hang in there, friend," I said, swallowing hard.

2 IN THE FIELD OR THE TRENCHES?

Mike's overall relaxed attitude about walking up to unknown properties stood in stark contrast to what I'd heard from many other animal protection officers, including in Canada.

"Ninety-five percent of the time, you have no idea what you're getting into," a Canadian investigator with years of experience said.

One of her coworkers agreed and elaborated. "You don't know how they're going to receive you or what you will be dealing with. Every hour that you are on the road, you are in defense mode."

"Nearly a decade in, and I still get that dropping feeling in my stomach as I walk up those steps or up to that door. I'm paying attention to everything."

"It's only a matter of time before one of us gets killed."

This last statement is especially unsettling, and it is a viewpoint not unique to this particular inspector. Her coworkers nodded in firm agreement. Officers across Canada and the United States have told me about being pushed off porches and into basements, and about people pulling out knives and guns. A female officer was down a gravel road out of cell phone service range with no two-way radio when a man swung a hatchet at her head. There was a warrant out for his arrest for murder, but this crucial information was unknown to her when she rolled up to his door.

A police officer was shocked about what the animal welfare officers in her area experience. "They are chased off properties with knives and other weapons—and they don't report it. They just think it's normal!"

Fear for their personal safety is something I hear expressed by officers of all kinds, but most commonly by those who work for nonprofits. They often do not have access to law enforcement databases that identify whether people being investigated have a criminal record or any outstanding warrants. Animal welfare officers may or may not have uniforms, personal protection equipment, reliable communications tools, and public respect. Some SPCAs have invested in proper vehicles for their agents, but there are still investigators who have to use a personal car or a vehicle donated by a local business or defunct agency.

"When I started, I remember loading raccoons into my back seat," a nonprofit worker explained. "Now I show up in this bright green car with the name of a car dealership on the side because that's what was donated. I'm not sure which is better." Neither am I, but I am certain neither is appropriate.

A recurring, international pattern is that inspectors who work for SPCAs and humane societies are paid far less than those doing the equivalent or same work in the public sector for a government-funded agency. Animal protection officers working for nonprofit organizations are more likely to be women than every other kind of law enforcement so face additional harassment and belittlement, especially since most people who purposefully abuse animals are men.[1]

The physical and psychological impacts of investigative work are connected. Most of us can't bear to look at photos of abused animals because it's too upsetting. Those on the front lines not only have to look but also have to stay and listen to, smell, and touch victims—repeatedly. It affects their lives in a full sense.

"I honestly don't take vacation. I might take a day or two here and there, but it's just too stressful. I'm supposed to be relaxing on a beach and the whole time I'm worried about the cases piling up. When I'm not there, there's no one," an investigator who works for a nonprofit said.

Her coworker agreed. "You feel really guilty being away. You can't just not check your email after 5 p.m. because your shift ended at 5 p.m."

Some officers have shown me vile insults and threats they've received, commonly from men who feel their rights have been infringed on, but sometimes from animal lovers who think the investigator didn't do enough for the animals. Officers' spouses and children are also threatened, including in person.

When resources are scarce, whether in public agencies like animal care and control services or nonprofits like SPCAs, officers are more likely to work alone. "Isoagents" is how one nonprofit deputy chief put it. Not being able to talk to people who understand what you're going through, who have seen what you see, is difficult.

"You don't have anyone with you at the door. You don't have anyone to vent with, to bounce ideas off. In my area we all communicate a lot and there's a great team, but we're still by ourselves, day in and day out. It takes a toll."

"I pull over and cry a lot."

"No one goes into this work because they want to euthanize animals," an officer who works for an SPCA said. Euthanasia may be the result if animals are deemed too physically or mentally damaged to be humanely rehabilitated. This is a recurring challenge in dogfighting cases, and in some large shelters where seized animals may end up, a lack of space could lead to an untimely death, even if they are deemed adoptable. People still have to want to adopt them, and animals who have been neglected or abused can be complicated. Some people are not able or ready to take on the work.

In 2015, University of Windsor criminologist Dr. Amy Fitzgerald and I surveyed inspectors in our home province of Ontario, Canada's largest with a population of nearly fifteen million. Only a small percentage of the inspectors were using animal cruelty investigations as the springboard to try to become human-focused law enforcement. The primary driver for the overwhelming majority was the desire to help animals. A few of them had actually been police officers and preferred dedicated animal protection work, despite its challenges and lower pay, citing toxic, macho work cultures in human-centered law enforcement.

"We put up with the shit pay and lack of pension and all the hate because of the animals. Because of them."

"And then once that door opens, sometimes you're the social worker, sometimes you're the parent, sometimes you're the law enforcement."

The crucial thing to remember about animal cruelty investigations is precisely that: they are *investigations* to determine if illegal harm is being caused, and if so, what kind, to whom, why, and what should be done. Officers can't rewrite the laws but instead have to follow them, even when they think the protections aren't sufficient or are limited by the steps they need to follow.

Officers still exercise their discretion in innovative ways and constantly make choices. In Germany, for example, where rigorous daily exercise for dogs is legally mandated, investigators don't just walk around spying on people to see if they're walking their animals. The law establishes and normalizes the expectation and can be used to help identify situations of more extensive neglect. Similarly, in areas with breed-specific legislation such as bans on specific breeds of dogs, officers often do not enforce those laws as a matter of ethical principle, but will if they suspect dogfighting.

Yet you can only really respond like a social worker and act with empathy if your employer allows you to, if your only two choices aren't to lay charges or make a suggestion but then walk away. When you have more options and tools in your tool kit, you can use them. A female inspector in Ontario shared this story:

> This man is a sweetheart. He has been diagnosed with severe depression. He gets $660 a month from the government to live on; $330 of that goes to his subsidized rent, leaving him with about $300. X amount goes to his phone, and x amount goes to his cable, and it leaves him with $66 at the end of the month, after he has bought food and litter for his two cats. [That's] $66 to feed himself for the whole month! This man loves his cats; he's got two. He saved from his $66 for seven months to get enough money to put his female cat through our spay and neuter clinic. Seven months!
>
> [But] his one cat has a tapeworm, so what am I supposed to do—write him an order that I know he can't comply with? And take his cat away so he falls further into depression? For what? He is a good owner. Thankfully we came up with a viable solution because he was crying on the phone. We are going to pay for the vet care under investigations, and we are going to go load up with a bunch of food and litter [to help him].

Stories like this don't make the headlines, but these smaller acts of compassion and problem-solving are central to animal protection, including as a direct result of cruelty investigations.

On the other hand, sometimes investigators find themselves in real-life horror shows. Emaciated animals who are near death. Abandoned animals trying to survive by eating wood, paper, their own feces, or the corpses of other animals. Animals frozen to the ground. Animals who have been violently assaulted or killed. Injured people, or the more subtle signs of family violence as kids peer around the corner fearfully. Animal protection workers often see the most damaged, vulnerable, marginalized, and forgotten members of our societies—human and animal.

An officer who covered a remote semirural area emphasized how what's really going on can be more complicated than a surface-level examination will reveal.

> I was called to an apartment, and the landlord said this old lady wasn't looking after her dog. I went, and the woman could barely walk; the place was a mess. Yeah, the dog had really matted fur, but this lady was in dire straits. The landlord's like, "Take the dog! Take the dog!" I said no, where are her people? Where is the help for her? I'll deal with the dog—and I did; I just took him to a local groomer and we paid for it. But this was a bigger problem. I was calling everybody trying to get them to help her, all the social services people, I was shaming some of them. I hate doing that, but I was like you can't just abandon her.

Hoarding cases are particularly difficult and damaging to the health of people and animals. Seventy dogs. Eighty rabbits. Hundreds of sheep. Twelve hundred mice. An officer who had to euthanize over a thousand pigs who were neglected to the point of starvation says that was the most difficult few days of their entire career.

"You get tougher with time, but it's never easy. It doesn't matter how much you think you've seen it all, there'll be cases that rock your soul. You just cope. You just find a way. You hug your animals and your kids and keep going. You keep getting up in the morning and doing it all over again."

Officers find the strategies that work best for them: time with horses, heavy metal, kickboxing, painting, or therapy. The burnout, depression, and other negative mental health effects experienced by people on the front lines, whether in the field or animal shelters, is recognized as secondary traumatic stress or compassion fatigue. These terms don't mean workers have gotten tired of being compassionate but rather reflect the psychological and emotional damage done by witnessing the suffering of others.

A growing number of workplaces, even cash-strapped nonprofits, now have at least some mental health supports available for staff. Whether such programs meet the needs of first responders who see situations civilians cannot even imagine is an important question. The answer is that it depends. Programs created by those who really understand what officers see and experience are more likely to really help.

Nonprofits in particular are contending with increased surveillance, and some people on the sidelines have strong views about how nonprofits should spend donor dollars. It is reasonable for people deciding where to donate their hard-earned money to know that it will be spent responsibly and effectively. But what may get lost is that animal protection depends on workers. The working conditions and well-being of those workers directly affect animals.

One officer laid the challenges bare: "This year I've got seventy calls in; that's not counting the ones left over from last year. If I'm at the south end of my territory and I have to go to the north, it's a 5.5-hour drive. So, I'm 11 hours in and I haven't got any work done, just going there and back. It's very difficult, and I cover all of those territories by myself. I just don't have the capability."

People who have massive caseloads, are disrespected, have trouble paying their bills, or whose personal relationships and family lives suffer because of their long hours and stress levels—these folks are stretched to the brink. Some will break. They are more likely to move on, creating a revolving door of new hires with less experience and knowledge. Plus overloaded and exhausted investigators are less likely to have the time and mental space needed to best apply their skills and intelligence. The workers suffer, and so do vulnerable animals.

Depending on what kind of organization it is, and then who is leading the organization, the degree to which investigators' working conditions are prioritized varies. This kind of work meets part of the definition of humane jobs: those that benefit animals and people. Animals benefit from the work, that is clear. But are these also good-quality positions for people? That depends. There are aspects of the frontline labor that can never be changed, and investigating suspected cruelty will always be mentally and emotionally difficult. This is true of emergency services, law enforcement, child protective services, and intensive kinds of care work, period. Yet steps can be taken to better protect and value the people on the front lines as well as support them as they undertake this painstaking and painful work. Fair pay, health benefits and insurance, proper equipment, and real mental health supports—these are not superfluous frills but instead workplace fundamentals and investments worth making that will also help animals. And frontline workers should have a voice in identifying and implementing what they need most.

In doing this research, I see a fraction of what frontline folks face, but I still bottle up a lot of it to spare those I love the gruesome details about what has been done to animals. Officers do the same.

At animal welfare conferences, I have seen animal lovers complain about even nongraphic images of abused animals being included in presentations. I fully understand that the topic is upsetting. The reality is far worse. Most people don't even begin to understand what cruelty investigators see and how profoundly disturbing some cases are. I would not suggest that graphic details be widely shared, but I do want people to understand that some in our societies do things to animals that are utterly horrific. There are violent, vicious individuals who are sadists, sociopaths, and psychopaths. Investigators on the front lines find these people and witness their reprehensible acts. Investigators do it for the animals as well as the safety of our shared communities. It is extremely difficult work.

Lesson #2: the physical safety, mental health, and work-lives of animal protection workers need to be protected so as to benefit them and animals.

Brad Nichols, director of enforcement and operations at the Calgary Humane Society (CHS), gets to the heart of the matter: "Take care of your people. Animal protection is an incredibly heavy mandate. The caseload is immense, and the secondary trauma experienced is significant. With proper compensation, mental health resources, training, and equipment, an agency can safely retain good people to do this important work."

Whether the organization responsible is a governmental agency or nonprofit, the well-being of investigators should be made a top priority and is highly worthy of greater attention and investment. Hiring more investigators means more manageable caseloads, officers working with partners, or both. Properly equipping and supporting those officers does not detract from animal protection; it augments it.

It's helpful to picture the cases frontline investigators see on the *animal harm spectrum*.[2] On the one end are the violent and heinous cases. On the other end are the cases like the man on disability described earlier who cannot easily afford the veterinary care his cats need. In between, there is a cross-section of cases that vary in their level of severity. Cases can also move along the spectrum for the better or worse. Some people's actions are intentional, while others result from ignorance or indifference. Laws often consider abuse and neglect as two sides of the same illegal coin. In practice, officers commonly see violent offenses and neglect differently, but the fact is that negligence can also cause serious harm to animals and be fatal. Hoarding is even more complicated. The animal harm spectrum is far from simple.

In some cases, the issue can be addressed with education and problem-solving. Comprehensive statistics about what investigators find on animal calls and how frequently are frustratingly difficult to obtain. But annual reports from the New Zealand SPCA, RSPCAs in Australia and England (the *R* stands for "Royal" in both countries), Irish SPCA, and Scottish SPCA suggest that problem-solving is used not only in some but rather in *most* cases. This is seen as a good thing by the organizations. It would undoubtedly be deeply concerning if the majority of calls led to the discovery of serious abuse.

Canada does not have a single, national agency investigating animal cruelty concerns rather a cross-section of different nonprofit and public organizations at work. The numbers from Canadian provinces and cities reaffirm this international pattern. Most often, the issues found are called *general neglect* or *passive neglect*, which means people who aren't caring for their animals properly. *Neglect* is an umbrella term under which different situations can fall, ranging from finding folks who are struggling and going without themselves, to obnoxious and power-tripping people indifferent to animals' needs or deliberately depriving them. Ignorance of proper welfare standards is not an excuse unto itself, but it shouldn't be treated like a violent crime when the problem can be fixed. That said, there are situations where firm directives or criminal justice tools are needed to mandate behavior change.

Which organizations are best positioned to do this challenging work as well as respond to those initial calls about suspected animal abuse or welfare violations? Animal-focused nonprofits? Animal care and control services? Police? Dedicated, public animal protection units that might be housed within a larger organization or separate from it? This is a significant issue I have considered from various angles for years because of its importance for animals and the safety of those we ask to undertake those ever-so-critical initial visits. The first contact also has implications for victims and evidence on-site.

There are arguments for and against each option. There are compelling reasons to view the law enforcement aspects of animal protection as a public responsibility and ethical duty. Law enforcement is a core, governmental responsibility funded by our collective resources: taxes. The public sector normally means more protections for investigative workers through higher rates of unionization, established mental health programs, and proper vehicles, personal protective equipment, and communication tools. Public sector agencies are expected and often required to provide more transparency along with undertaking comprehensive data gathering and management. Public enforcement agencies also have greater access to law enforcement databases that can provide investigators with crucial information *before* they arrive at a property.

At the same time, the public sector can have rigid policies. Even though opposition to animal cruelty is an issue that unites people across partisan lines, there can be fluctuating levels of funding depending on who is in charge of public priorities and spending. If public budgets are cut, animal units may be among the first to get axed (and this happened in Los Angeles in 2020). Plus the public sector is itself a constellation of agencies. What kind of public organization is best positioned to deliver robust investigations? Animal care and control, or police or another kind of specialized public agency that focuses on animal protection? Moreover, having a dedicated animal cruelty unit is different from simply assigning responsibility to a human-focused police service overall, especially if training on animal abuse and corresponding laws isn't provided.

Some nonprofits have struggled with investigative responsibilities, and some have done excellent work, despite their limited resources. When an organization's primary mandate is animal protection, more people motivated by animals' well-being will be drawn to such work. Yet nonprofits are dependent on donations and fundraising, which are volatile too. There can be worker safety issues, and private organizations doing law enforcement work raise oversight and access to information questions. In addition, some SPCAs and humane societies have liability concerns about sending their staff out to do law enforcement work that can be risky.

There are SPCAs that have ceased providing law enforcement services including the ASPCA in New York City, Edmonton Humane Society in Alberta, Canada, and the Ontario SPCA. Risks to worker safety and a belief that law enforcement should be a government responsibility were key catalysts in both Canadian decisions. The Ontario government could have downloaded primary responsibility for investigations onto local police or even the 444 local municipalities of the province. The government instead created a dedicated, public, provincial animal protection team and accompanying provincial hotline—a smart option for the specifics of the province.

Across the country, the volunteer-run board of the Edmonton nonprofit stated that it sees the organization as better equipped to play a supportive role, including by supplying care to animals from cruelty cases. This is an important reminder that while investigations into suspected legal violations are the front end, animals may be surrendered and seized. Having appropriate, safe, and secure options for transporting and housing animals is an essential part of protecting them, and hence not optional.

Similarly, the Columbia-Greene Humane Society/SPCA in Hudson, New York, began directing concerned citizens to the state police or sheriff's office in 2015. The nonprofit had three part-time investigators who were expected to cover almost thirteen hundred square miles. It continues to have trained staff who are appointed as peace officers but are not first responders. The staff play a supportive role, and the organization as a whole provides assistance, including with animal rehabilitation.

In New Jersey, the SPCA lost enforcement powers due to government action. A 2017 report by New Jersey's State Commission of Investigation, *Wolves in Sheep's Clothing: New Jersey SPCAs 17 Years Later*, raised concerns about the state's SPCA system, including poor record keeping, spending more on legal costs than animal care, slow response times, and civilians with firearms undertaking law enforcement work. The commission recommended that responsibility be reassigned to government agencies. A similar report had been written in 2000. Enforcement in New Jersey is now led by prosecutors' offices in the state's twenty-one counties, and local policing services were tasked with appointing trained humane law enforcement officers who will serve as first responders.

These important matters are being debated elsewhere too. In Britain, RSPCA investigators are the first responders. For the few cases that proceed through the criminal justice system, historically the charity would even pursue its own prosecutions. But recently the organization has begun exploring whether England's Crown Prosecution Service, a public sector organization, is better equipped to do the legal work of prosecutions.

For the last few decades, it has been more common to see governments selling off public assets and services to the for-profit sector—privatizing programs ranging from garbage collection to electricity. Animal investigations are an unusual case because in many areas, they have long been pushed off governments' desks and onto nonprofits. But when those nonprofits step back or governments want to take a proactive approach, the public sector must step in. Local or regional agencies can be created, or the mandates of those already at work can be expanded. National governments can also play a role depending on the jurisdictional particulars of the country.

So to return to the core question of what kind of organization is best positioned to be responsible, I do not think there is a one-size-fits-all model. What would be most effective in one area can be different from the best path in another. The animal harm spectrum further complicates the terrain. Not all kinds of organizations are well positioned to provide people who are struggling with the supports they need to care for their animals. Walking into a potentially dangerous property is never guaranteed to be safe, but it is safer when those we ask to take those risky steps are well trained, coordinated, and protected. In other words, police services do not have pet food banks, while nonprofit employees do not have bulletproof vests.

Lesson #3: no single type of organization can do everything, so collaboration helps people and animals.

Given the complex dynamics, partnerships among agencies are increasingly being used to share responsibility, deploy different skills, and broaden the responsive strategies available. Perhaps partnerships are what works best, most often. Some collaborations are shorter term and respond to particular situations. For example, many major animal protection organizations can mobilize rapid response teams to help in urgent and particularly challenging situations, ranging from hoarding to flooding to fires. Other partnerships are longer lasting and formalized. These efforts offer important food for thought.

3 PARTNERSHIPS AT WORK

Nestled in the trees alongside the Bighead River in Meaford, Ontario, is a little park home to a statue of a dog who welcomes visitors. It's the Beautiful Joe Park, a tribute to the real Beautiful Joe and the novel of the same name, written by Margaret Marshall Saunders in 1893. Like Anna Sewell's highly influential novel *Black Beauty*, this autobiographical story of a dog who experienced fierce human cruelty invites readers to empathize with abused animals and received global acclaim, including an award from the American Humane Education Society. Many of today's nonprofit animal protection organizations trace their roots back over a century to this fruitful time period when important questions were being asked about the normalized but unkind treatment of others, including animals.

The American Society for the Prevention of Cruelty to Animals (ASPCA) was founded in 1866. Whether it was installing water troughs for thirsty cart horses, creating an animal ambulance, or enforcing early animal cruelty laws, the ASPCA, like many major animal nonprofits, has long used a multifaceted approach.[1] Until 2014, that included bearing primary responsibility for the enforcement of animal cruelty laws in New York City. The nonprofit had fifteen to twenty agents working to cover all of New York City, but the ASPCA determined that this approach was not meeting the needs of the city's animals.

Conversations about moving responsibility for first response to animal cruelty concerns to the New York Police Department (NYPD) were initiated by the ASPCA and involved law enforcement leadership and the mayor's office. After a pilot in the Bronx, the initiative was spread citywide. In 2014, a distinct partnership was formalized. The first responders are now police, while the ASPCA has taken primary responsibility for training officers about animal cruelty. The ASPCA has created a small team of police liaisons that serves as direct support resources for NYPD officers and delivers that training to thousands of officers.

I have observed a number of different training sessions for police centered on animal cruelty. The sessions tend to be less than a day in length, and so concentrate on the basics and range in their levels of clarity. There are always audible responses to some of the images and descriptions of animal cruelty. Animal abuse resonates even with those accustomed to seeing social ills and harm.

What time of day it is, whether officers are attending directly after their shift, whether the training is mandatory or voluntary, the group dynamics, and the dynamism of the speaker all affect the levels of receptiveness. There are important larger conversations taking place about the relative effectiveness of many kinds of police training, including about racism and how to respectfully respond to disclosures of sexual violence and intimate partner abuse. Undoubtedly the leadership and larger organizational culture, and a host of other issues and dynamics, are also at play in significant ways.

"Those who have now had animal cruelty cases, they definitely take this issue more seriously," one of the police liaisons said as we were entering a Brooklyn precinct. "I'm seeing that more and more: officers in the room who have already had animal cases because of the partnership."

"In the past, if there was a dead animal found, that body was probably going to end up in the dumpster," another liaison said. "Now more officers know that body might be evidence. They may not know exactly what to do, but they know they can call us." The NYPD officers have been provided with a small, laminated resource card that summarizes animal offenses—misdemeanors and felonies—along with a dedicated 1-800 number that is staffed by the ASPCA to offer immediate support for officers in the field. The police liaisons can answer questions and assist on-site.

The NYPD added animal cruelty to its patrol guide for all officers as well as created a specialized detective unit, the Animal Cruelty Investigation

Squad, one of the city's Special Investigations Divisions. To put this in perspective, others include the Arson and Explosion Squad, Computer Crimes Squad, Hostage Negotiation Team, and Hate Crime Task Force. The Animal Cruelty Investigation Squad is smaller, but has a lieutenant and dedicated detectives. In other words, there are force-wide expectations for patrol officers to undertake the initial investigations as well as specialized experts with additional knowledge and skills who can become involved where there are more serious or complicated cases. Precincts also have animal liaisons among the community-based officers who serve as peer-to-peer leaders and resources.

The ASPCA has its own and partner veterinarians throughout the city's boroughs to care for animals in cruelty cases and has invested in veterinary forensics, which I'll return to shortly. The organization also employs a team of animal law experts who can provide support to the city's district attorneys' offices, most of which now have dedicated prosecutors who have animal-specific expertise.

Equally as important is that the ASPCA has expanded its own fieldwork significantly. These mobile teams involve social workers, veterinarians, and others with experience in human and animal welfare. When NYPD officers find something that does not seem to warrant law enforcement but rather another kind of assistance, they can contact the ASPCA and its teams will respond. The nonprofit can directly supply tangibles like food, no-cost veterinary care, or routes to adoption. The ASPCA has formed partnerships with social service providers and community agencies, so field-workers can connect people with channels for improving their own health, financial situation, and job prospects too, thereby helping their animals.

While out with the field teams, I saw hoarding, emaciated dogs without access to water, and people who peered nervously through their windows but wouldn't answer the door. I saw people who were treating their animals just fine, and others trying their best yet struggling. All of these require different responses, and the ASPCA's staff use their skills to determine the best pathway—or pathways—forward. And they can do so because the organization has invested in them and the sorts of supplies they'll need to access regularly like food, litter, enrichment items and toys, grooming tools, and turtle-friendly tanks.

An Animal Cruelty Investigation Squad detective emphasized the importance of this aspect of the partnership for providing options. "Last week we had an old lady with too many dogs. She was definitely over-whelmed, and it was not a great situation. But that's different from the guy who keeps throwing his dog down the stairs." If investigators' only tools are to charge someone or walk away, they are constrained. Having other options allows them to see shades of gray, think about the context, and pursue other routes that recognize the animal harm spectrum. I have seen cops wanting to demonstrate leniency with "suspects" who are struggling, while animal law experts were arguing for charges. I've also seen the reverse. These matters don't always proceed in predictable or tidy patterns.

Lesson #4: tool kits have different kinds of tools for a reason, and they should, including in animal protection.

Smaller issues and those that are clearly taking place for a specific reason do not warrant heavy-handed responses, and in my view, behavior that can be improved should be, whenever possible. More serious responses and prosecutorial routes should be reserved for those cases that genuinely warrant legal intervention. In New York City, the ASPCA can reinvolve the NYPD if problems persist or worsen. This aspect of the partnership allows for more nuance, and for the many cases that warrant problem-solving and/or empathy to be handled accordingly, even though the police are the first responders and don't deliver these kinds of services directly. The fundamental value of having different responsive options applies everywhere.

Both the ASPCA and NYPD have committed to collaboration and invested human and financial resources. Primary responsibility for investigations now falls squarely to the public sector, but the nonprofit is still subsidizing this work extensively. Whether nonprofit organizations should be subsidizing core governmental responsibilities like public safety is an open question, but

I understand the pragmatic reasons why the ASPCA has invested so much in the partnership. The multidimensional supports the ASPCA provides make it easier for the public sector to take on animal issues and help fertilize a culture change.

The exact model of this partnership may not be easy to replicate elsewhere since most places do not have only one police force and one major, well-resourced animal welfare charity at work. But key elements of the partnership are transportable and scalable, including the direct support being provided for police officers on the phone and in person, cards with critical animal crimes info, and creation of field teams that have the knowledge, connections, and resources to follow up with or handle cases that do not warrant charges.

How effective police are as first responders for suspected crimes against animals varies depending on the place, leadership and organization, and individual officers. Sometimes animal cases are mocked, at least initially and informally, and references to the *PAW Patrol* and "pet detective" abound. Police officers are expected to investigate promptly, which is beneficial, but their levels of commitment likely vary when on the scene. There are police officers who feel strongly about animals and treat these cases with the attention and professionalism they deserve. Others may technically respond, but simply look quickly and move on. This is a concern, and I've seen it firsthand. In New York City on a call about an extremely skinny dog housed outdoors, it was clear that the female officer was more concerned than her partner, who lingered aloofly by their vehicle while she attempted to make contact with the resident and spoke with neighbors (and no, he was not eyeing the houses for potential threats).

Police services are accustomed to learning about issues as research and new data become available. Intimate partner violence and child abuse were handled differently decades ago, for example. The same could occur for crimes against animals. The rates of turnover are normally relatively low in policing, and this reduces the need for constantly retraining the basics, and means that knowledge gained about animals and animal cruelty becomes part of the organizations' institutional memories. There are also prospects for sowing goodwill because of how strongly the public feels about animal cruelty.

At the same time, this issue is connected to important larger conversations taking place about the racial politics of policing and incarceration.[2] Some people do not want more policing. Others, even neighbors on the same block, may disagree and want police in their communities—police who uphold the standards of public service and trust, and who respect and reflect people across races, ethnicities, genders, and income groups.[3]

Animal defenders have different perspectives on these important issues as well. Some support the expansion of tough-on-crime strategies to animals including stiffer penalties, jail terms, and longer sentences for animal cruelty convictions, or simply want laws protecting animals to actually be enforced. Others are more persuaded by critics of the relative ineffectiveness of conventional criminal justice punishments like prison for deterring crime and rehabilitating offenders, and are concerned about the disproportionate representation of Black, Brown, Indigenous, and poor people of all ethnoracial identities in prisons not reflecting greater criminal activity but rather heightened policing and discrimination, both obvious and subtle. Still others fall somewhere in between and support criminal justice reforms to tackle the clear and inexcusable inequities present in the status quo, while not accepting simple slogans either for or against police or prisons, particularly without accompanying, feasible alternatives. They may support modest or major changes to existing structures, or see the policing status quo as beyond reform, and instead call for the creation of new publicly funded security services of different kinds. It is undoubtedly true that police have become a catchall for many different issues and responses, some of which, such as mental health crises, could be better handled by other public agencies.

Having police services trained in the fundamentals of animal cruelty and creating dedicated units that specialize in crimes against animals is not about more or less policing necessarily. It should be about smarter law enforcement and investigations. Having different responsive options for animal calls, like the ASPCA's field teams, allows police to redirect cases that warrant an individualized response yet do not belong in the criminal justice system. This makes sense for many reasons, including because the courts are already heavily loaded, and in some places, backlogged with cases. When there are other options, including pathways that might be more effective than simply fining or jailing people, they should be used.

People engage in actions that contravene the law for many different reasons. Dr. Randall Lockwood, who has worked in different spheres of animal protection for fifty years, including for the ASPCA, puts it this way: "Even when you have a relatively simple-seeming crime like shoplifting, some people do it because they're poor, some because they're bored, some because they like the thrill." In other words, the context and specifics are significant, and a larger debate is pertinent: Is crime is the fault of individuals or the result of social failures? On the one side, some believe that we are all equally able, equipped, and free to make choices and resist criminal possibilities. On the other, folks highlight the limits on real, positive opportunities in poorer communities; these dynamics are called the socioeconomic determinants of crime.

Undoubtedly the journey to (legal) prosperity is far easier for some than others. The contexts into which we're born and raised uplift, limit, and restrict us to different degrees. I suggest acknowledging the power of economic conditions to dramatically constrain the opportunities for accessing both education and income, but also not positing that economic matters *determine* people's behaviors. People are constrained in very real ways that do contribute to certain kinds of crime, and those constraints should be targeted whenever possible—by going upstream. Simultaneously, people should not be deprived of their agency—their ability to think critically and act accordingly—or entirely purged of having to take some personal responsibility either. A reason is not automatically a justifiable excuse.

Implicitly suggesting that low-income people who engage in illegal behavior have no ability to choose otherwise is problematic, despite being well-intentioned. Doing so discounts the fact that the vast majority of people in poverty do not commit crimes of any kind (and of course, the wealthy commit plenty of crimes). Plus it's reasonable to assume that even if as many legal job opportunities are created as possible, and we managed to create more supportive communities, certain people would still engage in crime and violence for various reasons. Interpersonal abuse, for example, is present in every income group. It is not caused by having too much or not enough money but rather by a range of other factors including insecurity, a thirst for power and control, misogyny, and in some cases, biological processes.[4]

Democratic countries like those in Scandinavia and northern Europe that have lower levels of violent crime, and where people feel the safest and happiest, have accessible education and health care, supports and interventions for those struggling, and more jobs and higher wages, not more people imprisoned. Taking these facts seriously means recognizing that feeling valued as well as having nutritious food, high-quality education, leisure, sport, and artistic opportunities, role models, and real prospects for a meaningful future significantly augment the likelihood of people of all ages choosing positive options. Such emphases won't completely eradicate crime, but investing in people individually and in communities makes everyone safer.

These facts underscore the crucial role that good jobs and income sources play in creating safer communities, preventing future crime, and therefore protecting animals. It is simultaneously big picture thinking and highly relevant in real, practical scenarios in the here and now. The influence of context needs to always be taken into consideration not only when investigating animal issues but when responding too, whether in the field or in legal circles when designing laws, reforming them, and determining what is legal and what is illegal. In other words, the value of investing in people's well-being is relevant both upstream and downstream.

Across the border and into Canada, a tale of two cities also offers food for thought when thinking about partnerships. Calgary and Edmonton are the two major urban hubs in the province of Alberta, which is located north of Montana and has a similarly breathtaking combination of mountains, foothills, wide-open spaces, and big sky. Sometimes called the Texas of Canada, Alberta's politics tend to skew conservative, especially outside the two biggest cities. The cities, linked by a two-hour highway drive as well as a long-standing and epic hockey rivalry, are home to animal protection partnerships with similarities and differences.

Alberta as a province epitomizes the enforcement patchwork, with different agencies having primary responsibility depending in particular on geography and the severity of the issue. In the city of Calgary, home to nearly 1.5 million people, the humane society is the primary responding agency for animal concerns, and its enforcement agents are appointed as peace officers who can enforce provincial law. The Calgary Humane Society is a nonprofit that has taken officer physical and psychological well-being seriously and invested accordingly.

But this wasn't always the case. "I look back at our officer safety program during my first few years as a field officer and I shudder. We were incredibly lucky that we survived those years understaffed, underresourced, undertrained, and underprotected," says Brad Nichols, director of enforcement and operations for the CHS.

In the last decade, this region has been rocked by two separate cases of law enforcement officers being killed when responding to calls, one being the barking dog complaint referenced in the previous chapter, and the other led to the deaths of four federal police officers in a multiple murder-suicide. Shootings, period, including those involving police, remain rare in Canada. These fatalities, combined with a harrowing close call for one of the CHS officers, were the catalysts for the meaningful organizational changes.

A key priority was hiring more investigators, and this translated into lower caseloads. Six peace officers work for the humane society including Nichols, so the number is better but still low for a large city. The officers have been equipped with GPS-chipped two-way radios, ballistic vests, respirators with ammonia filters, and a cross-section of animal handling tools. There are new check-in/checkout procedures and partnering protocols for known risk properties buttressed by additional defensive training. Crucially, the organization enhanced mental health supports and created a dedicated committee to help monitor and further develop these services. These are significant steps, and so are wages.

Nichols elaborates: "We've been able to get to the point where we're semicompetitive in salary structure with other peace officer positions. You can't pay peace officers like they're security guards. It's part and parcel of taking care of your people. Partnered attendance for officer safety and fair compensation are part of making all the shit worthwhile," he says frankly.

The city's animal services office is responsible for the local bylaw issues like barking dogs, bites, and strays, allowing the humane society's officers to focus on animal protection work, but there can be overlap and connections.

"Our dispatchers are trained to go a bit deeper, to ask probing questions," Nichols explains. Even if someone has called the CHS about a barking dog, something that would normally be the domain of the city's animal care and control services, the dispatchers will try to obtain more information about the context and possible causes, which could include problems taking place behind closed doors and opaque fences. "We always err on the side of caution. As long as we've got the minimum amount of reasonable and probable grounds of an offense, we'll go out and at least do a welfare check. We've found cases where barking was the result of horrific abandonment, a desperate attempt to get help in the final days or hours before dogs died."

It's deeply disturbing, without question. It's why the dispatchers work off scripts, but also are given the latitude to use their skills and experience to glean as much pertinent information as possible. The dispatchers have been with the humane society for many years—one of them for more than twenty—and are seen as central to the safety of animals and officers in the field. The dispatchers monitor the GPS chips and do check-ins every twenty minutes as well. "Dispatch is the first point of contact and it's our lifeline," says Nichols.

There are some situations that even well-protected humane society officers will deem too dangerous. During a case involving both human and animal victims of domestic violence, Detective Shawna Baldwin of the Calgary Police Service and CHS officers began collaborating. Nichols, Baldwin, and Dr. Margaret Doyle, Canada's busiest forensic veterinarian, also began presenting to veterinarians, social workers, and other pertinent professionals, aware of the lack of knowledge about crimes against animals and need for an all-hands-on-deck approach.

In 2017, when footage of a large dog being transported on a flatbed truck at highway speeds went viral, multiagency responsive collaboration brought another police officer into the world of animal protection, Constable Dennis Smithson. "Prior to that, during my years at Calgary Police and in the RCMP [Royal Canadian Mounted Police], I had never encountered or been taught about animal cases," he says. This is not unique to Calgary or Canada by any means. In fact, this is common in many police services.

When Baldwin moved to another department, Smithson became the unofficial liaison, taking responsibility for crimes against animals on top of his other policing responsibilities. He learned about the legal standards and obligations when animals are involved, and now serves as a subject matter officer who assists other units and branches within the police service. Smithson has prepared the standard operating procedures for how animal cases are to be handled and acts as a bridge between the humane society, veterinarian, and Crown prosecutors on files involving criminal charges. He has been diligently training service members about animal cruelty (close to a third of the officers at the time of this writing) as well as other agencies and levels of law enforcement.

"We've gotten really good at developing work-arounds," Nichols explains,

> but it would be really nice to have a dedicated unit at CPS [Calgary Police Service] that does not have to work off the side of their desk, with an associated budget to cover some of the diagnostics, forensics, and medical treatment of victims. Scarcity of resources is a reality in the world of nonprofits, and covering the caretaking and investigative expenses not only of CHS's enforcement operation but also those of the police is a significant cost on the back end.

Informal, collaborative working relationships are a good start and can serve as a stopgap. But when the particularly committed individuals are off work or move to different positions or places, there is a risk of the issues—and animals—falling through the cracks. Formalizing partnerships and investigative units directs organizational resources and officially establishes animals' well-being as a priority.

As is the case in New York City, this is another example of a nonprofit continuing to subsidize law enforcement work. In Calgary, this happens not only through the humane society covering the costs of crucial diagnostics and animal care but also by being responsible for the majority of first responses and initial investigations. "We are very lucky to have a donor support base that funds this important work and an executive that sees the merit in funding a robust animal protection program with quality investigations and care of victims," notes Nichols.

How the leaders of animal nonprofits that undertake law enforcement feel about the place of cruelty investigations—and investigators—within their organizations varies quite significantly. Some feel that showcasing the work and especially the results of investigations will bolster their organization's public image and fundraising opportunities given how strongly people feel about animal cruelty. Others have sought to keep investigations out of the media, fearing potential controversy and donor backlash.

Charges and convictions are both up in Calgary. This does not necessarily mean there is more animal abuse; rather, more of it is being recognized, investigated, and taken seriously. Charges are not the only measure of effectiveness either, although given some of the specifics, the details of which I will not repeat, serious, violent behavior has been identified that demands a comprehensive response for the protection of animals and women.

Reflecting on the multiyear journey from being uncoordinated, and in some cases, un- or ill-informed, it's clear how far this partnership has come, in part through trial and error, but primarily through perseverance. "If you've got a few key people who are motivated, an initial investigative service of whatever kind that has enough resources, a vet, a prosecutor, and a cop or two, you can replicate this model," Smithson says. As further illustration of the level of commitment, he adds, "And any one of us would be happy to help you do it."

In Alberta's capital city of Edmonton, the humane society undertook cruelty investigations until 2019, when the organization announced it would be ceasing investigations. The city council decided to create a small team of public employees—peace officers—within the animal care and control services to serve as the primary and initial responding body for animal welfare concerns.

In Canada, animals are protected by provincial laws and the national criminal code's animal cruelty provisions. "Provincial offenses don't require proof of knowledge or intention to commit any wrong," explains Peter Sankoff, professor in the faculty of law at the University of Alberta.

> The federal crimes are more serious, with higher penalties, including fairly lengthy jail terms. In addition, provincial offenses are restricted—both in enforcement and application—to the province in question. If you get punished, say prohibited from owning an animal, that punishment doesn't cross the provincial border. But federal punishments reach nationwide and go on a person's criminal record.

The new animal-focused peace officers in Edmonton were given the power to enforce the provincial animal protection law, which is uncommon for city workers in Canada. At the same time, even more ambitious plans were being developed. Two Edmonton Police Service (EPS) constables, Ilka Cunningham and Ted Dyck, were also getting educated and organized. I often find that when investigators are reflecting on what motivated them to do more for animals, they trace their path back to a specific individual whose experiences and suffering galvanized them. In this case, it was a young dog named Tucker.

On patrol in 2017, Cunningham and Dyck heard on the radio that someone was observed beating a dog in a parking lot. They immediately took the call, and with the help of witnesses, were quickly able to locate and arrest a man who, it turned out, had a history of domestic violence and drugs. They seized the dog too, just a puppy of only a few months old. Witnesses reported the dog had urinated and defecated from fear during the attack. The constables took the puppy to the emergency vet and named him Tucker.

"It was a challenge, but it also felt really good to be able to do something for this dog," says Cunningham. "But we had zero resources and no connections."

"At that time, we didn't know anything about the Animal Protection Act or Criminal Code charges involving animals. We didn't know our seizure authorities or what to do with the dog," Dyck adds.

The willingness of police officers in both Edmonton and Calgary to recognize their own and organizational shortcomings is refreshing. Maybe this kind of humility is a Canadian thing. In any event, being able to identify weaknesses and mistakes is important for law enforcement as well as essential for the process of genuinely changing and improving. Plus in addition to recognizing existing gaps, this pair of officers decided to do something about them.

Dyck is quick to give most of the credit to his partner. "Ilka really took the lead on this. She's studying the Animal Protection Act. She's having me read it. She's consulting with legal advisers. She's arranging a meeting with a law professor who specializes in this stuff." That was Sankoff, who happens to work in the same city. "He was good enough to sit down with two nobodies who knew nothing. Then he wrote a letter to the chief. In policing, if you stumble onto a file, there's almost always someone you can call, some expert you can contact, or you go see a detective. In the situation we were in, nobody knew. We had to build this from scratch."

The constables started talking more with the investigations team at animal care and control. "We learned a ton from them," Dyck says. Officers in both government agencies quickly realized they would be more effective with greater communication and cooperation. Edmonton's animal care and control services also has animal transportation and housing facilities along with in-house veterinary expertise. Collaboration made sense.

Cunningham and Dyck became known within the police service as the animal experts and began helping coworkers or taking over files. They were still patrol officers and were "really lucky that our patrol sergeants were supportive," says Cunningham. "They definitely saw the need. They would obviously read our reports, and we would brief them about what we were doing all day or all night. And our peers in our patrol unit were also supportive, thankfully, when we couldn't be out there responding to other calls and helping them with that workload."

Two constables who work a schedule of four days on, four days off, in a city of a million people seems insufficient. "Ilka does a lot of work on days off," Dyck explains.

Providing animal cruelty training was then suggested by their inspector. Initially reluctant due to an aversion to public speaking, the constables agreed to develop and deliver the training. Cunningham and Dyck supplied training to every frontline officer in the city's police service. That breadth of reach is highly unusual—and may be a global first. It is certainly groundbreaking and, as of now, uncommon.

The training was clear and well organized. It explained the key provisions of the laws, how to spot animal cruelty, what else to look for, and what to do when you suspect someone is hurting an animal. Often the answer is to contact Cunningham and Dyck to benefit from their deeper expertise.

Just before a break, Cunningham offered some unexpected information from the front of the room. "All of you know of Quanto, who was killed in the line of duty," she said.

Quanto was a five-year-old German shepherd on the Edmonton Police Service who had been stabbed multiple times in 2013 by a suspect—a man with long and violent criminal history. Quanto died from the injuries. This fatal attack led to the creation of the Justice for Service Animals Act, or what was informally called Quanto's Law for short. It further penalizes assaults on animals at work like police service canines and horses, military working dogs, and people's own service dogs, and includes a six-month sentence for killing one of these dogs. Prior to the changes, killing one of these animals was akin to breaking the headlight of a police cruiser.

"Quanto's handler, Constable Matt Williamson, is here with us today," Cunningham shared.

Hearing that was a shock. The training had included real cruelty cases. Security footage of a dog who had been thrown against the wall in an apartment lobby, a dog who had ingested oxycodone, and other disturbing cases, the specifics of which I won't summarize. Seeing evidence from animal cruelty cases is always difficult and disturbing so I was already feeling agitated. Hearing that Quanto's handler was in the room made my heart race.

Many German shepherds who have survived abuse and abandonment have been and are part of my family, so that is part of why I am extra emotionally invested in these dogs. People task them with dangerous work like policing, knowing there are greater risks to them. Some dogs pay the ultimate price protecting us. Without question, in that moment I also empathized with Williamson, who had to lift his dying canine partner's body into his vehicle, knowing that the dog was not going to survive.

I reviewed my notes and underlined some key sections to distract myself as the officers began moving out of the room for the break. A few people and a dog seated nearby remained in the room. Two officers from the province of Saskatchewan were also visiting to learn more about Edmonton's animal cruelty training; one of them was Sergeant Tia Froh of the Regina Police Service, the handler of Merlot, a highly trained and accredited justice facility dog who supports child witnesses and victims.[5] Merlot is a lovely black Labrador, and she had stood up for a stretch as Froh talked with another officer.

At that point I stood up as well, and Merlot noticed me. She specializes in supporting children who experience deep and complicated emotions as they are asked to share traumatic details about what has been done to them, including by family members. Merlot sits with the children, walks with them, or lays right across them as they speak with investigators and in trials, helping kids to find the courage to speak the truth. Merlot clearly knew that despite my masking efforts, I was feeling upset, and she moved toward me.

"Is it okay if I pat her?" I asked.

"Yes, absolutely," Froh replied.

I sat on the floor, and Merlot put herself in front of me so I could rub her face and sides. My mind and body were able to relax. Later that day in a meeting with members of the Edmonton Police Service leadership, Merlot said a quick hi to me, but them moved onto someone else who had caught her attention. She knew I wasn't upset or nervous sitting around a boardroom table with the police "white shirts."

Animals matter for their own reasons and deserve to be safe. But they also do remarkable work for and with us, and that is all the more reason why we need to protect them.

Training every frontline officer in Edmonton wasn't enough on its own and it wasn't supposed to be, Cunningham explains. In the same way that you can't learn how to properly investigate homicides in a day, you can't learn everything about the multifaceted work of animal cruelty investigations that quickly either. But her colleagues are more attuned to animals and potential animal issues now. Plus the city's animal-focused peace officers can get more information from the police before they visit people and properties—and can ask for direct police support on-site, augmenting their safety. This has proven valuable on many occasions, including when someone charged at one of the peace officers with needles. She happened to be speaking with Dyck. He was able to call for police support, and officers arrived almost immediately. The peace officers are unionized, which augments their workplace rights, but they have different protections and power than police.

Moreover, Cunningham and Dyck were organizing for a dedicated policing unit: having meetings, filling out extensive paperwork, and engaging their staff sergeant, Anna Sinclair, who also had to complete a mountain of paperwork and make the case for a dedicated unit. "We just kept pushing and pushing. More calls are coming in. The Crowns [prosecutors] are getting more files and wanting more files. People are getting it, they're seeing it. There were speed bumps, but we just kept pressing forward," Dyck says.

In late 2021, Edmonton officially announced the creation of the Animal Cruelty Investigation Unit within its serious crimes branch, Canada's first dedicated animal cruelty police unit. There are nearly twenty liaisons throughout the service who have committed to taking on animal cases and gotten extra training and experience. The investigation unit can second specific officers as well. There's still a lot of work on days off, and having at least two other uniformed officers and a full-time sergeant assigned to the unit to ensure seven-days-a-week coverage is a top priority for Cunningham and Dyck. But this city has made significant changes to how it handles crimes against animals, made animal victims a public priority, and made history in the process.

The wall of the constables' office is covered in photos of animals from their successful cases, mostly dogs who have benefited from their work who are now in "forever homes." A bearded dragon named Freddy is among the animals saved, and he lives in the police station.

Even with two city agencies responding to animal calls, they cannot help every animal. Some are found too late, too neglected, too diseased, or too injured to be saved. Dyck puts it this way: "We take our wins when we can, and we don't let our losses defeat us. You just keep going." That is a recurring theme on the front line. The Edmonton Animal Cruelty Investigation Unit's unofficial motto is "To serve and protect all of us." Serve, protect, all, and us stand out—words that should guide law enforcement everywhere.

Edmonton and Calgary have differently answered the question of which organizations should be the primary first responder for most animal concerns, with the publicly funded animal care and control team being responsible in Edmonton, and the humane society playing that role in Calgary. Both cities are examples of grassroots-driven efforts, of people on the front lines making the connections and getting things done. In contrast, the New York partnership was initiated by ASPCA leaders. Neither route is necessarily superior to the other, and this work can start at the top or bottom, but it must move through the organizations to be effective.

Partnerships can be planned and deliberate or can coalesce more organically. They always stem from people who make choices and act, who push and create, for the well-being of the animals. This is also what happened in El Paso, a city of nearly seven hundred thousand people on the western tip of Texas, directly on the US-Mexico border across from Ciudad Juárez.

A case from 2016 remains vibrant in Detective Vanessa Acosta's memory and heart to this day. This dog was a young Black lab cross named Raven. A collar was deeply embedded inches into her flesh and had to be surgically removed. Acosta was often sent cases with animal victims. "Supervisors would say, 'Vanessa likes dogs, let's give her this case.' No dogs from cruelty cases had survived until Raven, though." That warrants a painful pause, a moment to remember the stakes.

Acosta learned that other animal files seemed to be falling through the cracks due to a lack of knowledge and poor communication, especially with detectives erroneously thinking animal services was responsible for investigations. She knew she had to do something.

First, Acosta started paying for animals' veterinary treatment herself. People on the front lines often subsidize their own organizations and the criminal justice process. For example, some officers will obtain custody orders to take animals from cruelty cases into their homes when there are no other options, providing food, toys, and crucially, safety. Sometimes officers affectionately refer to their efforts as "witness protection," and there is truth to that. It's both witness and victim protection.

Acosta realized that paying for animal victims' care was not realistic or feasible in the longer term. It became clear that there was a greater need, both within the policing service and at the "back end" of cases to help the animals themselves. She met with local animal rescue organizations to see if one would commit to receiving the animals from cruelty cases, without success. She rescued Raven herself, and once Raven was healed and able to be adopted into a safe and loving home, this was a turning point for Acosta. She created the nonprofit Law N' Paws to help raise the necessary funds and provide care and housing for animals from cruelty cases. Here, the word *rescue* refers both to the animals who have been saved from horrific situations and the organization itself. It is a rescue that helps rescues.

Since its formation in 2017, Law N' Paws has helped more than 250 animals, mostly dogs, "the broken ones, the rescues many people think are unadoptable." Acosta explains that once the animal has been legally awarded or surrendered to the rescue, "we provide all the vet care. We will also spay or neuter, vaccinate and microchip them, and try to place them in a home. I require an adoption application, home check, and meet and greet to see if the canine is a fit for the family. If for some reason the family can't keep the rescue dog, we will take them back and try to find them another home."

Law N' Paws director and rehabilitator Veronica Chavez is at the facility 365 days a year, trying to provide some stability for the dogs and help them rebuild trust. The organization has successfully found permanent homes for most of these animals, although Acosta and her small but mighty team explain that there are certain dogs with especially complicated histories who have experienced particularly damaging forms of abuse.

"I have a few rescues that only like me and my volunteers that I know will probably have to remain at my rescue," Acosta says. Some animals who have suffered severe trauma will form extra deep attachments to those who provide them with the love and stability that stands in such stark contrast to their earlier experiences of people. I have witnessed this dynamic firsthand with my dog Sunny. "But at least I know they are safe, loved, and being cared for, and can live out the rest of their lives with us."

As she was establishing the rescue organization, Acosta began digging into the criminological and forensic psychology research about people who abuse animals, including the fact that violent offenders often begin with animals before moving onto human victims. She compiled her findings into a report for the police chief, Greg Allen, who decided there was good reason for a specialized unit. In November 2017, El Paso created the Animal Cruelty Investigations Unit, initially composed of a sergeant, four detectives, and an officer. The unit was immediately busy, with each detective having eight to ten cases in the first month. By 2021, it had grown in size to six detectives.

The city's animal services agency was providing essential assistance, but lacked tools, including fundamentals like sufficient X-ray technology, which is needed to help prepare evidence for trials. Acosta determined that Law N' Paws would also need to help cover the costs of involving outside veterinarians when cases proceeded through the criminal justice system.

As is the case in Calgary and New York, a nonprofit is paying for and providing a lot, as is Acosta herself. The current rescue facility is leased, and along with her aunt, Acosta has purchased land with the hope of building a permanent facility that can provide care, rehabilitation, and a sanctuary for the animals deeply damaged by human cruelty and indifference. Many local businesses donate food, supplies, and other resources. Finding people who can donate their skills and time to design and build a rescue facility is proving more challenging, but Acosta remains steadfast.

Acosta as well as Dr. Carolina De La Garza, a veterinarian at East El Paso Animal Hospital who has worked on animal cruelty cases, were recognized by the Animal Legal Defense Fund (ALDF) in 2021 on its list of "America's Top 10 Animal Defenders." Acosta is a woman whose work got a dedicated investigative unit created in her city and she simultaneously founded and oversees a nonprofit rescue organization to help the animal victims. By all measures, her commitment to the defense of animals is remarkable. And she wants to do more, including to help victims of cruelty in the rural areas around El Paso where there are widespread issues of neglect and abuse, weaker protections, and minimal enforcement.

Cases still haunt Acosta, the animals she couldn't help or who were found too late. "There's an emotional burden. But I have to keep doing this. . . . They say you can't save them all, but I can try."

Lesson #5: if something important for protecting animals doesn't exist yet, create it.

Whether it's a new policy, program, or entire organization, holes should be filled and future problems prevented.

The El Paso animal cruelty unit is intended to "study, investigate cases, and stop these offenders early in their development of violent behavior," explains Acosta.

Cunningham from Edmonton recognizes the same pattern: "It started with our love for animals, and then we realized there's a much bigger picture here and we quickly recognized the link to child abuse, to domestic violence. Animal abuse rarely happens alone."

In other words, crimes against animals are not a distraction from community safety. They are integral to it.

4 LINKED HARM AND PROTECTION

A female police officer responds to a call on a rural property and finds a Doberman drowned in the bathtub. The officer sounds alarm bells in her organization and is mocked by her mostly male coworkers because "it's just a dog." Later at the same property, a woman is murdered.

This scenario is from the feature film *In the Valley of Elah*, starring Tommy Lee Jones and Charlize Theron, but it could just as easily be describing reality, not fiction.

Animal cruelty can be the first visible indicator of antisocial behaviors that may escalate and expand—a red flag for future violent actions. Intervening effectively when someone is abusing animals serves the animal victims and can also help to prevent that escalation. Animal abuse does not occur in a vacuum. Investigating suspected animal cruelty can provide a window or gateway into other abuse that is already taking place or be the visible tip of a much more toxic and dangerous iceberg.

Some policing services and individual officers are still dismissive of animal issues or don't yet know about the human-animal connections, but the culture is shifting. The US-based National Sheriffs' Association has recognized the significance of animal cruelty for the protection of both people and animals and launched the Animal Cruelty as a Gateway Crime program. The association understands that "animal cruelty crimes can serve as a precursor to more violent crimes, as a co-occurring crime to other types of offenses, and as an interrelated crime to various offenses."[1] In plain language, animal abuse often occurs before *and/or* alongside the physical, psychological, and emotional abuse of people as well as before and/or alongside other crimes.

The pattern is known as the human-animal violence link, and it is a multidimensional social and political challenge. Animal abuse can be an early warning sign of aspiring serial killers and mass murderers, but analysts now understand that the violence link is even more widespread and complex. The webs of abuse, terror, and violence entrap people and animals. In addition to animal abuse being a potential warning of future violent behavior, people and animals are commonly harmed simultaneously, especially those in the same family.

Abusive men in particular will weaponize their partners', ex-partners', and children's love for animals as another tool of intimidation, power, and coercive control.[2] Abusers use animals to get people to provide sex or money, keep quiet, or stay or come back, either with threats or with emotional pleas about the animals' love and needs. Animals are used as pawns and proxies, and abusers will threaten to or actually harm them.

The National Link Coalition in the United States has an ever-growing bibliography of academic studies on these intertwined abuses. It includes more than fifteen hundred references and key patterns emerge.[3] Escalating abuse is common. Abuse regularly occurs simultaneously. Human victims delay leaving out of fear for their animals at least half the time. Studies of women with companion animals report that their animal was threatened or hurt by the abuser between 75 and 90 percent of the time, and children are almost always present.[4] Abuse survivors who escape may return to a relationship or property to try to help or comfort an animal and can pay the ultimate price. These are not exceptions or anomalies. This is a serious and widespread problem with real, lasting, and potentially fatal impacts for both people and animals.

Not every person who harms animals, directly or indirectly, will also harm people. Someone struggling with the costs of dog food because their hours got cut at work, or who lost their job, or who quit because their boss was sexually harassing them, or because they had medical bills, whose animal has slightly visibly ribs, is not more likely to become an abuser or murderer. The link should not be used as justification to treat every kind and type of animal harm as grounds for heavy-handed responses. Instead, awareness of the link means animal abuse and cruelty, particularly acts intended to harm animals, including serious neglect, should be carefully considered in their contexts not only as current problems but as indicators of other possible concurrent or future danger too.

Animals being burned or cut by men jealous because their girlfriend went out with her friends. Animal corpses being dropped off on women's doorsteps by abusers or mailed to them as retaliation for leaving. These are among the most difficult and disturbing cases, not only for their violence and depravity, but also because of the sheer depth of the psychological and emotional terror they cause.

Rather than including graphic details, I am going to focus on the responses, the work people across sectors are doing to confront the violence link—to really confront it by properly responding, and ideally, preventing as much violence as possible. The single most important dimension for confronting the violence link is collaboration. The abuse is linked, so protection must be.

Phil Arkow, Dr. Randall Lockwood, academic researcher Dr. Frank Ascione, and a handful of others have been collaborating on different aspects of human and animal relationships since the 1980s.[5] They've been exploring "the good side of the human-animal bond . . . like animal therapy and how animals benefit people and society, and the dark side, which is what we now call the link," Arkow says. In 2008, they approached American Humane, an organization that had distinct branches working on both child and animal protection for decades, about the need for more collaboration. American Humane assembled professionals from animal welfare, child protection, domestic violence, and elder abuse in Portland, Maine. The National Link Coalition emerged from the summit, and it serves as a national coordinating body united around a central fact: "When animals are abused, people are at risk. When people are abused, animals are at risk."[6] The initial members jokingly called themselves the G10; a G20 summit of nations was taking place at the same time as the initial meeting and served as the inspiration for this name. But there is something to that comparison. Like countries, the key players in the violence link landscape have things in common, but they also have differences, and they still need to work together.

Today the steering committee involves leaders and other professionals from prosecutors' offices, including domestic abuse and stalking experts, the judiciary, adult and elder protective services, the ASPCA, the ALDF, veterinary medicine and forensics, animal care and control, policing, and the academic sector. This exemplifies the cross-section of people who are collaborating to address the violence link—and who need to be.

"The link is bigger than any one field," Arkow says.

> People often overlook it in our increasingly specialized, silo-driven society. But when you introduce the link to them, many people have that aha moment, and the light bulb goes on when they see the connections. Whether your focus is child protection, elder abuse, or preventing domestic violence and gender-based violence, once you see that the animals are central, you get many new audiences. This gives each of the sectors cross-fertilization and additional people who can put these ideas into practice, into training, into legislation, and into policy change.

Lockwood explains that

> we realized the best way to reach out to groups that did not traditionally take this seriously was to go to their conferences and listen. I went to a lot of adult victim services conferences, a lot of domestic violence conferences, a lot of child protection conferences, a lot of police conferences, and worked out what can we do to help them. A lot of animal organizations will say, "This is the way it should be; you should be doing this"—but that doesn't get you anywhere, especially when you're dealing with social workers, police, or even veterinarians. So it was slow and gradual, learning what was important to them and learning their language.

Lockwood says that for some human-focused groups, preconceived ideas about animal advocates or the animal protection sphere can be limits but are not insurmountable. "I spent about three years going to prosecutors' conferences to see where we might have an entry point, getting to know people, and getting them to realize we're not just crazy animal people coming in, we also really care about people—and many people care about their animals."

In 2016, the US Federal Bureau of Investigation (FBI) began compiling data about animal abuse in its National Incident-Based Reporting System. Policing departments around the country are to submit their statistics, and the FBI tracks the specifics as a stand-alone data category. Prior to this change, animal cruelty statistics would simply get lumped into an "all other offenses" category There is no consistency across regions in how the offenses are defined, however. Some counties only use two groupings: neglect and intentional abuse. This does not properly reflect the spectrum of animal harm or illegal activity, and neglect means different things depending on the particulars. Plus not all regions submit. This has affected the quality and consistency of the process and results. But some patterns are emerging, thereby reaffirming broader and established trends, including that men are not only the majority of abusers but the large majority of violent abusers as well.[7]

In its data gathering overall, the FBI uses three categories: crimes against persons, property, and society. Notably, the FBI classifies animal cruelty as a crime against society. Animals are not made of metal or wood. Animals feel pain and fear. Yet in legal terms, animals are still defined as property. Although it is a statistical grouping, it is still noteworthy that the FBI did not define animal cruelty as a property crime but rather recognized the broader social effects.

Among the many individuals and groups pushing for years for federal involvement and tracking was veteran law enforcement leader John Thompson. In a violence link story in the *Atlantic*, he shared the following: "I spent 35 years in law enforcement and couldn't have cared less about animal abuse. I was stupid. No one was educated. It's how we used to think about domestic violence: 'If a woman is getting beaten up by her husband, why doesn't she just get out of the house?'"[8] It seems a willingness to recognize prior gaps in knowledge is not unique to Canadian law enforcement after all.

Thompson wasn't initially even an animal lover and thought animal cruelty was something for animal care and control services to worry about. But after first learning about the violence link from his daughter, he self-educated and began pushing for changes. He created the National Law Enforcement Center on Animal Abuse to educate officers and helped found the National Coalition on Violence against Animals, a network of more than sixty local, state, national, and tribal organizations that collaborate to combat animal cruelty and other forms of violence.

The violence link has been a central motivator for most of the police officers and leaders I've spoken with. "When thinking back, what stands out for me is the number of calls I missed not having had this information," Smithson from the Calgary Police Service says. "Whenever we go to train others, there's at least one person who will say, 'I wish I had known this for a specific file or multiple files because I would've done it differently.'"

Smithson knows this feeling firsthand.

> I had one of those cases and I think that's the reason I've become so passionate about why police officers need this information. I had this file—I was there after all the bad stuff had happened—but I had also been there prior to it escalating, when he was abusing the animal. At that point, I wasn't aware of the link. I look at that one and it bothers me. It really bothers me because he beat her bad and for a long time. Could I have prevented that early? Maybe. We have this information. Why are we not putting it in our officers' hands?

Dedicated animal cruelty units in city and county policing services around the United States have ebbed and flowed in recent years for various reasons, including because of shifting leadership and organizational priorities, uneven levels of commitment, and resourcing decisions. Los Angeles's dedicated animal cruelty unit was among the first to be cut during what was called the city's "fiscal emergency" of 2020. It may be an unfortunate effect of efforts to curb police excesses and brutality that these kinds of units—those directly helping the most vulnerable human and animal members of our society—are turned into financial casualties. But some persist, including in El Paso, of course, as well as in Austin and Harris Counties in Texas, parts of Arizona, and New York City. Interestingly, the current units are active in regions considered more liberal and progressive as well as in more conservative areas, in both urban and rural contexts. Prioritizing animals' safety through law enforcement is not unique to one partisan position.

This is also true internationally. Some cities in Norway have launched animal cruelty policing units, and the Netherlands created a dedicated animals branch within its national police services in 2011. Along with completion of a mandatory multiyear education and training, officers in this Dutch unit complete a specialized, ten-week course in animal welfare and abuse. Initial plans to have five hundred dedicated officers were replaced with a smaller number who are responsible for both investigating crimes against animals and general policing work. Concerns about animals are reported to the country's dedicated 144 animal hotline, an impressive communications tool, and nonemergency issues are dispatched to a national nonprofit's inspection services.

Communities around the world have created task forces or regional violence link coalitions, whether the policing service has a dedicated animal cruelty unit or not. These coalitions assemble law enforcers of various kinds, animal welfare workers, veterinarians, family violence shelter operators, prosecutors, social service providers, Indigenous leaders, and policy makers and political representatives of various kinds. Any of these people may be called on to respond to the immediate, interpersonal, or larger effects of abuse. They—and others like teachers—may be the ones who first see signs, including the more subtle or blurred manifestations. A child who is upset and reveals that her dad kicked their dog should be taken seriously—for the sake of the dog and the safety of the little girl.

Animal abuse as a red flag for potential future violence is more widely understood, while the frequency of simultaneous abuse and how animals are used to punish, manipulate, and control human victims are less well-known facts, even among those who see family violence regularly. As a result, educating and training people to, first and foremost, understand the full nature of the violence link is a central and significant goal. Paying attention to *everyone* increases the chance of seeing what's really going on or anticipating what may happen next if something—or someone—isn't stopped. Having more eyes and ears open increases the likelihood of seeing and hearing the truth.

Social workers, animal protection officers, police, and veterinarians are usually the primary target audiences for violence link awareness training and educational campaigns as these are the professionals who will most often encounter either at-risk or already victimized people or animals. Some violence link leaders are also reaching out to the broader collection of emergency services professionals and providing training to firefighting services and paramedics. In addition, many link coalitions are emphasizing college, university, and other training programs to reach people early. In a few places, including Calgary, domestic conflict screening teams now ask an animal abuse question, and dispatchers integrate a violence link perspective in their work. These efforts are laudable and worthy of significant expansion.

Intervening early and responding appropriately are crucial, and this frequently involves a combination of the social work / protective services sphere and law enforcement sector. Victims need to be protected, and perpetrators should be halted and held accountable.

Sometimes the entanglements of human and animal lives play out in unexpected ways. In 2018, a Florida woman discreetly slipped a note to the receptionist at the DeLand Veterinary Clinic that read, "Call the cops. My boyfriend is threatening me. He has a gun. Please don't let him know." The security footage was released to the media, and it is absolutely chilling to watch. But this Hail Mary worked. The abuser was arrested. He is in prison.

Every veterinary clinic would benefit from having knowledge of the many facets of the human-animal violence link, especially how to identify probable animal abuse and neglect, and how to spot the broader signs of family violence. Organizations like the World Small Animal Veterinary Association have recognized the need and expanded violence link training for members.

Dr. Melinda Merck, a respected forensic veterinarian based in Texas, shared a powerful story when speaking to the World Small Animal Veterinary Association in 2021. She had a woman visit her practice to obtain a behavioral assessment for her cat. When the woman's boyfriend would enter the apartment, her cat would freeze, urinate and defecate, and then run into another room.

"That is an extreme 'I'm going to die' fear reaction," Merck says. Merck was concerned about what had happened to cause the cat to behave with such existential fear and began carefully asking questions. The woman started to cry. She asked Merck to take the cat and find her a new home. "She said, 'I can't protect the cat and I need to focus on getting myself out of this relationship.'" Merck's empathetic and deliberate questions helped the woman realize that anyone who would hurt her cat was also a danger to her.

"Veterinarians will say, 'We're your other family doctor,'" Dr. Martha Smith-Blackmore explains. She is a Massachusetts-based forensic veterinary expert and was a visiting fellow at the Brooks McCormick Jr. Animal Law and Policy Program at Harvard University from 2020 to 2022. "We keep your pets healthy as part of keeping our community healthy. But when it comes to violence, most veterinarians don't yet recognize that violence to animals is also violence to their community." She worries that a lack of reporting is leading to the continuation of abusive situations. "We have a tendency to be somewhat fearful because we're caring individuals. We care and we heal. So when we see something done to an animal that isn't kind, it's just so far from our mindset that we recoil from it, rather than wanting to muster up the courage to confront it."

Smith-Blackmore's metaphor is noteworthy. "I've always seen my work as that of being a bridge that connects areas that may not otherwise interface. Veterinarian medicine is far removed from the criminal justice community and there needs to be a bridge. There need to be bridges." More and more veterinarians are learning about the link, helping others to learn, and propelling larger changes in communities and legal circles. This involves working upstream, downstream, and sometimes across the stream.

Veterinary schools in many countries have seen a significant gender shift in terms of their applicants and graduating classes. Whereas even thirty or forty years ago most veterinary students were men, today the majority are women—the large majority in some places. This may have an impact on how and how much the veterinary field approaches the violence link in the years and decades to come. Regardless of gender, all members of veterinary teams are valuable in the ongoing and concerted work of confronting the violence link.

It is true that many abuse victims don't want to involve law enforcement. This may be because they feel they won't be believed or respected by the police, or because they don't want intimate details of their life exposed in a courtroom. The abuser could be a police officer. I have had to engage police officers in situations of abuse and their aftermaths, and not as a researcher. The levels of empathy, knowledge, and respect varied significantly among them.

Author Margaret Atwood asked a male friend why men feel threatened by women when they are generally larger, stronger, and have more money and power. He told her, "They're afraid women will laugh at them. Undercut their worldview." She asked a group why women feel threatened by men. "They're afraid of being killed."[9] This has colloquially been condensed to "Men are afraid women will laugh at them. Women are afraid men will kill them."

Often victims of abuse just want to get away, and that is their only priority: to have freedom from fear and try to become survivors, not just victims. That might mean leaving with a backpack of only the most essential belongings or maybe even just the clothes on your back, with your dog right beside you or your cat in your arms.

Those fleeing might have a family member or friend to stay with, but that may not feel safe, especially if the abuser knows where they live. Whether a shelter can accommodate an animal is an open question. Thanks to the work of violence link task forces, the National Link Coalition, California-based Red Rover, and groups like Humane Canada, the answer is more commonly becoming yes. Domestic violence facilities are finding ways to safely cohouse human and small animal victims, or may partner with a local humane society that can provide temporary housing for the animals. The gender-based violence shelter might have developed a home-based foster program that places human abuse victims' animals in trusted residences until the full, multispecies family can be safely reunited. More and more communities are working to find solutions, but there are still many gaps. Rural and remote regions are particularly underserved, as are victims with larger animals like horses.

There are violence link coalitions being formed and already at work around the world, including in Australia, Bosnia and Herzegovina, Canada, Croatia, England, Estonia, France, Germany, Greece, Italy, Norway, Romania, Scotland, Spain, Sweden, and Ukraine. In 2019, a European Link Coalition was formed. A Latin American network has members in Brazil, Costa Rica, Ecuador, Mexico, and Peru so far.

Along with collaboration, translating knowledge of the violence link into tangible changes is central. This includes developing appropriate training resources, reporting and response instructions, questions and data categories to track patterns, housing plans, and educational materials for frontline professionals as well as members of the public. The process of moving from idea to action can be challenging. Sometimes laws are changed in compelling ways or created, such as to require reporting by veterinarians or mandate cross-reporting so animal protection officers have a legal duty to report suspected child abuse (and at times, vice versa as is the case in Connecticut, Illinois, West Virginia, and the District of Columbia). But then delays and gaps can appear at the stage of implementation if useful organizational policies aren't put into place and training provided. For example, if someone is required to report suspected abuse, they need to know what to look and listen for, and how to report it.

Larger debates about law enforcement and the racial inequities in the criminal justice system manifest in violence link circles. Social workers who serve marginalized communities and diverse people who have experienced police brutality may have different views about the causes of violence along with the preferred responses than the Republican sheriff in their region, and yet both may recognize the violence link and be ready to confront it. Social work responses are rooted primarily in an ethic of care and empathy, while policing may emphasize public service and/or patterns of discipline and punish. Coming together around the same table is not going to eradicate fundamental differences, but it can facilitate conversation and greater understanding.

"We've always seen the link as a bridge-building exercise," says Arkow, again evoking the water metaphor. When people understand that animal abuse can be both a red flag and a window, and so take it seriously, other species and our own benefit. When victims know they can take their animals with them, they are more likely to build the courage to leave and begin to navigate the long and uneven pathway to healing. There is more to be done, but important bridges are being built.

Confronting the root causes of interpersonal violence is challenging work. Many people and animals have been thrown in the river, and we still need to safely and respectfully pull them out. As a society we allocate significant energy and resources to reacting to harm, crime, and violence, and the need to respond to individual cases of abuse, whether the victims are people, animals, or both, cannot be downplayed. Responding to harm that has already taken place and the symptoms of deeper problems is, however, not enough on its own. Violence link action plans often include training and education designed to try to identify the risks and signs of future harm before it happens with the goal of intervening early. But looking even deeper than that, getting to the core of why people harm others is an even more profound challenge.

There is more than one answer, depending on the people and place. It often involves a combination of psychology and social circumstances—some nature and some nurture. Psychiatrists, psychologists, and sociologists have overlapping and distinct arguments to make. Social belonging or the lack thereof is at play. Feeling respected and secure, personally and financially, are factors. Respecting others and seeing their value, even if they are a different gender, ethnicity, or religion, is important. Biological processes in human brains, both inherited and environmental, figure in this equation. The fact is that two people with similar upbringings and job prospects may still treat others differently, and there can be both predictability and exceptions.

The large majority of abusers are men, and misogyny, which manifests in a continuum from the subtle and everyday to extreme acts of violence, is an undeniable and central propellant.[10] Abusers exist across the economic spectrum. There is much more work to do as a result, at various points along the river and in the broader landscape.[11]

Lesson #6: protecting animals is also about protecting people, and vice versa.

I spent many hours stuck in traffic with a retired police officer who now focuses on animal protection, so we talked a lot. As is always true when I am in the field in the United States, I happily answered many of his questions about Canada's public (or, single payer) health care. We talked at length about race, racism, and policing, the dangers of insecure, power-tripping cops and toxic occupational cultures, and whether more and/or specific postsecondary education training should be required for police (for example, librarians, who are not empowered with lethal force, normally require both undergraduate and specialized graduate degrees). We discussed how to balance response with prevention, what the police could reasonably be expected to do properly, and what should not be policing responsibility—those problems that instead require political and economic strategies, community-based programs, or both. We talked about why nuance and context matter, especially when lives are at stake.

"Getting some of these jaded cops to recognize that a little fluffy dog with matted fur might be a sign that someone else in the family is being neglected can be tough. Or that if the guy kicks the dog, there's a good chance he's going to kick the woman next," he said. "We've been at this for a few years now, and I'm seeing the changes firsthand. It's not one piece, it's everything together."

He shared a story, variations of which I have heard repeatedly from people on the front lines. "A woman who was too scared of her boyfriend to cooperate with law enforcement, well, he was also abusing her dog. So the charges were laid based on what had happened to the dog—we had all sorts of physical evidence. And the guy gets locked up for a month for animal cruelty. That gave the woman the time to get out. She's three or four states away now. And so's her dog."

5 SOCIAL HARMS AND PROTECTIONS

The recognition of deep human-animal bonds that informs violence link efforts is also propelling organizations that are working to help other vulnerable, marginalized, and at-risk animals—and people. Socially isolated seniors and persons with disabilities have crucial relationships with animals. Precariously housed people and those experiencing homelessness, especially women and youths, benefit from the companionship and protection afforded by dogs while trying to survive on the streets and in shelters. Poor people of all kinds love their animals dearly, but struggle with the costs of veterinary care or physically getting to a clinic. Animal welfare investigations find people who are affected by mental health challenges.

These dynamics are on the opposite end of the animal harm spectrum from those who purposefully hurt animals. Responses may involve preventing unintentional harm (like a lack of veterinary care) or animals from ending up in shelters, either because they were seized by law enforcers or heartbreakingly surrendered by caretakers. These situations may not actually be about animal harm at all either but rather about augmenting the level of care that can be provided and love that can be shared.

Animal protection can be fertilized by compassion for people—people who need support, resources, and services. The work can result from a welfare investigation or be pursued proactively—when people are struggling, this impacts their animals. These truths are another reason to go upstream to try to stop animals—and people—from falling or being pushed into the water.

Interestingly, some early humane societies focused entirely on helping shipwrecked people—and in certain areas, that emphasis persists. At the same time, many of the early "humane" organizations worked for reforms to benefit children, enslaved or formerly enslaved people, and/or women—as well as animals. *Humane* means treating others with compassion and care; the definition doesn't specify who is to be treated with kindness. The cultural and political association of the word humane with animal protection became more established over the twentieth century. In other words, there is a long history of people who protect animals working to support and uplift other people too. Often the two go hand in hand, or hand in paw, if you will.

The cross-section of animal protection approaches focused on working with and for lower-income people has no all-encompassing, tidy name. In many places, this work builds from the *one welfare* approach—a concept that highlights the interconnectedness of human, animal, and environmental well-being. One welfare is often linked to the concept of *one health*—recognizing the same triad but specifically for health care. These approaches reflect the fact that when one member of the trio suffers, so does at least one of the others, if not both.

In North America, this kind of work, particularly when it revolves around the struggles facing multispecies families in poverty, has increasingly been called the *pets for life* approach. Pets for Life is a specific program of the Humane Society of the United States, itself an affiliate of the global Humane Society International, yet a distinct organization with its own board of directors and leadership. The society is not an umbrella organization for local humane societies, and doesn't have (or seek) law enforcement powers. Amanda Arrington, a path-making woman who grew up in a conservative area of rural Texas, first began to see the power of proactive versus simply reactive work in North Carolina and founded an organization called Beyond Fences.

In many areas, it is not illegal to keep dogs outside year-round and 24–7 provided they have access to appropriate shelter. Some people choose to keep dogs outside for health reasons (such as allergies), or because someone in the home won't permit the dog to live indoors, the dog is happy outdoors, or doing so is their family or cultural custom. Living indoors with people is the reality for only a minority of the world's dogs.[1]

I tend to think many dogs are happier if they can spend much of their time living indoors, especially when the temperature inside is more comfortable, there are soft places to sleep, and love is generously given and received. But if the humans are always fighting, it is stressful for dogs. If the humans are rarely home, the dogs may be lonely and bored whereas outside they could watch people and other animals. If the dogs have grown up outdoors, perhaps even in groups with other dogs, that kind of life might be their preference. Some dogs get hot inside and like snow. There are many variables.

Whether it's legal to chain or "tether" outdoor dogs also varies. Is living on a chain outside the best life for dogs? Probably not. But yards need to be fenced for the dogs to be freed from those chains. This is where Beyond Fences comes in. The organization works to free dogs from chains by building fences, at no cost to the animals' caretakers, so the people and dogs can interact freely in their yards. It got Arrington thinking about taken-for-granted assumptions and inequities in companion animal welfare and whether a paradigm shift was needed. Pets for Life was developed in 2011, and Arrington is its senior director.

She is candid about the process. "Initially there were things that were not effective, appropriate, or respectful. So that had to become the North Star for us: How do we treat everybody with dignity and respect, and how do we start to shift the focus onto institutions and systems being the problem, not people?"

The Pets for Life approach stems from the significant inequities and tangible realities in the United States that constrain tens of millions of low-income people who consider their animals to be family members.[2] Due to longer patterns like slavery, segregation, and uneven regional development as well as ongoing issues with unemployment, underemployment, low wages, the cost and availability of housing, and discrimination, dramatic economic inequalities exist in the United States. These realities influence and are evident in all aspects of our lives, including animal care.

Having less money means purchasing the products your animal needs to survive and thrive is a challenge, as is paying for veterinary care. This is compounded by the geographic distribution of veterinary clinics and pet supply stores. Lower-income communities have far fewer of both. This makes it even more difficult to obtain what your animal requires, even just the basics, never mind if your animal has a special need or dietary requirement (and never mind advanced care services like physical therapy that benefit the animals of those who can afford them). You might have to take a bus, or multiple buses, with your cat, dog, or guinea pigs to reach a vet. Maybe animals aren't even allowed on the public transit in your community. Are the animals of people in poverty simply sentenced to suffer and die? Animal organizations are increasingly saying no.

Few among us would deny that animals are family, but to put it mildly, there can be an unkind double standard when it comes to poor people. "They can't afford to properly care for an animal." "They should focus on themselves instead of the animal." The comments are not always consistent but are no less damning. Some animal lovers and protectors make these kinds of arguments. Dogs in impoverished neighborhoods are disproportionately impounded. People experiencing homelessness have been harassed by people claiming the animal is being neglected, and some dogs have been stolen.[3]

Struggling to get by when financially strained, and ideally get ahead if possible, is challenging, physically, psychologically, and emotionally. Poverty is punishing enough. To also be denied the chance to care for an animal, laugh at their funny behavior, get exercise by walking together, and feel the unconditional love they offer—that is particularly cruel. Plus many animal shelters are already overcrowded. Is removing more animals from their homes, from the people they love, turning their worlds upside down and throwing them into the tense environment of a shelter from which they might or might not even emerge alive, actually good for the animals? Whether motivated by empathy with people who are struggling or even if only interested in the welfare of the animals, there are compelling reasons for trying to preserve and improve the care low-income people can provide, and attempting to keep human-animal families together.

The Pets for Life program begins from the premise that people should be able to share and benefit from love regardless of their ethnoracial identity, where they live, or their income. The lack of services, also known as the service gap or pictured geographically as pet care deserts, is why there is a demonstrable need to supply low-cost and no-cost veterinary care along with the items people need to care for their animals. The goals are even more ambitious, however.

"Offering services is an important part of the solution and certainly an immediate need. The direct care work of PFL is extremely important and will always be central to the program. But bringing about transformational change requires tackling the foundations of racial and economic injustice. . . . There is a difference between just offering services and creating equity in access," the Humane Society of the United States notes. It seeks to train and mentor local people to promote Pets for Life approaches in more communities. It also works to initiate and advance conversations with and among animal protection organizations, including law enforcement of different kinds, about the heavy reliance on the punishment side of the tool kit—fines, seizures, and criminal charges.

But this way of thinking challenges many entrenched social beliefs about poverty. Arrington considers it a foundational myth. "We receive messages from all different places that people who are poor deserve to be because they made a bad decision or are a bad person, that it's a personal fault if someone is experiencing poverty. That is a belief system that we must work to change. And it really impacts how people operate, the ways in which you build relationships—or don't."

Many US and Canadian nonprofit animal protection organizations (both local and national) now work to support low-income families with animals by offering a pet food bank, building doghouses, and/or partnering with the city or county animal services. This approach is not unique to nonprofits either, and animal services from Dallas to Oakland to Pima County to Rochester to Indianapolis to Calgary have programs.

How staff and volunteers interact with low-income animal caretakers who use these services varies. Some of these approaches are rooted in respect and even solidarity, while others are more judgmental, patronizing, and preachy. That leads to more or less positive experiences for service users, and affects the effectiveness of the services.

In Santa Cruz County, California, Todd Stosuy, the county's animal services field manager, emphasizes a problem-solving and dialogue-driven approach to calls, and the value of taking the time to really talk with and listen to people, even as the agency receives more than eleven thousand calls a year. "You always have the time," he says. He sees it as "working with not against people" and part of public service.

Stosuy argues that writing citations and impounding animals creates mistrust and doesn't necessarily solve the problem either. If people comply because they've been legally compelled, but don't understand the reasons why the change is better for the animal, they may simply repeat the problematic behavior. He believes that the more punishment-oriented tools should be used only if other, genuine attempts to solve problems have been exhausted and unsuccessful. The Santa Cruz County animal service also has a team of retired women volunteers known affectionately as the "granny squad" that will work with residents who don't want uniformed officers around to build doghouses. The county's shelter has an "open-door" motto and approach, and provides some low-cost veterinary services like spay and neuter as well.

Some areas' animal services have invested significant public resources into their facilities with the goals of better meeting the needs of low-income residents, protecting animals, and promoting public health. For example, the Miami-Dade Animal Services' budget has more than doubled over the last decade, and the public investment has meant considerable service expansion for the community. It is an example of an animal care and control service that seeks to provide everything pet related from cruelty investigations and licenses to adoptions and low-cost veterinary services.

The service employs more than two hundred people and receives more than thirty thousand animals a year. A welcoming new open intake facility (meaning there are no restrictions on animals being admitted or people surrendering animals) includes rooms decorated with couches so that potential adopters can picture animals in their own living rooms as they consider adding a new family member. A veterinary clinic offers care for residents' animals, especially low-cost spay and neuter services. A "tip the tipper" program focuses on the many free-roaming cats in the area. It provides compensation—and therefore incentive—for community members who humanely trap cats and then bring them to the animal services facility to be sterilized and vaccinated before being released. The tip of one of these cats' ears is also clipped off as a transnational sign for "this cat has been spayed or neutered." These strategies centered on the high number of stray and unwanted animals are about working downstream and upstream— preventing pregnancies before they happen, not just collecting the strays that result. Miami-Dade Animal Services has also partnered with the Friends of Animals Miami Foundation to bring medical services right into neighborhoods without easy access to vets through a mobile clinic.

Arrington has an even bolder vision. She emphasizes systems, not individuals. But what does that actually mean?

> Take housing. If you look back to what started with the New Deal, it created the American middle class and gave a lot of people the opportunity to own a home. Yet it was rolled out through a national appraisal system determining who got these government-backed mortgages and created opportunities for predominantly white people. That built generational wealth that still impacts communities today. If we don't have that context, that historical understanding of why there is a huge racial gap in home homeownership and what resources are in which neighborhoods, and the way that enforcement engages based on zip code, we are missing key information. We believe at Pets for Life that if we can develop more knowledge around what happened before leading up to today, then we will be much more effective in the solutions that are created and how we position ourselves to be of service.

They are thinking even further upstream, if you will, to understand both the legacies and ongoing impacts of inequities, and then working with understanding and empathy. Larger and longer patterns shape how people experience all aspects of life, right down to the level of animal care.

After Russia attacked Ukraine in 2021, reports emerged saying that the companion animals of white refugees were being admitted into neighboring countries more quickly than Black people were. This was far from the first situation of this kind, and the pattern has appeared around the world. It is another unequivocal indicator of the need for animal protection efforts not to reproduce inequities. In fact, more work should be led by people and communities of color.[4]

The logistics—and politics—of keeping people and animals together are even more challenging when those people and animals are without homes. Skid Rover is a program of the larger Homeless Health Care Los Angeles that provides food, collars, and leashes directly to people for their dogs in the city's Skid Row neighborhood. The organization states that by "working on a day-to-day, individual level, we are able to offer individualized care that improves quality-of-life and ensures access to critically needed services."[5]

I first learned about social worker Christine Kim's work because of the moving exhibit My Dog Is My Home that was housed in the National Museum of Animals and Society in Los Angeles in 2013. The exhibit evolved into a national nonprofit that assists organizations and service providers that work with and house individuals and families experiencing homelessness. Whether people and their animals were previously housed together before, or they joined up while trying to survive on the streets, what matters for Kim is that they are family now.

Certain shelters have developed programs that temporarily house animals while people stay in their facilities. A central goal of the all-volunteer team at My Dog Is My Home is the promotion of cosheltering: "'low-barrier' facilities that do not require people experiencing homelessness to separate from loved-ones in order to access services."[6] Not being able to bring your animal with you has been identified as a key barrier to people accessing shelters. Not only do shelters supply literal protection from harsh weather and the dangers of the streets, but they serve as hubs for service providers to engage with people experiencing homelessness to try to meet their immediate and longer-term needs.

My Dog Is My Home has provided support to local, state, and national human-focused organizations, including the National Alliance to End Homelessness, to help develop action plans and tool kits as well as share information. Some animal protection organizations were unsure about why cosheltering was important, but now most are supportive. "They understand the value of keeping people and their companion animals together, and that promoting cosheltering keeps animals out of animal shelters," Kim explains. "It helps keep scarce resources available to help animals who don't already have a family." In other words, stray and abandoned animals who have no human caretaker who loves them. "Your ability to pay for stuff is not an indicator of your ability to provide love for your animal."

California now stands out for its investment in services, including Los Angeles County, where many unsheltered people reside. "A few years ago even, the idea was unheard of, but now the county is not only recognizing the service gap but investing in accommodations for cosheltering [too]. That is a huge victory," Kim says. Communities around the United States including in Ohio, Indiana, and Florida have already implemented or begun to build their capacity to house animals within emergency shelters or in bridge housing. "It's not always the very formalized shelter providers but also churches and houses of worship that step forward when the conventional shelter system isn't meeting a certain need."

The idea that people experience homelessness because of a personal flaw permeates many societies. It's poor bashing on steroids. But the reality is that there aren't enough income sources and jobs, and the cost of housing can be high, especially in big cities, if it's even available. The pandemic has exacerbated many of the challenges. Yes, people are differently able and equipped to negotiate the hurdles life throws in their way, and some have stronger support systems than others. Some people face a lot more obstacles too. Those who end up without secure housing are not morally inferior. Addictions can play a role. They can be hereditary or the result of profoundly damaging experiences, including as a symptom of post-traumatic stress or effect of interpersonal abuse. The National Homelessness Law Center emphasizes that the lack of affordable housing is the number one cause of homelessness, though.

Research studies have found that relationships between people on the streets and their animals are in fact mutually beneficial. As Feeding Pets of the Homeless says, "The bond between pets and people isn't dependent on having a roof."[7] The animals provide nonjudgmental devotion and companionship as well as protection that can be lifesaving, especially for women and vulnerable youths. Researchers have consistently found that people experiencing homelessness not only ensure their animals receive love and food but also often become even more motivated to try to find more stable and safe housing. Dr. Leslie Irvine, a sociologist at the University of Colorado at Boulder, interviewed many people experiencing homelessness about their animals, and the resulting book title is a pithy synthesis of her findings: *My Dog Always Eats First.*[8]

Veterinary social work is another example of how the principle of shared well-being is being put into practice at a handful of vet schools so far as well as in communities and violence link spaces. Having a social worker in a veterinary clinic or animal shelter helps people access services they might need and/or negotiate challenging decisions about animals' lives and deaths, and the grief that can result. Social workers also help respond to compassion fatigue experienced by shelter and clinic staff, including veterinarians, and are now employed by certain veterinary schools, particularly in Canada.

The University of California, Davis, is among the schools with a clinic focused on the animals of those experiencing homelessness. Ohio State University's College of Veterinary Medicine has an outreach program that supports people and their animals. The University of Wisconsin's WisCARES is a collaboration among veterinary, social work, and pharmacy programs to help low-income people and their animals. Families struggling with the costs of veterinary care can be referred by a social services worker to the University of Tennessee Knoxville's AlignCare program, an initiative that promotes "Pet Health Equity."[9]

Equity is a noteworthy word. While *equality* refers to treating everyone identically and can be what's needed, *equity* underscores that at times, recognizing differences is essential to promoting equitable results. If some individuals or groups are disproportionately disadvantaged and excluded, additional or different resources will be needed to give them a fair chance (for instance, an accessible parking space benefits people with disabilities who can then access the facility or service, but isn't necessary for those without mobility challenges). When it comes to animal care, charging all families the same fees won't lead to all animals receiving the same care because of the vast disparities in people's incomes and ability to pay. Using the principle of equity to develop targeted programs and services, or a sliding fee scale, are the sorts of strategies that will lead to better and more equitable results for animals.

Collaborations between veterinarians and social service workers often provide medical care for the animals of people experiencing homelessness, and the people themselves, thereby feeding two birds with one fruit (which stands in stark contrast to killing two birds with one stone). Delivering these services, whether through mobile clinics or by inviting people into specific facilities, helps the animals as well as creates opportunities to engage with people and offer supports.

Community Veterinary Outreach is an example of the one health approach in action that recognizes the interdependency of human and animal well-being. The organization provides preventative veterinary care, resources, and education, and works in partnership with human health service providers to serve both people experiencing homelessness and housing vulnerability and their animals. Dr. Michelle Lem, the organization's founder, gets to the heart, and facts, of the matter. "Let's be clear, homelessness is the problem, not the people living homeless." This fundamental belief is shared by Arrington, Kim, and a growing number of animal defenders. To really help people and animals, and minimize the need for reactive, individual services, the root causes of poverty and homelessness need to be confronted.

It sounds good. It sounds really hopeful. But what does it actually mean? "People in animal welfare are in an important position," Arrington argues. "Companion animals are companions to people, and so we must be active participants in the challenges that people face. We hope that people will cross that divide into having care, concern, and compassion for other people, but even if you just love animals, advocating for these human-based issues helps the animals." Don't punish the animals of people in poverty, or people themselves, simply for being poor.

Lesson #7: animal protection can work with other movements promoting equity and justice for people, and it should.

Rather than operating in silos, these insights challenge animal defenders to see connections, especially between racial and economic justice along with animals' well-being. This means promoting and supporting affordable housing campaigns and policies, living wages, and the expansion of good-paying jobs, and challenging the high costs of educational pathways that open doors to a better standard of living in countries like the United States. In other words, acknowledging and then confronting the actual reasons people are poor. Animals will benefit, and so will people.

In many native communities around the lands we now call North America, dogs roam freely. They may be viewed as a risk to people's safety, members of the community, or some combination, depending on where you are and who you ask. Often called rez dogs, the animals are imbued with many different identities. Some native people themselves identify with the dogs as relatives and reflections, members of families, similarly hungry and rejected, and stubborn and wily survivors who are emblematic of the Indigenous spirit.

Dr. Michael Yellow Bird, dean of social work at the University of Manitoba, and member of the Mandan, Hidatsa, and Arikara Nation in North Dakota, shares this: "Whenever I visit tribal communities, I am always on the lookout for my relatives, the rez dogs. I want to know their stories: How did they get to where they are today? How did they survive? What happened to their babies, their parents, their friends, and their culture? What do they dream about? What hopes do they have for the future? What can they tell us about the fate of the human race and the planet?" He says that the lives of rez dogs cannot be uncoupled from human-human relationships, and particularly from the impacts of European arrival on native ways of living, learning, and honoring fellow creatures, including dogs. "The condition of dogs in our communities is a reflection of us. If they are sick, it is because we are also sick."[10] Often Indigenous people who work with animals make a similar argument.

Although unknown to many outside native communities, rez dogs have attracted the attention of some animal protection groups concerned about their health and safety, especially those in regions with harsher climates. These organizations have proceeded in a range of ways, and some have stolen the dogs right off the land. Others have reached out to the leaders in these communities and engaged in dialogue, asking whether the community would like assistance or to collaborate to protect people and dogs by bringing veterinary services, food, and/or other supplies, or rehoming the dogs outside the community.

Some animal organizations have been invited into native communities (usually called First Nations or Indigenous communities in Canada) to exchange knowledge. Of its successful and respected Northern Dogs project, the International Fund for Animal Welfare says, "First, we built relationships with First Nations across the country, to understand the challenges, then together we built comprehensive programs to address the issues. Today, we offer veterinary services, culturally relevant education, and real-life solutions for communities that would otherwise not have them."[11] The dialogue and relationship building must come first, particularly because of the longer pattern of outsiders telling native people that they can't take care of their own. This has not only happened with dogs but also with children. Native children have been taken into state systems or religious residential schools designed to assimilate and destroy Indigenous cultures and spirits. The children experienced harsh treatment, abuse, and disease, and many died. Decades of these patterns have created widespread and intergenerational trauma with psychological, social, and economic symptoms as well as mistrust. Understanding these truths, and working for reconciliation and healing, is difficult but necessary.

Many native communities have their own law enforcement and/or animal care and control services tasked with investigating potential harm and/or enforcing the communities' animal bylaws, which may permit free-roaming dogs or not. Native communities are diverse and have responded in different ways to rez dogs. Ermineskin Cree First Nation has developed a comprehensive law covering dogs at large, dangerous dogs, excessive barking, licensing, and protection. It begins from a place of respect, establishing that the nation "has a deep and abiding respect of the Creator's Natural Laws and a great sense of stewardship, with a long-standing traditional and spiritual relationship with domesticated animals, in particular dogs (*atimwak*), and holds such animals in high-regard and, as such, strives to ensure that matters related to such animals are carried out in a conscientious, respectful and prompt manner."[12] It also states that the regional Animal Protection Act applies on the reserve.

Animal services officer Norm Running Rabbit of the Siksika First Nation differentiates between dogs being "allowed" to roam free and being recognized "as free beings, as animals that should be without restraints." Speaking to the Alberta SPCA, he explains that this means dogs who are technically "owned" and cared for may be free to move about too. Some dogs have one family, while others, often called community dogs, may move among different families' yards and homes. He recognizes that many people are not accustomed to this approach, and that safety and animal welfare issues have emerged and will arise. The chief and council of the Siksika First Nation created an action plan, including building its own team and infrastructure. Running Rabbit works to enforce humane standards of care and responds to safety concerns—both animal protection and animal control.

He sees the dedicated animal services program with specialized officers who can handle issues responsively and work proactively as offering lessons for other native communities. Siksika has formed relationships with outside partner animal organizations, including to provide veterinary care, and Running Rabbit emphasizes the need for those who want to work with native communities and are guests on the land to learn and then respect protocols and local cultures, and get to know both leaders and community members. In a similar vein, Yellow Bird highlights the need to see the difference between being "a rescuer and a supporter," and central to this is not making assumptions. This kind of work is about mutual respect.

Diana Webster of the White Earth Band of Ojibwe founded the Native American Humane Society in 2014 to serve as a bridge between tribal and outside animal welfare organizations, and she works to empower native peoples as they respond to the animal issues in their communities. Speaking to the Reconciliation in Animal Welfare Symposium, a historic event organized by Alanna Collicutt of the Canadian Animal Task Force, Alison Cuffley from the British Columbia SPCA, Dr. Valli Fraser-Celin of the Winnipeg Humane Society, and Jan Hannah of International Fund for Animal Welfare,

Webster says, "When I first started in animal advocacy, it was all about rescue and spay-neuter. But I quickly realized that what it really was all about
was the relationship that people have with their animal. We were going into
communities and finding that people really love their animals, but they don't
have the resources or access to the services that their animals need." She
stresses that the work is emotionally difficult and can be frustrating. "A lot
of it is being done by women, by strong women. We need to build systems
and build onto existing systems." Based on her leadership experiences, she
offers advice for people wanting to help animals in native communities. She
suggests breaking big tasks down, taking the time to plan, and trying not to
get jaded. Webster also encourages people not to be obsessed with perfection
and instead be kind to themselves as they do their best.

The number of native tribes and nations that have their own animal
services agencies is growing. Some bring vet clinics into their communities.
Some work with national organizations like the ASPCA and the Humane
Society of the United States' Pets for Life as well as local or regional humane
societies.

Indigenous peoples are also creating their own grassroots organizations
such as Rez Road Adventures, the brainchild of Vernan Kee and Chantal
Wadsworth of the Navajo Nation, and Save Rez Dogs, founded by Leah
Arcand of the Muskeg Lake Cree Nation. They are working to help dogs,
inspire and educate others, build partnerships and community champions
for rez dogs, raise funds to make more work possible, and reclaim traditional
relationships that have been distorted and damaged by residential schools,
the reservation system, intergenerational trauma, and many other effects of
colonization. Arcand credits her role as a teacher, mother, and Indigenous
woman as to why she does the work, even though it can be emotionally
exhausting. Arcand and colead Craig Edes, who is Gitxsan and based out
of Treaty 6 (Saskatoon, Saskatchewan), emphasize the need to go upstream
when seeking to help the dogs. They highlight the value of understanding
history, share insightful tools for communities and individuals looking to
make a difference, and offer practical advice for people who have dogs. In
other words, the big picture and the little details.

Dorothea Stevens, a public health nurse with the San Carlos Indian
Health Service, began by transporting animals from her Apache nation in

southern Arizona to get the veterinary care they needed. But as the years passed, a group of other volunteers joined her to form the Geronimo Animal Rescue Team. Speaking to the Humane Society of Southern Arizona, Stevens said, "We work along with animal control. We just don't have the vets that we need and we don't have the enforcement as far as animal abuse. That's something we will be working on."

In addition to responsive work, she highlights the power of education. "As Apaches we respect all animals and we were raised that way a long time ago, but we don't see this happening anymore. We want to start with the little ones so they can teach the adults." Emphasizing the range of ways nation members can defend animals, the Rescue Team says, "Adopt. If you can't adopt, foster. If you can't foster, sponsor. If you can't sponsor, volunteer. If you can't volunteer, donate. If you can't donate, educate."[13] In recruiting volunteers, the group stresses essentials like physical strength, and twice it underscores the importance of mental stability, noting, "It can be really tough seeing the condition of some animals." This sort of work isn't about denying that problems can emerge and animals—and people—may need help. It's about doing so in a way that is rooted in respect for everyone.

There are many significant lessons to draw from this landscape and work, whoever and wherever we are. One is the importance of understanding history and context as well as asking questions and learning how things came to be and why, even if it's uncomfortable, and maybe especially when it is. Another is the need to question stereotypes, myths, and assumptions about Indigenous people. The value of creating but not imposing. The significance of dialogue, reciprocity, and respect. The interconnectedness of pain and healing. The interconnectedness of us all.

Changing how we think about harm and protection, and seeing how it is related to larger patterns in our societies, is challenging, and can be daunting.

Some might say, "I recognize the problems, but they're too massive and long-standing to confront." Organizations are overstretched and underfunded, especially nonprofits. People on many different animal protection front lines are exhausted. Is bold thinking just a fantasy, or can it really be translated into action?

"Start small," Arrington says.

> There are some things you can do that don't take additional human resources and that don't cost any additional dollars. The way you treat people, the way that you answer the phone, the way that you engage when someone presents at your front desk. It can have huge impacts in trust building and staff morale. Folks think it's going to be cumbersome, but when you change the narrative from us having to protect animals from 'bad people,' it lightens the emotional load. People being happy to see you [is affirming].

I began this book by sharing my concerns about being spit at when in the field with animal protection workers, because it happens. And it will always happen, because you cannot please everyone, and some people are going to be hostile, aggressive, or violent to others, humans and animals, despite all the best-laid plans. But not most people. By thinking about both causes and effects, we can identify ways to foster goodwill and collaboration while trying to minimize the hostility.

"Make a commitment to shift 5 percent of reactive work into proactive work and build on that," Arrington suggests. "Having that honest conversation with ourselves that if we don't change, if we don't say, "okay, what can we do differently, what have we done well, and what can we improve?" we're going to be in this place forever. We're going to be stuck in the cycle of responding and not really getting ahead and upstream."

A newspaper clipping from 1924 with two haunting photos of children with their animals encapsulates so much about interdependency, inequality, and the need to think thoroughly about the effects of our actions, regardless of how noble our intentions are, or we believe them to be.

On the left, a girl cries into her dog's neck. On the right, the two little boys look shell-shocked, and one of them is crying, as they stand with their dog. The images were captured right before the children and their families were forced to surrender their dogs because they couldn't afford the license fees.

"Dark Days for Little Dog Lovers: Bidding Her Pet a Last Fond Farewell; Sorrow and Resignation–Sentiments the Dog Shares." Photos published in the *Daily Mirror*, January 1, 1924 edition. The caption reads, "The New Year is a sad time for many young dog-lovers, compelled to part with their pets for want of money to buy a license. The above are typical scenes at Battersea Dogs' Home yesterday." Reproduced by permission.

Anyone, anywhere, who thought—or thinks—this is morally acceptable or good for animals possesses a darkness I cannot comprehend.

6 THE SCIENCE AND POLITICS OF INVESTIGATIONS–AND PROSECUTIONS

At the far end of the animal harm spectrum is another kind of darkness: violent crimes against animals. There are fewer of these cases, but they require careful attention. Challenging the taken-for-granted assumptions about fieldwork in animal protection and the prospects for working in collaboration with others who believe in a more just future has the potential to help many people and animals. But in even the most fair and caring societies, there will be serious and violent crime. Those who perpetrate the violence may be acting alone or as part of organized networks of crime.

Animal fighting, usually involving dogs or roosters, is a particularly horrific kind of animal cruelty. There are people who participate in fights as a "hobby," and professionals who earn income from betting, breeding, and selling animals. Dogs' loyalty is perverted in appalling ways. Roosters are infused with rage and literally armed with ankle blades. High-profile cases like the prosecution of former US football player Michael Vick in 2007 galvanized public anger, but animal fighting involves people of all backgrounds, races, and income levels.[1] Hundreds of fighting charges have been laid in more than twenty-four US states, and this is likely only the surface of the problem. Those involved in animal fighting almost always have one thing in common, though: their gender. An investigator who worked undercover in US dogfighting circles for two years saw hundreds of men but only one woman, and she was someone's relative. Another never saw a woman directly but heard that one was a prominent breeder.

Mark Randell worked for thirty years in British policing and retired as a senior detective. He has since led violence link training and supported public and nonprofit agencies across Europe as they build their capacities to protect animals, including in Ukraine. He has also led multifaceted undercover investigations in Greece, the Balkans, Serbia, and Bulgaria, in partnership with police and animal protection organizations. Randell estimates that globally, upward of a million dogs could be trapped in the dark world of fighting. "It is animal abuse that occurs in almost every country often with shared similarities but also with variations and unique differences dependent on the community involved. Animal fighting, specifically dogfighting, is linked to serious, organized crime and is often the pastime of serious criminals. It's rare for an animal fighting investigation not to recover guns, drugs, or both," says Randell.

Fights can take place in basements, on rooftops, or outdoors. Rings can be quickly erected and then immediately disassembled. Sometimes other kinds of dog competitions are used as fronts. Dogfights are highly secretive, and the locations of fights are known only to those involved and may change multiple times. Often pit bulls or pit bull–type dogs are used, and they may have scars or missing ears and tails. Heavily weighted bags or harnesses may be placed on the dogs while on outdoor runs to build up their strength and endurance, and/or they may be tethered on heavy chains. The dogs can have bodily deformities resulting from previous injuries that did not heal properly. Many of the signs of fighting, like treadmills, are hidden from public view at the back of properties or indoors.

Animal fighting is located in a liminal law enforcement space. Law enforcement agencies with the ability to effectively investigate may or may not take animal fighting seriously not only as a crime unto itself but also linked to many other kinds of offenses and criminal networks. Animal groups may care, yet are rarely qualified to safely undertake investigations. As Randell puts it, "The seriousness is exacerbated because it often happens under the radar of law enforcement who have other priorities and animal groups that rarely have the skills or powers to stop it." More law enforcement agencies are beginning to take animal fighting seriously in Europe and North America, and some large-scale arrests have been made over the last fifteen years especially, but more work is necessary.

Randell feels strongly that serious crimes and gang detectives need to be paying more attention to this clandestine world given their enhanced investigative powers along with the risks of undertaking this work, people who are involved, and dangers to public safety. He sees the potential for financial investigators to play a key role too. "If dogfighters' assets were seized suddenly, the landscape would change for the animals and communities affected by the violence."

After arrests and seizures, the work continues. In the case of roosters, they are usually automatically euthanized. What to do about the dogs seized is a recurring challenge. Professional assessments are necessary to determine the extent of the physical and mental damage done. Sometimes the dogs are deemed too injured or volatile because of their training and what they have endured, and a potential or likely threat to the safety of people and/or animals as a result. This was long the norm. When this happens and dogs are euthanized, there can be vicious backlash directed at the organizational staff and investigators involved, none of whom want to be ending dogs' lives, but who have professional and legal obligations, including to public safety. Nevertheless, they can become lightning rods for public anger, along with the actual abusers.

At other times, experts may determine that with proper care and rehabilitation, some dogs may ultimately be able to experience a good quality of life and not be an increased risk to others. The Vick case was a turning point in this respect. There are many variables and factors at play, including how long dogs have been trapped in the dark world of fighting and what specifically was done to them. Fifty-one dogs were seized from Vick's fighting operation. A handful of them died or were euthanized for health or behavioral reasons. The remaining dogs were eventually able to be rehomed either into families or sanctuaries. A number of rescue organizations offered their facilities and care, including Best Friends Animal Society and BADRAP. The dogs were given names like Handsome Dan, Jhumpa Jones, Little Red, Meryl, Gracie, Zippy, Sweet Jasmine, Cherry Garcia, and Teddles.[2] Initially scared of leashes and stairs, Jonny Justice became a therapy dog who would assist with children's reading programs and was named dog of the year by the ASPCA in 2014. Some of the dogs preferred quiet lives—understandably so. After eating a final steak and enjoying many years of love, Frodo, the last of these dogs, was euthanized in late 2021.

The ASPCA now runs a facility in Weaverville, North Carolina, focused on dogs with extreme fear, most often those from hoarding cases or problematic backyard breeders, usually known as "puppy mills." The process frequently takes thirteen weeks, after which the dogs are placed in partner shelters or with rescue groups that work to find forever homes. But it depends on how fearful the dogs are, and how they respond to people's attempts to help them learn, change, and trust.

The ability for some animals who have been abused or neglected, and are victims of human cruelty, greed, or indifference, to also become survivors, friends, family members, therapists, ambassadors, and a host of other identities is truly remarkable. Those who cannot, who are too damaged, are not flawed. It is our species that has failed them, and it is up to us to honor their memory, try to make amends for what we have done, and work to stop future violence.

Animal fighting and other kinds of violent cruelty cases require professional attention and expertise. Upward of a hundred of those professionals gathered in St. Pete Beach, Florida, in 2018 at the International Veterinary Forensic Science Association conference.

I chose a seat at the back of the conference hall near the water pitchers so I could replenish my glass often. It had been an intense night trying to keep up with the hard-drinking forensic veterinarians and law enforcement officers who were assembled to learn and share information. This is a global collection of people whose lives are essentially *CSI: Animals*. At work in the United States, England, Scotland, Taiwan, Colombia, Australia, Canada, and elsewhere, they use the intricate methods of forensic science to help uncover the truth about what has happened to animals.

"A nonambulatory dog had been found at the end of a dead-end street," Dr. Martha Smith-Blackmore said from the front of the room as her presentation began.

Nonambulatory.

Unable to move.

A dog unable to move at the end of a street. Near a playground.

My heart rate sped up. Most of the presentations had created more distance between the living animal and data being examined. Every single one was still about an animal who had suffered. Each case was difficult to hear. But the earlier presentations had been more focused on a particular part of the body or piece of evidence, and that made it possible to concentrate primarily on the science being explained, such as a specific wound and its composition, or a sample of saliva. It was easier to mentally compartmentalize.

Smith-Blackmore proceeded to explain the case, in methodical scientific detail, yet the dog was also described vibrantly. There were photos. The dog was present in her own story. The dog turned out to be a young female pit bull who was named Puppy Doe because her identity was unknown. All the broken bones and other injuries, including stab wounds, were identified in sequence.

It took a while.

"Do not cry. Do not cry," I kept saying to myself. Even though I was at the back, I did not want to look emotional in that room full of scientists and law enforcement agents.

A larger investigation had been launched. The media had amplified the story of Puppy Doe, and people in the Boston area had become truly enraged. Investigators began to piece together details from the dog's journey. She had most recently belonged to an elderly woman. It turned out that it was this woman's hired caretaker who had been abusing the dog and possibly the woman herself. He was ultimately convicted of twelve counts of felony animal cruelty.

Forensic veterinarians can determine certain things unequivocally through their diagnostic and analytic methods. In other instances, they can narrow things down to a specific range of possibilities. Forensic veterinarians can identify nonaccidental injuries. Puppy Doe had nonaccidental injuries. She had not fallen or been hit by a car. She did not have bone cancer. The extent of her injuries was extreme, and the injuries were intentional.

Veterinarians had decided that she was too injured to ever be able to recover or walk again, and euthanasia would be the most humane option given the depth of her suffering. Smith-Blackmore showed a photo of the dog wrapped in a blanket. "She was patted and cuddled in her final moments. She wagged her tail. She felt love."

At that point, the tears fell. I couldn't stop them. The final moments of all the dogs in my life who have been euthanized flashed through my mind like a movie reel. Their confusion. The brightness in their eyes dissipating as their bodies fell still. Overwhelming sadness washed over me, knowing that this sweet, innocent dog had been so systematically terrorized by a human. He was going to be punished, but that did not bring her back to life. And despite months of torture, she still forgave our species. She was still able to express joy as she took her last breaths.

Late that night after all the formal proceedings, informal discussions about the vets' experiences collaborating with local politicians and violence link coalitions gave way to fierce debates about the future of health care after one southern vet arrived with moonshine. The night ended with demonstrations of how to get out of a choke hold, and me shocked that there were people around the table with guns on their ankles. These people were from different parts of the country and world. They held wildly different political views on almost all issues. But they were linked by their commitment to using their intelligence and skills to help try to get justice for animal victims, to let animals' bodies speak, as Dr. Julio Aguirre, Colombia's leading forensic veterinarian puts it. It is painstaking and painful work. I felt grateful that they do it.

I just couldn't stop thinking about the dog who had become Puppy Doe. And all the dogs like her.

Shows like *CSI*, *Bones*, and *NCIS* have dramatized forensic sciences. In reality, there are field investigators, technicians, and experts on certain kinds of diagnostic tools or subject areas ranging from insects to ballistics. They work methodically at crime scenes and in laboratories with microscopes, specialized computer programs, mass spectrometers, sophisticated cameras, and revealing light sources.

Forensic investigations are not reserved exclusively for humans. Veterinary forensics is now an established and growing field. Scientific papers authored by British researchers in the late 1980s and early 1990s began to identify the forensic potential of animal DNA, and in the decades since, veterinarians, scientists, and other analysts on both sides of the Atlantic and beyond have been doing more research, publishing papers, diligently diagnosing their findings, and getting organized—such as by forming associations, creating journals, holding conferences, and doing all the academic and logistical work needed to establish a new area of thought and practice. Forensics is taught at a small but growing number of veterinary schools, and a master's program at the University of Florida allows professionals to deepen their knowledge and skills.

Dr. Ranald Munro, a professor of forensic veterinary pathology at the Royal Veterinary College in London was the first British veterinary surgeon to obtain a diploma in forensic medicine. He and Dr. Helen Munro wrote a seminal book on forensic veterinary pathology; pathology is a subspecialty concentrating on disease origins and diagnoses through the analysis of tissues, whole organs, bodily fluids, and at times, entire (deceased) bodies. Veterinary pathologist Dr. Beverly McEwen, who is officially retired from the University of Guelph but still teaches in the University of Florida's graduate program, was one of the first people to help me navigate this scientific landscape and understand its role in animal protection. I almost immediately asked if it is emotionally difficult to be sent dead animals who may have experienced a violent or painful death, and have to write entire research papers with excruciating details about topics like suffocation, strangulation, and bodies taken from water. "You focus on the results," she said. "You focus on what you can do. That's how you help animals and find the truth."

The veterinary field is grappling with a serious mental health crisis, including a high prevalence of suicide.[3] Burnout among veterinary doctors, technicians, and nurses is increasing, and leading to clinic closures, reduced hours, and less services. Some people are leaving the field altogether. The difficulties of having to euthanize many animals, being asked to end the lives of healthy animals, being doubted and harassed, and carrying large debt loads—there are many factors at play. The pressure on forensic veterinarians, many of whom take on criminal investigations on top of their regular patient care workloads, is even greater. Those who do forensics full time, such as in the ASPCA's labs in New York City led by Dr. Robert Reisman and the Veterinary Forensics Science Center in Gainesville, Florida, headed by Dr. Rachel Touroo, spend their working life looking closely at the serious and fatal effects of human violence. The educational process is long, expensive, and challenging. The cases are difficult and time-consuming, and the work is not glamorous. This career path is not for the faint of heart or easily distracted.

Forensic veterinarians may be called on by law enforcement agencies to assess an injured animal, crime scene, or dead body—like an autopsy, but called a necropsy when the victim is an animal. They perform many necropsies. The goal is to determine with significant scientific objectivity what happened. Forensic veterinarians work to establish things like the cause of the injury, injuries, or death, types of wounds, and types of weapons used—the painstaking details about what happened, or to rule out possibilities such as accidental death or the actions of a natural predator. Their services may be paid for by a nonprofit or government agency. The Clark R. Bavin National Fish and Wildlife Forensics Laboratory in Ashland, Oregon, is a publicly funded center that helps determine the cause of death and whether a crime has been committed against a wild animal.

In the United States, where animal abuse trials are more common, forensic veterinarians are called on to further explain their findings and face cross-examination. There have been cases where their analyses were refuted. Certain veterinarians with forensics training serve as consultants and expert witnesses for the defense in animal cruelty trials. There are calls for a standard of ethics to be created for veterinary forensics.

Smith-Blackmore would like to see medical examiners' offices and criminal investigation agencies have open conversations with veterinarians who are willing to help them. "When they respond to a murder-suicide and they see that there are animals there, [they should] bring in the veterinarian to make sure that the animal issues are addressed because often when there's a bad crime against people, animals are also harmed. I wish that there was representation for the harmed animals in those scenarios as well, because that's part of the whole story." Some forensic vets think the animals of human abuse victims should automatically undergo more examinations to determine if they, too, were being physically hurt.

Dr. Melinda Merck, who is considered a matriarch of veterinary forensics and is the author of another influential early textbook, had a light bulb moment in 1990 after a couple brought a kitten in for examination, claiming the tiny patient had gotten accidentally injured. But Merck's analysis revealed otherwise, and she reported it to the police, initiating further investigation and ultimately animal cruelty charges. Today, more than forty states require or permit veterinarians to report suspected animal abuse—a pattern increasingly common around the world (for example, in Canada, all veterinarians have a legal duty to report). At the time, it was not required, but Merck saw reporting suspected cruelty as a moral imperative and commitment to the patients she had sworn to serve. After setting up her own practice, she began to notice more and more cases. Plus when police investigated, they were finding other abuse in the homes—the violence link in action. Many forensic veterinarians also do violence link work, from delivering training to serving on local and national coalitions, out of a commitment to animals, vulnerable people, and public safety overall, trying to build and solidify those crucial bridges.

Canada's busiest forensic veterinarian, Dr. Margaret Doyle, who is now an essential part of the Calgary partnership, began her journey into forensics after having a humane society worker give a talk on animal behavior at her practice for clients. Doyle asked how she could reciprocate, and was invited to join a shift in the field to provide her expertise. On that first shift, Doyle and the officer discovered and ended up seizing a dog who was badly neglected and abused. "I'd never see anything like that. I distinctly remember being heartbroken by what had happened to this dog, but she still wagged her little tail when you patted her, she was still happy to be with people despite having had a horrific experience." This dog was named Patches. The similarities to Puppy Doe are remarkable, but Patches was found in time and survived.

Doyle spoke with the peace officer about what would happen next, and the officer was surprised at her interest, having found that other vets were less keen to assist with cruelty cases. Certain vets are still hesitant to report suspected cruelty, particularly if not legally mandated to do so, fearing the potential loss of business that can result from bad reviews (although anyone can post lies anonymously online claiming anything they want). Doyle did not have that concern and sees the ethics as clear-cut. "Protecting animal abusers is not why we became vets."

After looking into training on how to be an expert witness, things snowballed, and Doyle ended up completing the University of Florida's master's program in veterinary forensics. She co-owns clinics and works in regular veterinary practice, yet makes time for both delivering violence link training and cruelty cases, of which there is a growing number—animals who are alive and need assessment as well as necropsies. Bodies that ten years ago would not have been assessed are now regularly being considered as potential evidence of wrongdoing.

Doyle vividly remembers when an armed suspect threatened to kill her and the peace officers on the scene during an investigation, reinjecting the importance of frontline safety, including for veterinarians. "I was there with my stethoscope and clipboard, and he's threatening to kill everybody. Now I stay in the car until people are in handcuffs."

Reports written by Doyle are so detailed and persuasive that she rarely has to physically testify in court. She often receives around thirty subpoenas a year, and normally only needs to testify at trial once. And Doyle sees the trial side as only one part of the animal protection landscape. "In cases that really deserve it, successful prosecution would be a measure of success, but if there were a way we could quantify how we've improved animal welfare, I think that would be the real measure. I think we are continually setting a higher standard for how animals are cared for in the city."

Cases involving forensic veterinarians often involve violence against animals and their deaths, so are more likely to involve not only charges but the other wheels of the criminal justice system and law too. It's helpful to unpack what "the law" really means and involves. Constitutions provide the fundamental governing basis and legal principles of countries. Elected legislators make laws and change those that were created by earlier politicians. These laws reflect social priorities and values, and govern many aspects of society, including what is permitted in both the public and private sectors as well as in private spheres like homes (for instance, abusing children is illegal, wherever it happens). Legal systems then exist with judges and lawyers who differently focus on criminal cases, civil cases (disputes between parties), and other specialized aspects of the law. In other words, the law actually means different things, and involves a range of people and organizations.

All of them are relevant to animal protection in some way. Four groups are particularly pertinent. First, there are the democratically elected representatives who create and debate legislation that affects animals' lives and those of the people who defend animals. Then there are the animal protection organizations trying to shape lawmaking. Third are the animal legal organizations and staff therein who file suits, appeal, intervene, and otherwise advocate for animals in criminal and civil cases. And finally, there are those within the criminal justice system who investigate suspected crimes and prosecute the offenders (insert *Law and Order* drum sound here). Laws are not some abstract, external, neutral, natural, or unchanging entity. They are social, ethical, and political creations, and depend on people to not only enforce them but also come up with them in the first place, interpret and apply them, change or replace them, and fund each of these spheres of work.

Elected representatives are introducing new laws or amendments to existing legislation all the time. It is impossible to keep up with the developments in this arena of work, and that is a good problem. Examples of specifics are integrated throughout this book. Laws are being passed to ban particular practices, reconceptualize animals, establish higher standards in workplaces where animals are present, and enshrine new protections. These changes usually result from the efforts of animal protection organizations, many of which have concerted government relations strategies and regularly work with individual politicians across parties. When regressive legal changes seek to reduce or eliminate protections for animals, this kind of political work is crucial too.

Aguirre was among the dozen veterinarians working alongside forty assistants in Colombia's largest public animal protection and welfare program, which has a shelter housing close to a thousand animals. "The work consisted of checking on your patients first thing in the morning, scheduling surgeries, making euthanasia decisions, and receiving more animal victims at a rate of about twenty cats and dogs per day. There I was a young veterinary doctor with a passion for emergency and critical care. After three years in this program, I had a change of consciousness," he shares. "Vulnerable animals were treated only as 'patients' when they were also or really victims."

This is an interesting insight. In some country's laws, including in other parts of Latin America, animals' health is protected, but not their welfare or well-being. In Colombia, however, the "law now recognizes that chordate and vertebrate animals share with humans the way they perceive external and internal sensations, and that therefore there must be a joint duty between the state and its inhabitants to protect animals against the pain and suffering by commiseration and empathy. This gives them the characteristic of sentient beings and also subjects of special protection by the state," Aguirre explains. In other words, not only legal sentience on paper, but accompanying investment.

Colombia is many things, including the second most biodiverse country in the world. Its landscapes, including tropical forests, mountains, and rich grasslands, are home to a remarkable range of wild animal species, especially birds. The national law applies to all kinds of animals, whatever the physical environment in which they are found or live, and the phylum *Chordata* even includes some slinky sea creatures like lancelets and salps. The country is composed of thirty-two departments (which are like states or provinces), and protection efforts vary depending on the specific area and city in question, but national regulations set the standard, including "approximately fifty situations in which animals can be victims of abuse or animal cruelty." The country's domestic animal protection policy says, "All lives (human or not) are sacred and must be protected. It is not about prioritizing one over the other, but about making efforts for the well-being of all."[4]

Aguirre felt the animals he was working with at the clinic were being made "more vulnerable to episodes of institutional revictimization and even to traumatic adoptions with families that did not understand their emotional distress." This launched a change in his ideas and career path. "I began to implement the first versions of a forensic clinic for evaluation of homeless animals who were victims of abuse and cruelty." Aguirre credits Merck as helping him to deepen his knowledge and understand what education was needed to become a specialist. He formed a veterinary forensics unit involving more than two dozen people that has been contracted by governments to undertake investigations and provides services for people directly. "Our veterinary forensic unit attends free of charge to 35 percent of animal victims who come from families that do not have economic resources to finance the investigation process. We recognize that we must bring science closer to justice, and for now in our context, the best strategy is to finance the team's work through additional activities such as offering continuing education, consultancies to cities, etc." In other words, generate revenue from those sources with money and provide services without cost to those in need without the financial means. Cases run the gamut and have included sadistic violence against animals. Aguirre's team works diligently to understand and document what has been done to animals of all kinds.

In 2016, Aguirre launched the Colombian Association of Legal Veterinary Medicine and Forensic Sciences with about thirty associates—the first of its kind in the country. Two years later, he founded the first veterinary forensic unit with Remington University in Medellín. The unit has worked on nearly six thousand cases in South America since, and in 2020, Aguirre was appointed dean of the faculty.

It is not only veterinarians but also political leaders, animal organizations, and members of the public who have been pushing for protective infrastructure in Colombia. The national law, first written in 1989 and then amended in subsequent years, allows for "many additional regulations that prohibit the fighting of animals as a show, the use of animals in circuses, and the hunting of wildlife and its commercialization; regulate the use of animals in research; and raise animal abuse to the category of crime including custodial sentences. A number of additional determinations give meaning to our political constitution as a tool that protects biodiversity and seeks the welfare of animals and citizens," Aguirre says.

When people want to report suspected cruelty that is not considered life-threatening, Aguirre explains that they contact "the urban police inspection office that is in charge of receiving the complaint, verifying the situation, and taking action when necessary. In some larger municipalities, there are immediate reaction units that work exclusively to deal with these complaints with air-conditioned vehicles and trained personnel to comply with the national indication to deal with reported cases within a maximum period of twenty-four hours."

When a wild or domesticated animal has died or is in severe danger, a specialized team becomes engaged. In 2019, the attorney general created the Grupo Especial Contra el Maltrato Animal, or Special Group for the Fight against Animal Abuse, consisting of 138 prosecutors, 38 investigators from the technical investigation corps, 44 agents of the national police, and 16 canine teams focused on wildlife trafficking. The country's 123 emergency line and 122 complaint line can be used.

An entire unit of the national police, the Policia Ambiental (nature police), with hundreds of officers, is responsible for the enforcement of ecological laws. Wildlife policing units are increasingly common across Latin America, as countries strengthen their legislative protections for animals of all kinds, or create new laws and provide funding for enforcement. In Colombia, specific environmental taxes are collected and help fund wildlife assessment and care facilities, because wild animals are in danger from not only trafficking and other kinds of human cruelty but also vehicles.

Many of the eleven hundred municipalities are investing in prevention and one health programs, including rabies weeks during which free vaccinations are administered. Free surgical sterilization of animals is often made available as well. Aguirre notes, "We have recognized that there are other health services that should not be provided free of charge because of the false sense of comfort that this offers irresponsible landlords or criminals. And it is true that public money is not infinite, and more so in a country with high levels of corruption. For a decade, we have emphasized education and the strengthening of the capacity of the communities to deal with risk situations with their own infrastructure and workforce."

There are, adds Aguirre, "local programs that have high operating budgets for the comprehensive care of domestic fauna [animals] in risk situations. For many years, we have confirmed that if a city allows itself to permanently protect animals, its citizens feel safer and more at peace. There are policies that seek to guarantee sufficient economic resources and infrastructure."

Colombia's animal protection landscape, including its legal dimensions, public investment, and frontline services, offer significant food for thought and fodder for further examination, and challenge many ideas about what is possible when animals and people are understood as connected.

Lesson #8: valuable knowledge should be shared–and exchanged–within and across borders.

Courtrooms have become busier with animal-related cases of many kinds over the last decade. Within the criminal justice system, even in the United States, the country with both the highest total number of prisoners and largest proportion of its citizens incarcerated (as of 2021), courtrooms are not as busy with animal cases as you might expect. Specialists in animal law are divided over whether this is a good thing or not. Some argue that incarceration does not help animals, has minimal deterrent effect, and disproportionately punishes Black people, Indigenous peoples, and people of color, with certain critics joining with others to call for an end to prisons altogether. Others want animal abusers to know that crimes against animals will be taken seriously and prosecuted, and hurting an animal can result in not only fines, community service, or prohibitions on owning animals but also lengthy jail time. Many animal defenders fit somewhere in between.

The rage many people feel when animals have been abused is potent and undeniable. The desire for punishment can be powerful. But legal decisions, including those that will fundamentally influence people's futures such as by affecting their employment prospects and removing their right to vote (as is done in Armenia, Chile, many parts of the United States, and Belgium in certain circumstances), should be based on facts and carefully considered.

"I certainly don't think animal cruelty should be decriminalized, and I do want people to be held to account for suffering they cause to animals," says Camille Labchuk, executive director of the Canadian animal law organization Animal Justice. "One of my biggest concerns with the penal system is its current emphasis on harsh punishments, which have been shown by a large body of research to be ineffective in reducing offending and addressing harm caused. There is no reason to think this would be different in the context of animal cruelty offenses."

Labchuk does not see the criminal process as irrelevant but rather in need of changes. "Part of this concern can be mitigated by crafting sentences in a way that is not designed simply to punish harshly for the sake of retribution but that incorporates evidence-based principles that can help reduce future animal suffering, such as counseling and sensitivity training, restitution (keeping in mind a person's means), and prohibition orders designed to keep people away from animals." But prosecutions should be understood as one part of longer and larger racialized and classed patterns, she argues.

> I recognize and fear the structural inequities that are built into every stage of the penal system, from initial biases in police investigations and charging decisions, onerous bail/release conditions, the devastating impact of a criminal conviction on job prospects, travel, and more, and perhaps most strikingly, the inability of most people to afford legal counsel and the shortage of publicly funded defense lawyers. I do have concerns that there is an overreliance on the penal system, coupled with relatively few government resources devoted to proactively preventing animals from suffering.

Building the capacity of prosecutors and other criminal justice actors to thoroughly understand animal cruelty cases, including their link to the future or concurrent abuse of people, and what legal responses are available, is a priority for many defenders of animals. This has resulted in a range of pathways, including the creation and expansion of educational opportunities for lawyers. In 2011, the National District Attorneys Association joined with the ASPCA and ALDF to create the National Center for Prosecution of Animal Abuse to educate and train prosecutors. In 2019, the ALDF launched a partnership with the National Council of Juvenile and Family Court Judges to bolster judges' knowledge for cases related to animal cruelty. The National Link Coalition and members of local coalitions also regularly offer and deliver training. In Canada, the National Centre for the Prosecution of Animal Abuse, an initiative of Humane Canada, provides resources and offers training as well. Similar initiatives are being pursued around the world.

Around a dozen US states have created dedicated prosecutors or prosecutorial units focused on animal crimes, in both red and blue states. Animal files are not normally their only area of concentration, but these attorneys have deepened their expertise and will take on most, if not all, of the cases with animal victims. Within the United States and beyond, individual prosecutors have also chosen to learn more about crimes against animals, either by attending formal training or through their own digging and persistence.

Another example of a nonprofit organization investing in or subsidizing the public sector is the range of legal assistance the ALDF provides free of charge. The organization has expanded its services, including the delivery of a suite of trainings for lawyers, judges, frontline law enforcers, and veterinarians along with funding for expert witness testimony, legal research, and grants to help cover the cost of animal housing and care in criminal trials. In 2016, the ALDF officially launched another approach, funding a dedicated resource prosecutor for the state of Oregon who is available to assist with or prosecute cases for any of the state's thirty-six district attorneys. Of his new position, Jake Kamins said, "Animal cruelty cases are technically and factually complex. Every animal is different, and I am often dealing with dozens or even hundreds of victims. District attorneys throughout Oregon are facing substantial budget challenges. Focusing one prosecutor's resources entirely on the issues of animal neglect and abuse ensures that these defendants are held fully accountable."

The United States is atypical because many district attorneys are directly elected by voters. Ministers or secretaries of justice are commonly appointed by parliaments or the top elected leader (the president, prime minister, premier, etc.) from among those who were elected, but the lead, practicing prosecutorial role is widely seen as one that should not be tied to public opinion and politicized but rather rooted in legal qualifications. US district attorneys and those aspiring to be in that role are increasingly pledging to get tough on animal abusers, or highlighting their records when it comes to prosecutions, convictions, and the resulting punishments.

This kind of "tough-on-crime" approach is most often why animal abuse registries are created at the local and state levels (although these are not unique to the United States). Like sex offender registries, the intent is clear: identify those convicted of offenses to help people protect themselves and those they love. The registries could be used as part of assessing potential purchasers or adopters of animals, and this was the intent in Greece. In 2021, as part of a package of new animal-focused laws, the country established a database of people who have been sentenced for torturing animals. Managed by the Athens prosecutor's office, individuals seeking to register as pet owners are first cross-referenced to check for prior convictions. This approach differs from posting photos, names, and other details online as is done in a number of US regions.

Registries could also be used by vigilantes, unsatisfied with how the legal system handled specific cases or how animal abuse is handled overall. This is one of the reasons the ASPCA has established its opposition to animal abuse registries. It also notes the expense of creating and maintaining them, and the potential for more plea deals and lesser charges to result as perpetrators seek to avoid being placed on the registry (that is, pleading guilty, but to a lower-severity charge). The ASPCA argues that "well-enforced no-contact orders, mandated psychological assessment and inclusion of pets in orders of protection, provide a response that is more effective in preventing harm to animals and people."[5]

In contrast, the National Humane Education Society promotes the establishment of animal abuse registries, identifying states with legislation pending that would create new registries and encouraging animal lovers to contact their legislators. PETA has also issued statements in support of registries.

As a result of an animal cruelty charge or conviction, people can be issued fines ranging in size and/or be required to cover the costs accrued by others, including the humane society, shelter, or other organization that housed the animals as well as provided or paid for veterinary care. There may be probation or a suspended sentence. Offenders may be sentenced to community service, or imprisoned for weeks, months, or occasionally years. There can be mandatory counseling or treatment. No-contact orders and orders of protection can include animals, and people can be prohibited from owning or residing with animals for a set period of time. As is the case with all criminal proceedings, legal responses and penalties are affected by a host of factors.

I am not an expert in penology (the study of criminal justice punishment and prison management), and the data vary among countries. It is clear, however, that prison sentences are often more heavily applied to people of color. And the core question about whether "prison works" seems to have different answers depending on how you define "works." It does seem reasonable that dangerous people not be permitted to walk around freely, able to hurt and terrorize others. In my own experience, I have seen people fail to change their behavior due to lesser penalties, but a short jail sentence served as the catalyst for dramatic personal change. Yet I have also seen people engage in criminal behaviors that if convicted, could result in serious penalties, and those potential punishments did not give them pause.

Animal-loving people often have a strong eye-for-an-eye philosophy about animal abusers, to put it mildly. Sound public policy and serious legal decisions with lasting consequences should not be based on our gut reactions or anecdotes, though. They need to be grounded in evidence and robust data. The rage felt when someone abuses an animal is real and visceral. It is a powerful impulse, and one I not only acknowledge but also feel directly. Hurting the innocent is abhorrent. So it's easy to want to grasp onto and push for simple solutions, without really digging into whether the status quo is effective.

Why people harm animals is a crucial matter to consider. Criminologist Dr. Angus Nurse has studied types of animal offenders at length and found that people hurt animals for different reasons. Particularly for men who participate in criminal behaviors and networks as a source of power and status, Nurse argues that the risk of prison may have minimal deterrent effect. Instead, it may be seen as "an occupational hazard as well as reinforcing their male identity and confirmation of society's lack of understanding of their needs."[6] Penology experts point out that prison is not especially good at preventing recidivism (the recommitting of crimes), and it can trap people into a cycle of poverty by significantly constraining their postsentence rights. It can also increase the chances of them hardening and reoffending due to being exposed to more violent criminals and criminal networks inside prison walls. In other words, incarceration can stop criminal behavior in its tracks or add fuel.

"You get all kinds of offenses for all kinds of motives, and often there are overlapping issues of past abuse, substance abuse, many factors that enter into it," notes Dr. Randall Lockwood. "So even if it's very similar crimes—say two sixteen-year-olds who set fire to a cat—they might be coming in from very different doorways. One might be coming from substance abuse, while another may have been sexually assaulted by his uncle."

How to recognize the causes of behavior, including acts deemed illegal, and then how to appropriately respond are fundamental challenges within and beyond the legal system. When people who are victimized become victimizers, what is an ethical and appropriate way to respond? These are deeply important and challenging questions.

The dearth of reliable and comprehensive data about animal cruelty compounds the problem. There is a shortage of data on how often animal cruelty offenders reoffend, the impacts of different sentencing routes (incarceration versus treatment, for example), and whether prohibitions on the ownership of and contact with animals prevent future crimes, among other crucial dimensions.

Justin Marceau, a professor and director of animal law at the University of Denver, has raised questions about the prevalence of and reliance on tough-on-crime responses, particularly given the lack of evidence of their effectiveness.[7] He questions the taken-for-granted place prosecutions and prisons play in some animal protection spheres, and in turn, how little investment has been allotted for investigating and implementing alternatives.

When I read figures showing that animal neglect is on the rise in many communities and the response is to say we need more police and prosecution of neglect, I am left wondering how much better we could do by the animals and the people if we invested more in programs like Pets for Life. . . . This is not to suggest some sort of magic or silver bullet approach, but the focus on law and order as a vehicle for curing animal harm is, at the very least, underrepresentative of the realm of options.

Neglect is an umbrella under which both serious and more modest things take place, and animals do die from neglect. I have not observed a widespread push for the prosecution of minor neglect, especially when it's obvious that the person is barely keeping their head above water. Depending on whether it's police or animal services or a nonprofit investigator who finds it, neglect might or might not actually register on their radars. But a desire to prosecute even more minor issues, including when it's clear the people are suffering too, does appear in certain areas, particularly those regions in the United States that employ zero tolerance and extra-tough-on-crime approaches. Few animal cruelty cases end up being tried everywhere in the world, and when they do, a comprehensive picture of what results is among the data we lack. Based on the rulings and sentences data I have been able to find and piece together, I suspect it would be prudent to say "certain" animal cruelty charges result in jail or prison, but not "many," and rarely those for neglect. Most animal defenders I've observed who argue for higher prison sentences do so specifically for cases of violent animal cruelty and serious or fatal neglect.

Yet it is undoubtedly true that alternatives to incarceration are not well researched, nor are they widely implemented. Some Indigenous communities stand out as exceptions and have developed community-led and community-based programs rooted in restorative justice. The Centre for Justice & Reconciliation explains that restorative justice has four essential components: inclusion of all parties, encountering the other side, making amends for the harm, and reintegration of the parties into their communities. Admittedly, I balk at the thought of victims and survivors of abuse, especially women and children, being asked to encounter the abuser and consider their side. Some may value the opportunity, but many survivors never want to see the abuser again and live in constant fear that they will—in a grocery store or park, or on their doorstep. The premise of restorative justice challenges my thinking about interpersonal abuse, but this area and related strategies are nevertheless worthy of greater study and attention. Restorative justice would not need to be a one-size-fits-all model applied to every case and type of crimes either. It may or may not be suitable for interpersonal abuse.

A growing number of animal defenders are striving to move beyond simplistic analysis and proposals on either side of this debate. I might even say many animal defenders are not simply calling for more imprisonment at this point. Seeking to repair the harm caused by crime rather than simply punish, especially if the punishment may or may not prevent future harm, is somehow both challenging and compelling. It is easy to translate anger into a desire for vengeance, particularly when people have hurt animals—very easy and understandable. I feel it and grapple with it a lot. I want people who hurt animals to be punished, to face consequences. But I have been challenged to reflect on whether punishment is enough unto itself.

"I think we're really just beginning to look at alternatives to incarceration," says Lockwood, reflecting on this question and what he has seen over his decades-long career in animal protection. "Part of the problem is that anything else that actually addresses the many needs of people who get in trouble is costly and time-consuming." Prisons are also expensive. Perhaps societies need to accept that creating safe communities is going to cost money and are investments worth making, and then choose the pathways that are most likely to benefit people and animals.

"What I've seen, now having been looking at this for twenty or thirty years, is that the pendulum keeps swinging between the social service approach and the punitive approach," Lockwood observes.

And hopefully it will swing back again. The reality is that the best things to prevent harm and violence are supportive parents, providing developmental resources to kids, good mentorship, things like that. The things that don't work are just putting people away. And yet we are still in the midst of this focus on retribution and incarceration partly because it's big business, it's private business that controls a lot of the prisons [in the United States].

That approach speaks to basic human need for revenge or retribution, but it's not data based. And what works is the social service–type stuff that is time-consuming and lifelong. Maybe the pendulum will swing back.

More than thirty US states either recommend or require judges to include treatment and counseling programs as part of animal cruelty sentences. A small number of programs exist, including the AniCare Approach, an initiative of the Animals & Society Institute developed by Dr. Kenneth Shapiro, Dr. Mary Lou Randour, and Dr. Brian Jory, combining "cognitive behavioral, psychodynamic, attachment, and trauma-based theories" into a model for practice. Shapiro and Dr. Kimberly Spanjol have more recently created BARK (short for behavior, accountability, responsibility, and knowledge), a group-based diversion program for adults who have abused animals that builds from the AniCare Approach. They are piloting and evaluating its impact, and once refined based on the feedback and evaluation, hope to expand its usage across the United States.

These issues are inextricable from larger social patterns, including those connected to gender, especially masculinities. Lockwood points to some of them:

> Under California law, if you're convicted of animal cruelty, it's mandated that you go through psychological assessment and treatment, and I had an inquiry about what kind of treatment is appropriate for a dogfighter. I said, they're not mentally ill. They're criminals. They're assholes. That's the shortcoming of blanket law. Likewise, we are still battling a reality involving men that some don't realize. So if someone is cruel to a woman's companion animal and they get convicted, they might get sent to anger management. But it's not an anger issue; it's a power and control issue, and that is not the appropriate therapeutic intervention.

Lockwood has also been documenting the behavior of some animal hoarders for more than two decades as they move across state lines and enlist aliases to try to avoid prohibition orders. Hoarding has a complicated underlying psychology and is difficult to address.[8]

Because of her work on many criminal cases and the bridge-building roles she plays, Smith-Blackmore has seen many facets of this important debate. "There are passionately outraged animal activists and animal lovers who want to put the perpetrators in jail and throw away the key. But if you're caring and loving, then some of that caring and understanding has to spill over to the perpetrator." It's a tough yet important dimension to consider. Smith-Blackmore still sees prisons and the risk of a prison sentence as playing a range of roles in animal law enforcement, as being "one of the tools in the tool bag." In other words, not as the only or even primary option, but as one of a number of potential outcomes based on the specifics of the situation and context. Having a real range of responses to convictions and evidence-backed options seems particularly important.

As one example, she highlights a case involving a dog named Coco. A woman brought Coco's body to a veterinarian for cremation. "The veterinarian reported it, and that opened an investigation. The dog ended up coming to me; I was able to tell her story." Smith-Blackmore determined that the dog had been beaten to death.

The case involved a young man—the son of the woman who had brought Coco's body for cremation. He had already gotten into trouble with firearms-related offenses and been mandated to get psychotherapy as a result. "After one of his appointments, his mother asked the psychotherapist, in front of her son, if she should be afraid of him. And the psychotherapist said, "Well, it's not like he's killed the family dog or anything," Smith-Blackmore explains. Later that day, the son insisted on staying at home when his mother ran errands. While she was gone, he killed Coco.

Smith-Blackmore continues:

He very clearly wanted people to be afraid of him and to know that he wanted them to be afraid of him. It was like a recipe book. Somebody gave him the recipe, and he said, okay, then. If this is what I have to do to prove to you that you should be afraid of me, I'm going to do it. When we have people inflicting violent harm on animals so we know they are dangerous, we should listen to them.

Ultimately the young man was sentenced to "five years of mandated residential psychological hospitalization because he's that sick, he's that violent, and he's that dangerous." This sentence resulted from a plea deal. "I'm certain that if seven years of being in jail wasn't on the table as a possible outcome, he wouldn't have accepted the hospitalization as treatment. You can't abandon the carceral response when it helps to influence people into having to accept help," Smith-Blackmore argues. The sadists, sociopaths, and psychopaths, the perpetrators of organized crime—some of them hurt and kill animals, so cannot be ignored.

The animal law field of practice is expanding. There are animal lawyers who defend people whose dogs have been deemed "dangerous" and sentenced to death. The place of animals in divorce proceedings is an increasingly hot topic, including how custody decisions can integrate animals' best interests. Related to the criminal realm, the inclusion of animals in protection orders, particularly in cases of domestic and family violence, is becoming more common.

In 2019, a dog named Campeon in Costa Rica garnered attention when he was brought into the courtroom during the trial of his former abuser (who was eventually acquitted). More substantive and concerted efforts by animal lawyers are working to have both the law and its interpreters, like judges, view animals as victims whose interests need to be thoroughly considered. A federal judge appointed Rebecca Huss of Valparaiso University School of Law as a guardian/special master in the Vick case. The ALDF states that

> Huss was tasked with making independent recommendations to the court for the disposition of each seized dog after considering their well-being.
>
> While many dog fighting rings had been prosecuted prior to 2007, this was the first prosecution where an attorney was appointed by the court to advocate for the animal victims. Her appointment made a critical difference—not only were the lives of individual dogs saved, it fundamentally shifted the default for victims of dog fighting from euthanasia to rehabilitation.[9]

Advocating for animals can be and is done in different ways at trials depending on the jurisdiction and its legal system, including as part of sentencing. The organization Animal Justice obtained intervenor status in the appeal of a dog abuse case in Edmonton, Canada, at the province's superior court, for example. In Connecticut, another strategy was inspired by the fundamental question of animal representation, awareness of the human-animal violence link, and brutal killing of a dog named Desmond who had been severely beaten and starved. Jessica Rubin, director of the University of Connecticut Law School's Legal Practice Program and its Animal Law Clinic, notes that there was also evidence that the accused had strangled his ex-girlfriend.[10]

The prosecutor recommended a prison sentence, but the court opted for the Accelerated Rehabilitation Program, a diversion pathway open to certain nonviolent offenders and/or those who are considered unlikely to offend. The conditions may include doing community service, paying restitution, taking part in a hate crimes diversion program, getting psychiatric or psychological counseling, and/or getting alcohol and/or drug treatment. After two years of the program, the accused's record is expunged of the charge, meaning there is no legal trace of it. Not surprisingly, there was significant public outrage that this was the result for the person who had killed Desmond so violently.

A report by the Connecticut Office of Legislative Research found that there were 3,723 offenses under the state's animal cruelty statute between 2006 and 2016. This is the number of charges laid; the number of complaints reported and investigations undertaken would be far higher. Forty-six percent of those charges were not prosecuted, 34 percent were dismissed, 19 percent resulted in guilty verdicts or pleas, and 1 percent ended in findings of not guilty. The report notes that of the 1,267 cases dismissed, 1,012 of them—80 percent—were dismissed after the offender successfully completed a diversionary program such as the Accelerated Rehabilitation Program. Animal defenders are split about whether this is a positive or negative set of findings, for the reasons already outlined.

Rubin was a central engine in the political and legal response, which led to the introduction of legislation by Representative Diana Urban and ultimately the passage of what is known as Desmond's Law. It establishes the right for a courtroom-appointed animal advocate to "represent the interests of justice" in cases involving cats and dogs.[11] Originally, the bill didn't specify that it applied only to these kinds of animals, but it was amended after pressure from agricultural groups in particular. The advocate can provide information to the prosecution, yet is not required to be affiliated with either the prosecution or defense. The advocate's primary responsibility is to the animals. The advocate may be a supervised law student or lawyer volunteering their time who can gather additional research, analyze specifics, present briefs, and otherwise work to represent the animal's interests in the service of justice. A handful of other states have followed suit or are considering similar legislation.

Rubin highlights the value of this approach because animals are not able to describe their victimization. Necropsies are one way animal victims' bodies speak (after death), but courtroom advocates also consider details such as the number of victims and their experiences, length of time they suffered, what the motives were, and whether the act was intentional, among other factors. The appointment of an animal advocate in trials does not automatically lead to any specific outcome. Rubin says that "a just outcome can include many components—a conviction, incarceration, monetary payment, education, counseling, surrender of animals, orders preventing future animal contact or ownership, community service and/or ongoing monitoring."[12] It doesn't mean more or less of any particular response is assured. "The Advocate functions in the trenches of a courtroom, sorting out the realities of cases with victims who are unable to describe offenses. . . . An Advocate's goals are nuanced, varied, and specific to each case."[13] The need for nuance and context-specific analysis is paramount and refreshing. Comprehensive data about the effectiveness of this program are not yet available, but it is an approach worthy of further study.

This is a constellation of serious issues that demands the thoughtful attention of those concerned about the future of people and animals alike—experts not content with either the status quo or utopian visions. We need the mental power of those committed to the hard work of finding real solutions in the real world, with all of its messiness and violence. In addition to critique, we need solutions and alternatives.

The full story of Puppy Doe cannot be properly understood without Smith-Blackmore, who initially expected she would be a companion animal veterinarian. As part of her training, she served at the Massachusetts SPCA and "found that more fulfilling than I ever expected. It was very soothing for me to be able to rehabilitate and help rehome animals." She decided to become a full-time shelter veterinarian. Shelter veterinarians work for and with animals at shelters, not with people's pets.

While serving in that role, SPCA law enforcement officers were increasingly asking Smith-Blackmore for her perspective on injured animals and whether the story they had been told matched up with the animals' injuries. She wanted to ensure her analyses were robust and saw potential to expand not only the science but its role within the legal system too. With foundation funding, she created "a fellowship in forensic pathology, with a veterinary twist," to deepen and strengthen her knowledge, and then founded Forensic Veterinary Investigations LLC. This path ultimately led her to Puppy Doe.

A woman in Quincy, Massachusetts, was waiting for her friend to pick her up for lunch and heard a car so headed for the front door, but the vehicle was pulling away as she stepped outside. Across the street by the edge of a forest she saw something white, which she initially thought was garbage that had been dumped. "She went out to investigate and found that it was a puppy who couldn't walk," Smith-Blackmore explains.

> The woman's friend then arrived, and the two of them carried the dog to the front lawn. They fed her and gave her water, and found her to be eager and friendly. The women called animal control [officers], who responded and said this dog needs emergency care; they thought she was probably the victim of dogfighting. At the emergency hospital, the dog was seen by Dr. Amanda Duffy, who is one of my favorite emergency veterinarians in the world. She said, I can't even begin to list all the injuries this dog has. I don't think she will ever be able to walk again.

Based on the severity of the damage done to this dog's body, it was ultimately decided that euthanasia was the most compassionate option.

"She didn't have a microchip. She didn't have a tattoo. She didn't have a tag. She was just going to be an unknown dog that would go to general cremation," says Smith-Blackmore. "But Dr. Duffy wasn't content with that idea, and she asked if I could do anything. She wanted there to be an investigation. She wanted to get answers."

Puppy Doe's body was brought to Smith-Blackmore, who conducted the necropsy. The exam report was delivered to the prosecutor's office, which then went public with the dog's story to elicit help from members of the public to try to identify who she was—or rather, who she had been. The exam played an essential role in piecing together Puppy Doe's past and eventually finding the man who had tortured her. "I needed to make sure her story was told, clearly, accurately, and with some volume, so there would be a response," Smith-Blackmore says. "There was such tremendous public outrage, and then there was the actual criminal investigation response that was appropriately broad and deep that solved her case. And then there was the legislative response that followed, where people demanded stronger laws to protect animals."

Smith-Blackmore emphasizes the series of people who together carried this dog and her story forward. "It was at the emergency hospital where she was being treated where she was euthanized, where she wagged her tail in her final moments and received love. That was part of her story that came to me. It was important enough for those who carried her body physically to me that they also wanted to carry the essence of who she was as a dog." That somehow, after everything that had been done to her, Puppy Doe still could feel and give love.

It would be a deepening of injustice if individual animals were forgotten in either the broad strokes or the intricacies of human legal debates: All the animals, including Puppy Doe and the dogs like her. The hidden. The abandoned. Those deemed disposable.

"It was a chain of caring that brought Puppy Doe into the light," Smith-Blackmore says.

Because the women who first saw her cared enough, they wrapped her in their love. She was surrounded by that when she was carried to the emergency hospital. Then she was wrapped in love in the emergency hospital. And then even after she passed away, I think it helped to propel the science and the criminal justice response to what had happened to her. It was because everybody who had contact with her, everyone who was at a point of influence in the case, cared about her and cared for her.

Rather than simply being an unknown animal victim at the end of a dead-end street and then a pile of ashes, Puppy Doe inspired so many, and a circle of care formed around her. "I had the intellectual knowledge that people can be sadistic and torture or harm animals intentionally for their own reasons of depravity. But I had never before witnessed it like I did with Puppy Doe. It's almost as though . . . ," Smith-Blackmore pauses to consider her words and feelings, "she made an indelible mark on my soul. It was the etching of animal pain that became part of my more spiritual reason for doing the work I do. I think maybe she became a conduit to other animal souls."

Puppy Doe is gone, but her impact lives on.

7 · CONSERVING WHAT AND WHO WE LOVE

In 2018, the image of armed conservation officers standing guard around Sudan, the last remaining male northern white rhino on the planet, sent shock waves around the world. Likewise, the footage of a lone orangutan trying to push back a bulldozer recorded by International Animal Rescue is utterly devastatingly. There are countless wild individuals and species, and how people close by and far away feel about them varies. How people feel about animals affects whether and how they are protected.

Wherever we are, wild animals live around us (or maybe we live around them). This creates protection challenges and opportunities. Close proximity can involve human-wildlife tensions, as wild animals try to survive around our infrastructure. Our buildings, roads, mines, farms, and other infrastructure have led to steep declines in animals' habitat, caused entire species to vanish, and put thousands of others at risk of extinction. More animals will disappear off the planet if things don't change—specifically, if we don't make changes.

Work focused on wild animals often operates at the species and/or ecosystem level. It's normally about saving larger numbers and areas for them to live in with minimal human interaction. As a result, sometimes individual animals or groups are sacrificed or considered necessary casualties, such as when groups of animals are culled or private hunting is allowed. In some contexts, however, both the larger group and individual members thereof are the focus of protection efforts.

Conservation is widely recognized as a practical science, but also as fundamentally about legal protections, politics, economics, and organizational work, both with the animals and far away from them. How exactly organizations acknowledge or integrate those different areas varies. Conservation organizations come in all shapes and sizes. Some are global powerhouses with robust fundraising departments and prominent spokespeople. Others are smaller, targeted, scrappy organizations. The people involved may view this work as different from the world of "animal protection," which tends to revolve around domesticated and companion animals, or they may see distinctness as well as connections.

I see the latter. Conservation is a key route people use to defend wild animals from harm. Sometimes the same animal protection organizations even have programs and campaigns focused on domesticated animals close to home and wild animals around the world. Plus a number of parallel themes emerge when examining what people do to help the wild and tame. These include how poor people are differently affected or involved in various strategies, the risks of the frontline work, and the potential for not only protecting other species but simultaneously promoting the well-being of our own.

Along with the growth of conservation science, which centered on building a comprehensive understanding of animal species including their diets, behaviors, and engagements with their environments, the creation of large, protected areas of land, either private preserves or public parks, was a primary protective strategy used for well over a hundred years and especially in the mid- to late twentieth century.[1] The rationale is clear: since wild animals need their habitats to survive, and their habitats are in danger, you help animals by protecting those habitats. Particularly beautiful and/or humanlike wild animals who garner great interest and sympathy from members of the public, such as elephants and great apes, are often referred to as "charismatic megafauna." When you protect their habitat, you protect many other smaller species therein, especially those less likely to elicit human attention—or attract the donor dollars that make so much conservation work possible.

Yet the strategy was also criticized for excluding and damaging local people, including Indigenous peoples who had long lived among and subsisted off plants and animals, but who were not the reason for species becoming endangered. This tension was particularly salient when the conservation organizations were from the wealthy Global North. As the economic pressures on countries in the Global South—home to many animal species—deepened, local people who had engaged in small-scale hunting and farming or waged work were pushed further into poverty, and had fewer opportunities to subsist or earn a basic income. Consuming what had traditionally been a miniscule proportion of a species changed, as the total number of those animals plummeted, upping the significance of each life lost.

Along with protected areas, governments began creating laws to protect native endangered animals. This meant certain kinds of subsistence hunting became crimes. As local and international markets for keeping wild animals as pets or using their body parts expanded, international agreements and restrictions were also put into place, like the Convention on Trade in Endangered Species of Wild Flora and Fauna. Some animals can legally be removed from their natural habitats and shipped around the world for sale, but a busy black market continued too—and continues—and there can be overlap between the legal and illegal wildlife trade. People with few economic opportunities will poach protected animals so as to eat them, market them locally, or sell them to international networks, including some involving organized crime.

In other words, the taking and killing of endangered animals, or their movement across national borders while still alive, involves local poor people, local rich people coordinating poaching rings, and transnational networks. Dr. Vanda Felbab-Brown, director of the Initiative on Nonstate Armed Actors, codirector of the Africa Security Initiative, and a senior fellow at the Brookings Institution, has studied wildlife trade and trafficking extensively. She explains that the people and networks involved in collecting and then moving animals or their body parts across international borders are varied in structure, with many concentrating entirely on animals or animal products, and some on particular kinds of animals. Certain crime syndicates that traffic in narcotics and/or weapons have also expanded to animals. These networks vary in size, ranging from a few people to hundreds, and Felbab-Brown notes that it is much easier to smuggle things that are dead in comparison to animals who are alive.

Smugglers expect to lose many animals in transport if moving live individuals and so take even more of them from the wild. "If the goal is to sell ten rare parrots in China, often one hundred birds or more will be taken because smugglers know many will die. It can be upward of 90 percent," Felbab-Brown explains. "Smugglers build in those losses, sometimes enormous losses. Traffickers can be very indifferent to animal deaths, and see them as a cost of doing business." Some parrot traffickers stuff the birds into plastic bottles and then toss them out to sea in order to reclaim the bottles from the less monitored ocean. Not surprisingly, many birds die when this is done.

Images of interceptions and the resulting seizures of pounds of ivory, rhino horns, or pangolin scales often make the media, but "are the least effective enforcement strategy and can actually be counterproductive," Felbab-Brown says. "You might have seized the ivory, but those elephants are still dead." Instead, she underscores the need to focus on the front and back ends of the trafficking network: the enforcement and prevention of animals being taken from their habitats, and the retail markets around the world, ranging from China to the United States. "It's far more effective to try to prevent the taking of animals in the first place. But effective enforcement also needs to dismantle the network. That can mean not seizing the animals or animal parts, but rather following the chain."[2] In other words, working both upstream and further downstream.

There is some debate among conservation researchers about the unintended effects of declaring particular species endangered or highly at risk. When animals are known to be rare, it can heighten their worth on the black market; their very vulnerability increases their monetary value. When protecting specific areas, it's almost as if a neon sign is erected proclaiming "high-value animals here." Yet it hardly seems prudent not to identify the species in need of extra protective attention, so the enforcement of local, national, and international protections is crucial where the animals live.

Conservation players also differ in their views of the legal wildlife trade. Some see it as an essential income-generating source for local people that prevents more animals from being taken, and work to facilitate commitments from corporate purchasers to buy and at times pay more for products provided by Indigenous hunters (the logic of the latter is to reduce the overall number of animals killed). For example, based on efforts by the Wildlife Conservation Society to help strengthen an Indigenous group's territorial rights, Gucci ended up agreeing to pay more for caiman skins (an alligatorid) from the Tacana in Bolivia.

Other conservationists highlight overlaps between legal and illegal trades, and emphasize that the legal trade is still damaging to animals. When poaching methods involve practices like killing the mothers and taking the babies, whose cuteness generates more in "pet"-buying markets, this is particularly upsetting. There are also health risks to humans when circulating, handling, keeping, and consuming animals who may possess pathogens that do not harm them but instead are dangerous or fatal for people.

Because those exacerbating the risks to some endangered species in their home habitats are a combination of low-income local people with few job prospects and wealthier criminals, multiple strategies are needed. Major global organizations like World Animal Protection, the International Fund for Animal Welfare, the Wildlife Conservation Society, the World Wildlife Fund in North America and World Wide Fund for Nature internationally, and TRAFFIC (originally an initiative of the World Wildlife Fund and International Union for the Conservation of Nature, but now a distinct organization) are actively partnering with local and national agencies in countries from which wild animals are taken to try to prevent trafficking through education, particularly by inspiring and supporting future generations of conservationists and citizens committed to protecting their animal neighbors. Law enforcement partnerships of many kinds also exist, and this frontline defensive work is undoubtedly essential.

Countries and organizations have tried both similar and distinct responses when local people violate the law and endanger animals, especially those being suffocated by poverty. Some have focused on enforcement, and sought to charge and prosecute these crimes and their perpetrators. Others have recognized that poverty drastically constrains people's options and that the need for a basic livelihood is real and often what is motivating people to kill, take, or otherwise harm others, and have therefore prioritized the creation of income-generating alternatives to poaching and trafficking. Frequently a combination of strategies is used.

In every country, there are always poor people who do not choose animal harm as their route to attempt to survive or climb up the economic ladder ever so slightly. This is important to recognize, and it is not about painting any economic group with a single brush. But it is crucial to understand behavior in context, and see what else is going on that limits and directs people toward particular pathways. The strategies that see local people, specifically in situations of widespread and extreme poverty (earning less than two dollars per day), not as enemies, but as allies, as current or future nature guardians and conservation leaders, as having their own right to a decent life, and as having valuable skills and knowledge—those are compelling paths that warrant significant attention. People not Poaching, a joint initiative of the International Union for the Conservation of Nature and the International Institute for Environment and Development, has compiled more than a hundred case studies of community-based approaches to the illegal wildlife trade.

Outsiders from rich countries can play a role, particularly in generating desperately needed funds, but should do so with respect, and serve as partners and facilitators. Mostly white people walking in and trying to tell local people and governments what to do replicates the longer damaging history of colonialism and hardly fosters goodwill or presents a recipe for successful conservation. Telling people who are in poverty because they lost their traditional livelihood patterns, governments and companies from already-wealthier parts of the world extracted valuable resources, and international financial institutions imposed debilitating conditions on their nations that you care only about the animals in danger—not people's suffering—is wrong on every level. The damage third world debt does to endangered species is salient as well, and liberating low-income countries from the demands of international financial institutions or at least reducing the size of the required payments would help people and animals. Earlier global campaigns like Jubilee 2000 pushed for such changes, and while this emphasis is less common today, the foundational issue has not vanished.

On the ground, important conservation strategies involve creating humane jobs—alternative options for people to earn a living not by harming animals but rather by helping them. These include law enforcement jobs defending animals and their habitats, feeding two birds with one fruit, as it were. In such instances, not only are people gaining employment but their jobs also directly benefit endangered animals. Who is hired into these roles varies, and can include former poachers or hunters who use their knowledge of the landscape in the service of animals while providing them with a non-lethal income-earning alternative. Moreover, hiring can focus on groups in particular need to try to enhance equity in a community.

In other cases, humane jobs created may not be directly working with the animals but instead by providing alternative income sources that do no harm, thereby minimizing the risks to endangered animals and their habitats. So I would not suggest that livelihood-centered conservation strategies and sensible law enforcement be seen as entirely mutually exclusive. Together, both give the animals and local communities a stronger chance of coexisting sustainably. Indeed, many animal defenders in the world of gorilla conservation share this view.

When I was a student, Dr. Jane Goodall, Dr. Dian Fossey, and Dr. Biruté Galdikas, the "trimates" as they are sometimes called, really captured my interest as I was first learning about the lives of animals and work people do to protect them.[3] They undertook groundbreaking and controversial projects with chimpanzees, mountain gorillas, and orangutans, respectively, and helped generate global attention for the plight of these apes, all of whom are at risk due to habitat loss from forestry and encroaching agriculture (major palm oil plantations in the case of the orangutans), war, poaching, and mining. Two of the three, Goodall and Galdikas, continue to be active. Fossey was killed in 1985, giving her life trying to defend animals.

I devoured Farley Mowat's biography of Fossey, *Virunga* (I own two copies), and Fossey's own *Gorillas in the Mist*. Both books provide a fascinating journey into an extraordinary and complicated place where local people live alongside these magnificent and often misunderstood gentle giants, the gorillas, who live in family groups and spend most of their time filling their bellies with leaves, fruit, bark, wild celery, and ideally, bamboo shoots.

In fact, there are four subspecies of gorillas: western lowland gorillas, eastern lowland or Grauer's gorillas, the more recently recognized cross river gorillas, and those Fossey focused on, the mountain gorillas. All wild gorillas live in and across different countries in Central Africa, and the especially furry mountain gorillas are concentrated entirely in the high-altitude regions of the Bwindi Impenetrable National Park in Uganda, Volcanoes National Park in Rwanda, and Virunga National Park in the Democratic Republic of the Congo (DRC). Essentially, the mountain gorillas live in and among the Virunga volcanoes, the eponymous title of Mowat's book, and the name of a riveting, Oscar-nominated documentary that won film festival awards around the world in 2014. In many ways, these two "texts" together animate not only the specifics of mountain gorilla protection but provide a compact synthesis of how conservation, particularly in the African continent, has changed too.

Fossey, from the United States, began her journey with scientific observation at the Karisoke Research Center between Mounts Karisimbi and Bisoke. Like Goodall, Fossey raised many (largely male) scientists' eyebrows when she recognized the gorillas' individuality by naming them, such as Effie, Puck, Nunkie, and Digit. Multiple generations of gorillas live in these lush and steep mountain ranges. Poaching had become a significant threat to the mountain gorillas, whose lifeless bodies would be found without heads and hands, the latter often being taken to serve as ashtrays. This fueled Fossey's anger, understandably. And although some local people were involved at Karisoke as staff, Fossey also engaged in controversial tactics that made local tempers flare.

The Dian Fossey Gorilla Fund recognizes this history. It highlights her extra fondness for one gorilla in particular, a young male she named Digit. The fund states that he had

> no playmates his age in his group. He was drawn to her and her to him. Over time, a true friendship would form. Tragically, on Dec. 31, 1977, Digit was killed by poachers. He died helping to defend his group, allowing them to

escape safely. He was stabbed multiple times and his head and hands were severed. Eventually, there would be more deaths, including that of the dominant silverback Uncle Bert, and Group 4 would disband. It was then that Dian Fossey declared war on the poachers.

She would wear Halloween masks to try to scare them away, dismantle and burn the snares intended to capture other wild animals, and spray paint cattle in an effort to deter herders from moving their animals into protected parkland—all unpopular tactics that agitated local people. Fossey was brutally murdered in 1985, and the cause and details are sources of great speculation about why, how, and whether her death was related to her approach to conservation, local people, and area governments.

The Dian Fossey Gorilla Fund continues to operate to this day, and its approach has evolved along with the world of conservation overall. The organization still foregrounds the scientific documentation and analysis of mountain gorillas as well as Grauer's gorillas, monkeys, birds, and plants. The fund continues to operate the Karisoke Research Center, now located at a newer facility. In 2018, actress Portia de Rossi surprised her wife, comedian Ellen DeGeneres, with a major gift to the fund to help build the Ellen DeGeneres Campus of the Dian Fossey Gorilla Fund in Rwanda, a permanent hub for conservation work. That work includes programs to help train future conservation scientists who herald from Central Africa and promote sustainable agriculture. The family trees of mountain gorillas have been kept for more than fifty years by the fund, which also conducts a census to determine population numbers. In 1981, there were only 242 mountain gorillas left on the planet. Due to intensive protection efforts, the numbers have been slowly climbing. In 2019, there were close to 1,100 mountain gorillas—a significant increase, but still an alarmingly low number.

Some threats to the gorillas have remained, and new ones have emerged. These threats include war and armed conflict; the mining of coltan, which is used to power cell phones, gaming systems, and computers; and ongoing extreme poverty. Protected areas continue to be central to gorilla conservation in all countries where the mountain gorillas live, and nonprofit organizations and government agencies increasingly collaborate. In some cases, carefully planned private ventures are being pursued under the umbrella of green, sustainable development and ecotourism to combat poverty, promote peace, and protect biodiversity.

The publicly funded Institut Congolais pour la Conservation de la Nature (Congolese Institute for the Protection of Nature) oversees the Virunga National Park, Africa's oldest. It employs nearly seven hundred park rangers, including twenty-six women at the time of this writing, and they have responsibility for law enforcement in and around the three thousand square miles (seventy-eight hundred square kilometers) of the park. Today, the institute says the total distance covered by its rangers is larger than the circumference of the earth. Rangers undergo six months of intensive training to prepare and be ready to cross paths with antigovernment rebels and illegal loggers as well as poachers. Some lead tourists to view the animals and especially gorillas—a strategy that has long been both controversial and used because of the funds it generates. Some rangers work with bloodhounds and spaniels, whose powerful senses of smell help identify poaching (and can be used when people, including children, go missing in surrounding communities too).

Aline Masika Kisamya Kisamya, one of the first female rangers in Virunga, knew little about the gorillas, but was mesmerized by the forest. She told the *National Geographic* that "you see it from the outside, and it's so beautiful—I wanted to know its secrets." She loves to lead groups of tourists to see some of the three hundred mountain gorillas who live within the park. "They're very rare animals, and so big, so robust. I love to watch visitors' reactions—they're amazed by them."[4]

The work is popular, particularly when it provides reliable income, but it is still dangerous in many countries, including in the DRC. The Virunga Alliance reports that two hundred rangers have been killed in the area over the last century, most of them since the mid-1990s, when violence in the area surged, and especially in the mid-2000s. This danger is not unique to the DRC or gorilla conservation. The International Ranger Federation was formed in the early 1990s to strengthen, support, and promote knowledge exchange among rangers globally to help make the work safer and improve the quality of jobs. In 2019, the Chitwan Declaration reaffirmed the need for protecting, valuing, and diversifying rangers, including by promoting Indigenous and women rangers.

Lesson #9: protecting people on the front lines is also about defending animals, everywhere, and especially where it's most dangerous.

In 2020, a number of international conservation organizations formed the Universal Ranger Support Alliance to collectively respond to the rangers' concerns, including by establishing global welfare standards and a code of conduct. The World Wildlife Fund, one of the members of the new alliance, said,

> The global community is asking rangers to protect 30 percent of the planet from poaching, habitat destruction and other threats to the ecosystems that keep the planet healthy. Rangers are currently on the frontline of the COVID-19 emergency, and are the key to safeguard[ing] the ways of life of people whose lives and cultures are inseparable from nature. They take on a myriad of roles: environmental scientist, tour guide, firefighter, law enforcement officer, political ambassador, community liaison, teacher, first aid responder, communications specialist, land manager, sociologist, historian, moderator, building manager and the list goes on.
>
> Despite their critical profession, rangers work without adequate pay, often without suitable contracts, equipment, training or insurance.[5]

Rangers need to undertake multifaceted work, possess multidimensional skills, and put themselves in physical and psychological danger; the commonalities between animal cruelty investigators and conservation rangers are undeniable, although the physical risks to park rangers, particularly those in the Global South, are even greater. Six Virunga rangers were killed by members of an armed militia in January 2021. A dozen were killed a month later, another in the fall, and more were injured. The stakes are high, and the dangers are real. The violence has a direct impact on the animals too. Not only can animals be injured, but when parks must close to tourists or prospective visitors are deterred by the threat of violence, that means less revenue for conservation efforts.

People from poor communities across the African continent and around the world are literally losing their lives to protect animals. Their well-being needs to be taken even more seriously, and their jobs need to be made truly humane.

The Gorilla Doctors, originally formed in 1986 as a realization of Fossey's belief in the need for a veterinarian to be on-site, provides direct veterinary care to both mountain gorillas and Grauer's gorillas. It is a strategy that some see as controversial, but the impetus behind it, particularly given the shockingly low numbers of gorillas who remain, is nevertheless clear. It is a form of emergency, extreme conservation. Yet it's also now part of a multifaceted and proactive approach to multispecies care. Providing care to individual animals as part of species defense is becoming more common.

Today, the Gorilla Doctors collaborate with half a dozen other gorilla conservation organizations, government agencies, and the Karen C. Drayer Wildlife Health Center at the University of California, Davis, Veterinary School, among others. Most of the veterinarians are from African nations, and the organization is another example of the one health approach in action. Gorillas will wander outside the official park boundaries and be close to local residents and their animals, including dogs and cattle. The Gorilla Doctors deliver routine health care, education, and screenings for people who live near the park, offer rabies vaccinations for cats and dogs, monitor for potential zoonotic (animal-human) diseases, and create opportunities for local veterinary students and doctors.

The services provided to the conservation staff and their families are even more extensive, and include annual physical exams, immunizations, referrals to medical specialists and government programs, treatment for intestinal parasites, and family planning education. Four hundred park employees and close to two thousand of their family members have accessed these services, and the Gorilla Doctors also report that more than a thousand dogs have been vaccinated against rabies. A smaller organization, Docs 4 Great Apes, furthers the support for veterinary and human health education and work, including eye care, in and around the park. It is a comprehensive approach to health care for animals and people alike as well as workers' well-being and work-lives in a full sense.

The Virunga National Park is home to the Senkwekwe Center too, currently the world's only orphanage for mountain gorillas. Andre Bauma, who gained global prominence due to the film *Virunga*, originally began conservation work focused on elephants. But after a massacre of gorillas in 2007, he and others were able to rescue two young survivors, Ndezi and Ndakasi, who were five and two months old, respectively, and still clinging to the bodies of their dead mothers. The center's staff strive to provide orphans with the kinds of essential care they would otherwise have gotten with their mother and family groups, rehabilitating them for release when possible, or ensuring them a life of safety within the protected forest areas of the sanctuary.

Speaking of Ndakasi, Bauma describes her as an explorer but also an individual who wants her own way. She and Ndezi both remained in the sanctuary since there were no group members left to return them to. In fall 2021, a powerful and deeply affecting photo of Ndakasi in her final moments of life was released. She died in Bauma's arms, the man who had lifted her off her mother's body fourteen years earlier. Reflecting on this gorilla, this individual named Ndakasi, Bauma said, "I loved her like a child. Her cheerful personality brought a smile to my face every time I interacted with her."[6] It is the essence of conservation and animal protection overall really: looking backward and forward, oscillating between joy and pain.

Dr. Kerry Bowman, a leading conservationist who is also a bioethicist at the University of Toronto, worked to protect orangutans in Asia in the 1980s and then expanded his work to Africa. He founded the Canadian Ape Alliance in the late 1990s when war was destroying many human and nonhuman lives in the DRC. "There was massive loss of the Grauer (eastern lowland) gorillas, and it was a nightmare. The park guards were hanging on by a thread, and they hadn't been paid in a long time. My approach at that time was to simply raise money [in the Global North] and then pay the park guards."

In the ensuing years, as outright war ended, the work evolved. Attuned to the diversity of local cultures, the Canadian Ape Alliance pursued a mix of strategies, including the development of local agricultural projects for Batwa people, who had traditionally been hunters and gatherers but lost that option when the Kahuzi-Biega National Park was created. The alliance facilitates a women-led cooperative that tends to chickens whose eggs are fed at the local nursery school and helps fund an environmental school whose students are primarily children of park rangers.

Today, Bowman collaborates with many partners, including a Congolese NGO, Strong Roots, which is led by Dominique Bikaba. Bowman stresses that the Congolese are leading the current efforts and that true partnerships are essential. "The directions of these programs and the meaning of these species are really in the hands of the Congolese, as they should be. And in the area, there are many different ethnic groups that are distinct culturally and linguistically. But among the vast majority, gorillas are tremendously respected and not hunted."

Bowman and Bikaba argue that land is still critical to conserving species like the eastern lowland gorillas, but that communities need to be actively engaged in the protection. They have seen the fragmentation of gorilla groups, and are pursuing the creation and protection of corridors connecting protected spaces to allow the groups in heavily forested areas to move around. Local Indigenous leaders have been central to these efforts as well as to interweaving newer concepts like "forest health and community forests" with traditional, precolonial practices like not hunting pregnant animals and reestablishing sacred sections of the forest where many animals go to give birth. Major rain forest–focused organizations are partnering to support this work, and Bowman recognizes that when you're protecting large, charismatic species like gorillas, you're also protecting "frogs, turtles, the biosphere itself, and species people may not have even identified or named yet." Indigenous-managed forests can complement publicly owned national parks, and in parts of Latin America constitute significant amounts of land—upward of one-third of Amazonian and other forests in some countries.

The DRC is no longer considered at war, but it is a fragile situation. Unlike in some parts of the world, Bowman doesn't think that the militias in the DRC are antienvironment or target conservationists. He has seen compelling progress in the area, even throughout the pandemic. Remarkable developments, such as learning that groups of forest elephants (who are different from savanna elephants, including in their social organization) are alive, protected deep among the trees, spread hope.

As a bioethicist and someone who has worked in tropical forests around the world for forty years, Bowman's analysis is both local and global. "These are spectacular species that will be lost, and it's just fundamentally wrong. Not just because humans of the future won't be able to see them, but because we share this world with these animals. The lack of respect for nonhuman life is what has gotten us into this mess, and respect for nonhuman life is what will get us out of it."

Bowman notes the increasing emphasis on "ecoservices" or "bioservices" in conservation—a move toward trying to quantify the economic impacts of animals and nature through things like pollination and carbon dioxide processing—and the financial losses that would result if species and natural spaces (forests and plankton) were removed or disappeared and thus no longer provided those services. He sees that these frameworks can play a role and recognizes the pragmatic realities of economics in conservation spheres, but also doesn't want the ethical dimensions to be lost. "The destruction of forests and the commodification of animals are a danger to every species. Respect for nonhuman life is fundamental." The species and the individual animals matter.

Lesson #10: we can't change the past, but we must learn from it as we shape the future.

"We almost entirely focus and fund strategies focused on the effects, and rarely do we fund and focus on what's going on upstream," Bowman says. He wants to change that in a range of ways. When the idea of the environmental school was first proposed in the early 2000s, some said local customs will mean only boys attend, ethnic groups like the Batwa will be excluded, and children with albinism will be ostracized. "It posed an ethical challenge for me, but I said, 'It's Canadian funds, it's a Canadian university, those kinds of exclusions are not possible,'" Bowman explains. "And it wasn't the end of the world. We've had equal numbers of girls, and the Batwa are included in the school. Fast-forward to today, and an increasing number of park guards are women, and they do an incredible job. The Batwa were involved as guides, and now there are more of them. I can't say for sure, but I think it must have had a positive influence." Reciprocity, inclusion, and equity benefit people within and across national borders.

Speaking to the International Union for the Conservation of Nature and Natural Resources in 1968, Senegalese forestry engineer Baba Dioum said, "In the end, we will conserve only what we love, we will love only what we understand, and we will understand only what we are taught." I would add the word *who* to this compelling statement. We will conserve only who we love. We will love only who we understand.

"The school is a stone's throw from the edge of the park—twenty feet from the school is the forest wall," Bowman says. "There are times when the gorillas will wander out right into the backyard of the school." Diverse, healthy children learning together about nature and our place within it, who can grow up to have humane jobs protecting animals, as families of gorillas forage nearby—it's an inspiring image.

On the other side of the world, International Anti-Poaching Foundation founder Damien Mander along with sergeant and squad leader of Akashinga Ranger Team One Vimbai Kumire spoke to two thousand people in southern Ontario. Mander is a former Australian navy diver and sniper in an elite hostage recovery unit. He had spent years in war zones, and "seek and destroy" is tattooed across his chest. Seeing the lifeless body of a bull elephant who was literally faceless because his tusks had been cut off to obtain the ivory was life changing for Mander. He describes it as the true defining moment of his life. He used his life savings to create the foundation and channeled his energy into the preservation of wild animals. Many conservation rangers are trained by current or former military members, but the International Anti-Poaching Foundation is one of the few organizations focusing entirely on women. Akashinga—Women Protecting Nature—was Zimbabwe's first all-female conservation unit. *Akashinga* means the brave ones in Shona, a language spoken by 7.5 million people.

It started with sixteen rangers. Now there are hundreds. Potential rangers in each new cohort are tested, and the strongest are selected. The rangers are trained with a special forces model and must endure "the four pillars of misery—hunger, exhaustion, cold, and wet." They are organized based on military principles, and then armed and outfitted accordingly. Given the intense physical and psychological demands of the job, these dimensions are understandable.

But potential rangers are deliberately recruited from marginalized circumstances—survivors of domestic violence, single mothers, women in extreme poverty, and/or women who were orphaned by the AIDS epidemic. "I will teach you to use your power," Sergeant Petronella Chigumbura says in the short documentary *Akashinga: The Brave Ones* directed by Maria Wilhelm. The challenges the women have already experienced and survived are a testament to their strength.

And while the women must have physical strength, endurance, combat skills, and mental toughness, the approach is not a "full-on armed assault against poachers" but rather emphasizes community buy-in. The rangers eat an entirely plant-based diet and do almost all of their work without actually firing their rifles. They receive information from community members, patrol, and fight the fires used by poachers to "herd" animals into snares and traps, and the Akashinga rangers make arrests. The levels of poaching in the areas where they work have decreased significantly, some by rates of 80 percent. Mander sees women as less likely to accept bribes and better at de-escalation, thereby reducing the risk of corruption and violence. He highlights research showing that women in developing countries invest 90 percent of their income in their families, whereas men invest about one-third. "Wildlife is worth more to the community alive than it is dead at the hands of poachers," he says, particularly if carefully planned ecotourism programs are in place. And women are central to helping current and future generations understand why peace and protection are better for all species, including our own.

Vimbai Kumire, one of the original recruits, shared powerful stories about the struggles in her life as well as the "meaning and purpose" she feels by defending wildlife and earning her own money. "This work has made me see that I am someone." She concentrates on the Phundundu Wildlife Area in the Zambezi Valley, a 115-square-mile former trophy-hunting zone. The women normally come from the very communities that surround the animals in need of protection. Having to investigate and potentially arrest neighbors or even relatives can be challenging for frontline law enforcement everywhere in the world, but that does not deter Kumire. "If you harm my animals, I will catch you," she says. The women receive threats, and every day, they unsettle assumptions about what they can and can't do.

After the moving formal presentation, Mander and Kumire were in the lobby of the theater, and audience members, especially women, lined up to speak with them. Mander largely kept to the side, and people, me included, wanted to express our gratitude and admiration for Kumire. Awe, inspiration, guilt, and humility—I expect these feelings and more were at play.

"The women are now the leaders. I'm expendable. They are the ones taking this program forward," Mander says, aware of the legacy of colonialism, the neocolonialism of some conservation strategies, and the limits of white saviors.

The Black Mambas, all women, are also busy in South Africa. Founded in 2013 by Transfrontier Africa NPC, the group initially focused on the Olifants West Region of Balule Nature Reserve. But the women were quickly invited to extend their work and now protect all boundaries of the reserve in the Greater Kruger Area in South Africa, a 620-kilometer (240-mile) area that is home to rhinos, elephants, leopards, lions, buffalo, and many other species.

The rangers are mostly in their twenties. Patrols are undertaken day and night, on foot and with vehicles, to identify and remove snares as well as disrupt both bushmeat poachers and traffickers. The Black Mambas "want their communities to understand that there are far greater benefits to them through rhino conservation rather than poaching."[7] They run the Bush Babies educational program in local schools to help shape the hearts, minds, and goals of future generations. In fact, there are a number of programs revolving around young people, including an educational program specifically for the children of people employed within the nature reserve, and one addressing kids' immediate needs (like footwear and clothing). There is also a knowledge-sharing program specifically for grandparents.

These multidimensional, intergenerational, and award-winning strategies caught the attention of the Unbound Project, an initiative of We Animals Media, cofounded by acclaimed animal photojournalist Jo-Anne McArthur and visual arts scholar Dr. Keri Cronin of Brock University to highlight the work women are doing around the world protecting animals. "The Mambas are the eyes and ears of the reserve," shared Felicia Mogahane, a member of the Black Mambas. "We do visual policing. We look more carefully because we're not carrying guns." It's another of the noteworthy aspects of the Black Mambas: they are not armed. The Black Mambas want the areas they patrol to be seen as difficult and unprofitable terrain by poachers. Their presence is a source of power. They pay careful attention to the protected spaces and animals, engage neighbors and community members, watch and listen, and serve as role models. "We are the best," Leitah Mkhabela, another Black Mambas member, told the Unbound Project.[8]

Women-led conservation programs exist around the world. Some are small and informal and will never gain the attention of large organizations and international sponsors. I wish I could do them justice. From the 'trimates' to local conservation leaders like Kumire, women have been central to conservation. Supporting, learning from, and empowering women benefits them, their families, and animals.

8 THE WILD THINGS AREN'T THINGS

It was a warm summer evening when I spotted a furry little brown and black body curled up on the side of the road. My stomach dropped, and I quickly pulled over to see what had happened, as did another woman. We found a young raccoon with blood on her face, alive but barely moving. Raccoon mothers and babies will stay together for close to a year, but mom was nowhere to be seen, and I feared the worst.

The other woman's husband lost patience quickly and left, but she gently cradled the youngster in her arms while I contacted two wildlife care and rehabilitation centers that had accepted animal patients from me before. Neither would take raccoons.

I was frustrated but unwilling to leave an animal in pain on the side of the road to suffer and die. The woman and I put the little creature in a bin, which I placed in a quiet area at home. I consulted the government of Ontario's list of recognized animal rehabilitators and called every single one within my area code. They were all either full or not accepting raccoons.

"I'm way overfull, but I can send your name and number out on the listserv if you like," one rehabilitator offered.

"Yes, please," I said. I was losing hope, though. The little raccoon was alive but laying still. Her soft snores sounded like our dog Sunny when she sleeps.

I contacted all the local veterinarians I know personally and searched online, trying to find someone who could assess the young raccoon and provide care. I took to social media. "Why is it so difficult to get care for wild animals in this country? Is this the best we can do?!" Followers near and far offered suggestions and asked to be kept in the loop. They were rooting for this little raccoon and sharing my frustration.

I finally called the local emergency veterinary clinic. Its hours have fluctuated because of staffing shortages, but it was open that night. While the clinic could not treat a wild animal, it could euthanize one. Given that I seemed to have exhausted all possibilities, sadly, that appeared to be the most humane route.

Ten minutes into the drive, my phone rang. It was someone from a rescue that specializes in raccoons, and they had seen the details sent out over the listserv. They wanted to assess the raccoon! My husband and I did not drive the young animal to her certain demise. After quickly arranging for dog care, we instead embarked on a 3.5-hour drive to the raccoon rescue center. En route, we named the raccoon Regan, after Regan Russell, an animal advocate who had been killed after being struck by a truck hauling pigs into a slaughterhouse just days before. It seemed like a fitting tribute to a woman who had lost her life bearing witness to animals' suffering.

It was nearly midnight by the time we arrived at Mally's Third Chance Raccoon Rescue and Rehabilitation Sanctuary, but the furry patient was stirring and more alert. The rehabber met us on his front porch and apologized for his "COVID hair." He put on gloves and picked up little Regan.

"Hi there, little one," he said, examining her body gently.

He had to get up early for his day job and had another raccoon due to arrive just after midnight; still, he answered all of my questions and promised to keep us posted. The dogs were thrilled to see us when we finally got home after 3 a.m. We were exhausted but felt cautiously hopeful.

The next afternoon, my phone buzzed. When I opened the message, my heart sang.

The little patient was doing much better, and the prognosis was good. This young raccoon would likely be able to return to the wild, where she belongs.

I am someone with extensive knowledge of the organizations involved and protocols to follow, and it took hours of me relentlessly negotiating a labyrinth in search of somewhere that could provide care, combined with a seven-hour round trip, only possible because one rescuer checked their

email on a Sunday night and called me, literally minutes before the young raccoon was to be euthanized. My frustrated question sent out on social media remains: Why is it so difficult to get care for injured wild animals?

Many Indigenous people have long seen themselves as one part of a larger, multispecies community and sought to defend the water, land, and forests.[1]

Tensions can emerge between Indigenous people seeking to engage in traditional practices like trapping and hunting, and non-Indigenous people who want to protect animals. Indigenous people assert their rights to such practices, whether for subsistence or seeking to generate income. Some people argue that there are animal protection battles within non-Indigenous cultures that should be the focus for non-Indigenous people—and some animal defenders agree.[2] Others disagree, prioritizing animals' lives and suffering, regardless of who is causing it.

How non-Indigenous communities view and treat the animals who live in their own neighborhoods also varies. As noted in the previous chapter, most efforts revolving around wild animals concentrate primarily on species as a whole. Both nonprofit and governmental natural resource management and conservation agencies exist the world over. Frontline workers including rangers, guides, and educational officers are tasked with delivering programs and enforcing whatever the laws of their area dictate is permissible and prohibited, including when it comes to permitted hunting, fishing, and trapping. Policies may require them to kill some animals directly. There are species-specific programs that preserve animals of all sizes; some have brought species and places back from the brink, some have failed, and some have net-neutral or still-to-be-determined results.[3]

But many individual wild animals become injured because of us. Birds crash into windows. "House cats" allowed outdoors stalk, maim, and kill chipmunks and songbirds. People drive into and over frogs, lizards, squirrels, rabbits, deer, skunks, gophers, raccoons, opossums, foxes, badgers, and countless other species who are simply trying to live their lives, care for their young, find food and water, and escape predators in terrains that our species has made even more challenging with high-rises and concrete, not to mention droughts and fires.

What exists to help those animals, if they survive? It varies, depending on the type of animal and where they live. Publicly funded animal services may or may not receive wild animals, or that responsibility may fall to fish and wildlife agencies or equivalent government bodies. Most of these agencies do not provide therapeutic health care for the animals. As a result, many wild animals simply suffer in pain until they are killed or die in the cold, wet, and heat. Yet there are people committed to protecting animal neighbors by helping individuals in need: wildlife rescuers and rehabilitators.

Some rehabbers work within or have formed organizations, while many provide care out of self-built facilities, often on their own property. Most do not receive any government funding for their work, but instead rely on donations or simply self-fund. Mally's Third Chance Raccoon Rescue and Rehabilitation Sanctuary, where little Regan raccoon went, receives donations, but the founders spend close to C$200,000 (approximately US$160,000) of their own money each year to cover the costs of staff, food, veterinary services, medication, utilities, and facility maintenance.

Rehabilitation work involves nursing wounds, or feeding youngsters every two hours, 24–7. It includes treating skin conditions, other infections, and frostbite as well as creating splints and casts. It may mean freeing animals from tin cans or bottles. In some cases, especially when a relatively larger organization has a veterinary clinic, surgeries are performed.

I have gotten advice from wildlife rehabilitation experts, including about what to do when one young chipmunk who had been expelled from mom's burrow (which is what happens after a few weeks) was simply clinging to the wall in fear (the answer was to do nothing right away—and the wee one did come down and move on the next day). Some animal patients I have brought to rehabbers have survived. Rereleasing a young dove after he had spent a week healing at the rehabilitation center was wonderful. Some injured animals I tried to help were euthanized, like a finch whose wing had been broken in two places and could not be properly repaired with a cast. "They will never be able to fly again and are in a lot of pain," the rehabber explained. It still hurt. I had watched the bird working to survive on the ground for two days before I was able to reach the rehabber and obtain approval to collect the feathered patient and bring them in. I had witnessed the bird's will to survive.

This health care is provided while trying to keep the animals as wild as possible. At times, this is easy—and administering the care is the challenging part with evasive, skittish, and/or defensive animals. In other cases, the animals, especially if they're young, are desperate for affection and warm touch.

Rachel Parsons is a licensed rehabber in Maine with more than a decade of experience. "I always wanted to work with wildlife but didn't know this career existed until I found a skunk hit by a car in January of 2008," she says. "I called Maine Fish and Game, and they directed me to a wildlife rehabilitator who became my mentor." She created a 501(c)(3) charitable organization and works from her home. Parsons exemplifies the multidimensional nature of this labor, working "closely with fish and game wardens, animal control officers, animal damage control personnel, and the veterinarians who agree to help take care of wildlife in need," guiding members of the public about animals they encounter, and providing appropriate housing, food, and treatment when animal patients are admitted. She specializes in small to medium-sized mammals, including squirrels, voles, moles, woodchucks, opossums, porcupines, skunks, raccoons, and foxes, not necessarily popular or beloved species, but each with their own distinct attributes and worthy of care in Parsons's view. A mole we named Vanderbilt has lived behind our house for two years. Moles have limited eyesight and can only see light and movement. Vanderbilt's ability to avoid roaming house cats, hawks, and owls, and survive through all seasons, is inspiring.

A useful resource has been developed to assist people seeking to get help for wild animals in the United States. In 2012, the Colorado-based nonprofit Animal Watch created Animal Help Now, a centralized, searchable database accessible online and through an app that streamlines the searching process. On the rehabber side, the highly uneven patchwork of regulations, laws, and funding is a concern, understandably so. "Each state has different standards for licensing and training rehabilitators, and there is no base standard for the level, quality, and maintenance of education regarding raising, treating, and releasing wildlife," Parsons says, and that situation is compounded by the lack of data about many aspects of wild animal care. Neither of these problems is unique to the United States.

Wildlife rehabilitation is challenging but also affirming work. "It's incredibly rewarding to watch an animal that would otherwise have died return healthy to its home," Parsons says. "The harmful effects of humans on this planet are evident everywhere, and often it's the connection between wild animals and humans that enables us to educate people on that effect and how to make a change for the positive."

The people at Mally's Third Chance argue that "the word *overpopulation* floats around, but we have not found where real facts or studies can validate this." They suspect instead that

> people may not want to coexist with some species. But if we reduce populations of coyotes or foxes as some may feel they are "overpopulated," then the number of rats and mice may increase. When this happens, now rats and mice become "overpopulated" so people use poison. The poison then spreads up and down the food chain including to raccoons or birds that may eat the carcasses, then offsetting the balance of nature even more. Not to mention the pain and suffering caused. Everything is connected.

And everyone.

Despite the challenges, it is remarkable what rehabbers are able to do for animal neighbors. For example, parasitic mites that cause intense itching and hair loss and weaken animals significantly (called mange), thereby endangering their ability to seek out food, can be treated successfully in rehab facilities and the wild in certain circumstances. Rabbits, chipmunks, and birds who suffer from cat attacks can sometimes be successfully treated and rereleased.

Some organizations directly engage folks who want to proactively assist animals, including insects, and provide guidance or even free seeds to help people build humane yards and grow beneficial gardens. In my country, for example, the David Suzuki Foundation's Butterflyway Project helps train neighborhood volunteers who encourage the development of plant "highways" for butterflies, bees, and other pollinators through their communities.

There are also growing "rewilding" movements around the world.[4] The importance of having more spaces for wild animals to survive and thrive with minimal human contact is clear. The premise is that areas that have been damaged can be allowed to regenerate, and animal and plant species can repopulate. At times it can be guided, and can include the deliberate reintroduction of particular species and/or the work of other animals, such as donkeys to help trample seeds. At times rewilding simply happens, when people leave areas for any number of reasons (natural disasters, human-made disasters, or economic closures). As is the case for all work considered in this book, there are different visions of how rewilding can and should occur. I relish images that are captured when animals move back into places formerly dominated by people and when green plant life erupts from the cracks in our concrete. It is a powerful illustration of survival and the will to live.

Anne Lewis had long served on the board of the Washington Humane Society, including as president, but her concerns for animals' well-being extended beyond cats, dogs, and other household companions. "I learned that all sick, injured, or orphaned wildlife had to be transported an hour away to the nearest rehab facility in Maryland. As a result of this delay in treatment, many of these animals didn't survive." In addition to this upsetting dimension, she recognized that having local vehicles in transit for more than two hours wasn't an efficient use of local resources either.

Ultimately she cofounded City Wildlife, DC's only wildlife rehabilitation facility. After raising private funds, sorting out the legal requirements, finding and equipping a suitable facility, and securing a financial commitment from the city, the organizers opened the center. The facility now admits more than two thousand wild patients a year, employs six staff, and depends on dozens of volunteers. The staff all play important roles, including cofounder Jim Monsma, who serves as executive director and provides organizational and administrative leadership, along with a veterinarian, other animal care staff, and a front desk responder who offers lifesaving information and advice, and asks callers questions to determine if a wild animal is truly in need of help or should be left alone. The public funding covers a portion of the organization's budget, and other revenue sources are essential. But receiving any government money is rare in the world of wildlife care, even though many of us feel deeply for the injured, orphaned, or sick wild neighbors we encounter.

Lewis argues that wildlife rehabilitation also plays important public health roles, and Parsons agrees. "Wildlife rehabilitators are often the first to bridge the gap in knowledge about how to live with our wild neighbors. As humans encroach further and further into animals' territory and affect ecosystems at all levels, rehabbers are often the first to see the effects of that in the wildlife." Rehabbers have valuable knowledge about new or worsening viruses and patterns of disease, including potential animal–human or animal–other animal pathogens. Plus if no qualified rehabilitator or clinic is operating, people can try to care for wild animals themselves. Lewis points out that this can lead to public safety concerns as well as mounting health costs if people are injured in the process.

Organizations like City Wildlife provide a broader social service too, leading efforts to track—and combat—fatal bird–window strikes in its area. "Citizen-science programs like our Lights Out DC project—which documents bird–glass collisions in DC—create databases that can support the work of those in a position to effect change through policies or legislation," Lewis says. The number of birds who become injured or killed by crashing into the windows of our houses and tall buildings is staggering. Migrating birds also become confused by bright lights at night, causing them to become exhausted and vulnerable. These factors affect both individual birds and their species as a whole.

Lights Out initiatives that seek to minimize the threats to birds who migrate at night by reducing light pollution, even for short periods of time, are coordinated throughout the United States by the National Audubon Society. Initiatives like FLAP Canada and the American Bird Conservancy provide information about decals, films, and types of glass that make windows more visible to birds, thereby reducing the strike rate, so people, including builders, can make a positive difference right now. These kinds of organizations are also working for important legislative change to make it mandatory for future buildings to be constructed in ways and with glass that automatically reduce bird deaths so as to address the problem upstream and in a more systematic way.

"Treating the individual animals at our center is our core activity," Lewis explains. "However, since many, if not most, of these animals come to us because of some human-caused activity, it is necessary to address the root causes of their distress. Animals stuck on glue traps, attacked by free-roaming pets, orphaned by nest disruption during pruning, tangled in discarded trash, stunned by collisions with glass, and run over by lawn mowers—these are all human-caused activities." For this reason, City Wildlife emphasizes the importance of sharing knowledge with people of all ages as well as collaborating with environmental groups that prioritize habitat preservation and the protection of biodiversity. Knowledge exchange with other rehabilitators and wildlife veterinarians through conferences and formal networks like the National Wildlife Rehabilitators Association and International Wildlife Rehabilitation Council are particularly valuable, and Lewis contends that coordinated information sharing has helped improve care and professionalize the work. She recognizes other rehabilitators that are setting a high standard and leading the way, including the Toronto Wildlife Centre and the Tri-State Bird Rescue & Research based in Delaware (created to help birds damaged by oil spills).

"I would like to see rehab education formalized and standardized," Parsons says. "I would like to see more money put into research to better the rehab process on all levels from nutrition to husbandry to ideal release conditions." She highlights a practical issue of particular concern: formula. "Formula is the f-word among rehabbers. If you want to start a fight in a room full of rehabilitators, ask about formula! What would be a huge benefit would be an up-to-date large-scale study of mother's milk composition of the many species that we treat, and milk powders that aim for accuracy and excellence over marketing and the bottom line."

Many rehabilitators make some determinations about which animals they will treat. Some focus on particular species groupings, rule out rabies vector species or large animals, and/or will refuse to treat legally defined "invasive species." So-called invasive species may have been around for so long that most people don't even know which ones they are—and it can be surprising. For example, the house sparrow is deemed invasive in North America and many places outside Europe, while other kinds of sparrows are not. At no point was it the fault of the birds that they were brought across the Atlantic. Plus given the small number of individuals of these supposedly invasive species who would be brought to a rehabilitator, denying them care seems negligible in the grand scheme of native species well-being, not to mention cold. Lewis explains that like conservationists, rehabilitators can emphasize an environmental imperative focused on species as a whole, a humane philosophy prioritizing the elimination of animals' suffering, or both. Clearly, so can policy makers and lawmakers.

To help duck neighbors, City Wildlife also assists people who own properties that are popular but unsafe nesting spots to encourage the birds to choose other, more suitable locations. When ducks do nest in high-traffic and heavily populated areas, trained volunteers are available to help mama and her ducklings get to water safely. Efforts like these invite us to think differently about community and being a good community member in a full sense.

Speaking of water, there is a remarkable number of individuals and organizations focused on wild turtles and tortoises. Stories of the particularly aged turtles are awe-inspiring, like Jonathan, a Seychelles tortoise who lives on the island of Saint Helena and is at least 190, identified by the *Guinness World Records* as the oldest chelonian (tortoise or turtle). He reportedly enjoys napping and carrots, cucumbers, apples, and other fruits, and still mates with other turtle residents.

At the same time, images of sea turtles ensnared in fishing lines, wrapped in six-pack beer rings, and being strangled by plastic bags have not only won awards but also painfully illustrate how much harm our species causes. Lonesome George was a giant Pinta tortoise who lived at the Tortoise Breeding and Rearing Center in Puerto Ayora on the Galápagos Islands.[5] He died in 2012, and was believed to be the last of his kind, but a 2019 discovery has raised the prospect of a related subspecies continuing to exist. When it's down to one or a handful or even a few hundred members of a species left on the entire planet, that's an alarmingly powerful indication of the damage humans have done.

Many kinds of turtles and tortoises are endangered, both close to home and around the world. Those on land are in great danger when trying to cross roads, even though their slower pace should make them highly visible to drivers who can plan accordingly. Nearly all US states have at least one person or group that will help turtles, and some, like California, have close to fifty. I marvel at the work that the nonprofit Ontario Turtle Conservancy Centre does to repair broken shells and incubate eggs for later release. Many turtles struck by cars are females on the move to egg-laying destinations. The conservancy also works upstream (the metaphor is even more apt here) to protect precious habitat that turtles need to survive. It has one of the few wild-animal-focused hospitals that has been accredited by the College of Veterinarians of Ontario and operates at a standard akin to those serving people's pets and companions. Volunteer turtle taxis are coordinated when individuals are in need of transportation to the hospital, and people of all kinds donate their time to drive these reptiles to get care. Networks of people who drive animals in need exist in many places, and although ad hoc, are salve for the weary—and wary—spirit.

There are actually a few turtle hospitals at work. The village of Warm-inster near Orillia, Ontario, is home to the province's second facility. Some aquarium clinics can and will treat wild patients. The nonprofit Turtle Hospital in the Florida Keys concentrates on sea turtles. It has its own ambulance, accepts emergency calls seven days a week, twenty-four hours a day, and employs two dozen people. Its primary focus is to treat and rerelease as many turtles as possible who are injured by boat strikes, fishing lines, sharks, and other hazards. Sea turtles are also at risk of contracting fibropapilloma, a tumor-causing disease that appears to pass among turtles and be connected to environmental damage and ocean pollution.[6]

Along with diagnostic suites and sophisticated technology, there are smaller and larger tanks for physical therapy as well as to test the swimming abilities of patients before release. Some of the patients are deemed unable to safely survive in the wild due to the loss of a flipper, or when air pockets are formed beneath their shell after they are hit by boats that make them too buoyant and unable to dive to escape dangers (like other boats). These turtles have permanent homes at the hospital, with names like Chance, Bender, Montel, and Kent. The clinic posts updates on their health—and personalities. Brianna doesn't like to share her space with other turtles, but she wants to be able to see them. Some of us can relate, Brianna.

Many, if not most, wildlife rehabilitation centers do not have a high volume of public traffic moving through their spaces to reduce the stress levels of the animals, who are already tense enough about being held by humans and at various states of pain and healing. But the Turtle Hospital takes a different approach, and guided educational tours are offered daily. Gabriela Queiroz Miranda, a high school student at the time, became aware of the dangers of boat strikes and the resulting life-endangering subshell bubbles at the hospital. As a result, she developed a 3D-printed vest to help turtles plagued by the condition, which continues to be researched.

The Galápagos Islands, now a UNESCO World Heritage site due to their rich wildlife diversity, have long been an important spot for turtle and tortoise research and conservation. Many proactive and responsive programs are run through the Galápagos Conservancy centers, including breeding, rearing, and rereleasing turtles, and working to safeguard the ecosystems where turtles still live freely. The conservancy also works with local farmers and landowners because tortoises, like all wild animals, do not see a difference among public, protected, and privately owned land. The tortoises move around in pursuit of what they need at any given time of the year.

The Galápagos Conservancy notes that some farmers work to keep tortoises off their land, while others do the opposite, seeking to take advantage of tourists' fascination with the giant shelled creatures. The Giant Tortoise Restoration Initiative works to "reduce these types of conflicts, to ensure the health and well-being of the tortoise populations, and to work toward consensus with the local landowners on how the tortoise-human interactions are managed."[7]

Paso Pacífico is a US–Latin American organization concentrating on the Pacific Slope ecosystems in Central and South America, especially Nicaragua and El Salvador. It partners with and is supported by donations from governmental and nonprofit conservation organizations from around the world. The organization exemplifies the multifaceted nature of more and more conservation work. First, the organization staff observe, listen, and develop relationships. Then they strive to understand the context in a full sense, including the historical, cultural, political, biological, and economic factors at play. Once those are understood, solutions can be designed. "Since problems usually have several factors, we launch solutions that incorporate several approaches. We apply technology and scientific procedures, incentivize best practices in the community, and implement social programs that involve and empower local communities," the organization states. This process is precisely that—a process; it's not a destination. "Because we are trying to fix a constantly changing system, we are always assessing current conditions and looking for new ideas and ways to improve."[8]

A turtle-specific example of this perspective is the organization's ranger program, which involves community members, including former poachers. These individuals' knowledge of the landscape is enlisted to help turtles, not harm them. The people gain paid work, and the turtles have human protectors—another example of how humane jobs are essential to animal protection. Rangers monitor beaches 24-7 that are key nesting locations including for the critically endangered hawksbill and leatherback sea turtles. Due to poaching, natural predators, tourist disruption of traditional nesting spaces, and environmental changes, few eggs will actually become adult turtles. This makes guarding the nesting areas particularly crucial. The rangers work with and help educate hotel owners and staff so they, too, can be partners in protecting nesting sites. "In the past 10 years, Paso Pacífico's rangers have protected more than 50,000 turtle eggs," the organization declares, proudly.[9] GPS-equipped eggs, "InvestEGGator" decoys, invented by Dr. Kim Williams-Guillén, are also being used to help identify trafficking networks.

One of my research assistants, Dr. Erin Jones, participated in a program coordinated by the Latin American Sea Turtles Organization, a Costa Rican conservation organization. Along with employing locals, including former poachers, as research assistants and guardians, the organization invites international assistants and volunteers for "voluntourism" as it is often called. The strategy is used in many places globally by some conservation organizations, animal sanctuaries, and orphanages to generate income and benefit from the volunteer work of people who want to contribute to animal care and conservation. Conservationists and researchers have varied views on these kinds of programs, but they are popular, and like every strategy in the world of animal protection, there are different iterations.

This organization works primarily in a coastal area near fresh water, home to diverse land species including sloths, monkeys, and raccoons as well as aquatic animals from dolphins and manatees to crocodiles. The area's beaches are also popular nesting spots for a number of endangered sea turtle species. Poaching turtles and their eggs is illegal in Costa Rica, as is any trade in wildlife, in fact. But as is the case everywhere, laws remain aspirational words on paper unless enforced.

The Costa Rican staff work in collaboration with the international guests to undertake overnight patrols and guard the hatchery where eggs laid in vulnerable locations are moved. Once the babies are born, they are released to the wild with the hope that as many of them will survive as possible, despite the environmental and especially human-rooted risks. Jones recalls the "pitch black and relentless humidity" while on patrols, and how much she learned about coexistence and turtles themselves. "They have extraordinary internal navigational systems. They use the earth's magnetic field as a source of navigational information during transoceanic migrations, and the females will often return to nest on the same beach every single year, even thousands of kilometers from their normal feeding areas." We see these kinds of epic migrations—the ability to understand and navigate extensive distances—among other animals like birds and elephants too. For some it is an innate ability, while others learn from older members of their family and social groups, or some combination.

"I will never forget that first time I was snorkeling and came face-to-face with a green sea turtle quietly eating in the warm Pacific waters," Jones says. "Turtles have a lot to teach us, but also have some truly extraordinary abilities far beyond the scope of what we could even imagine."

Turtles, tortoises, and terrapins—the shelled reptiles who may thrill, intrigue, or repulse people—live in so many places, and the strategies being used to defend them vary. The fact that tortoises in particular can outlive multiple generations of people, not to mention their immense resilience in the face of extraordinary obstacles and change, is simultaneously humbling, inspiring, and galvanizing—as are they. Don't they have as much of a right to be on this planet as humans do?

Reptiles don't normally attract the same levels of public attention and adoration as gorillas and elephants, but there are exceptions, like the turtles and tortoises. Regardless of an animal's perceived cuteness, they all feel pain, are capable of suffering, and play important roles within their ecosystems. Frogs and toads have long been recognized by herpetologists (the scientists who study amphibians) as bellwethers whose health mirrors the overall state of an ecosystem, and who play a central role in environmental balance (eating insects, for example). As a result, these little animals serve as powerful red flags, and oh, the flags they are a-waving. The National Wildlife Federation deems amphibians "the most threatened class of animals in nature."[10] This class includes frogs, toads, salamanders, and newts. These cold-blooded, ectothermic (their body temperature is not autonomously self-regulating but rather affected by the environment), tetrapod (four-limbed) vertebrates (with spines) spend part of their life in water and part on land (*amphibian* is rooted in a Greek word meaning "double life").

These little animals are in grave danger. They have been on earth for hundreds of millions of years and survived through seismic planetary changes, yet now their numbers are plummeting.[11] That really warrants a pause.

From habitat loss to pollution and disease, the wildlife trade to climate change and vehicles, these animals face many threats. Emergency efforts, both on the ground and through policy changes, are underway to try to protect the amphibians who are still here. The Association of Wetland Stewards for Clayoquot and Barkley Sounds in British Columbia launched the fantastically named Society for the Prevention of Little Amphibian Tragedies. It focuses on the high mortality rates that result when these animals must cross busy roads as they migrate between forests and wetlands, including through the creation and maintenance of tunnels and culverts to allow frogs and salamanders to migrate more safely.

Every year, for a couple of days, the air all around my home is enveloped by the hauntingly beautiful song of frogs, which some people call nature's most sublime announcement that spring has arrived. I don't want a future without spring or frogs.

Individual animals and whole species should both be protected, and the services available to provide health care to wild animals should be more than a loosely knit patchwork of individuals and nonprofits that have chosen to take up this work. Colombia's Wild Flora and Fauna Attention Center (Centro de Atencion y Valoracion de Flora y Fauna Silvestre) can serve more than two thousand animals who are victims of trafficking, illegal possession, or accidents. The building is equipped with state-of-the-art technology as well as spaces for appropriately delivering and managing the care of animal patients who have been extracted from their natural environments. At the center's launch in 2021, Secretary of the Environment Carolina Urrutia said investment in the facility helps pay "a debt to wild animals." For public health, environmental, and ethical reasons, strategic public investments should be made to fund wild animal care—and create humane jobs to deliver it.

9 THE ANIMALS IN BETWEEN

Before the Netflix docuseries *The Tiger King*, there was Ming the Bengal tiger, seized from a Harlem apartment in 2003. In 2002, Susan Orleans wrote in the *New Yorker* about a tiger who walked through the streets of Jackson, New Jersey, and the woman who had more than a few other tigers at her home. A tiger roamed the streets of Houston for a number of days in spring 2021.

In 2012, an image of a monkey in a shearling coat waiting at an IKEA store in Toronto, Canada, emerged and circulated, inspiring memes, concerns, and questions. Why is there a monkey in a coat in an IKEA? Is it legal to have monkeys as pets? Is the monkey okay? All are good questions.

The reality is that individual animals who are members of wild species are kept far away from their ancestral homes, in people's houses and backyards, stores, roving displays that pop up at festivals and malls, and cages and tanks. The animals' real homes may be in the same country or on the other side of the planet. They may have been taken from their lands themselves or born from a mother who was. They may be birds, reptiles, or mammals. Their stories vary, but the risks to their physical and mental well-being and very survival are consistent.

These are some of the animals in between—in between places, in between legal categories, in between wild and tame, and in between their rightful homes and hell. Often they are called captive animals to recognize that these are not members of domesticated species, those animals whose lives and reproduction have been governed by humans for centuries or millennia. The majority of the members of these species are still in the wild, but these particular individuals are in captivity. When their species is not native to the country in which they're being held, these can also be called *exotic animals*, although questions have been raised about this term given its racially loaded history and connotations.

In certain cases, decimation of the wild members of the species in combination with the sheer number of captive individuals unsettle the definition. The claim that "there are more tigers in captivity in the United States than there are wild in Asia" circulates periodically. Given the lack of precise data about how many captive animals there are, it is hard to definitively determine the statement's veracity. Even proactive attempts to use freedom of information requests, as the international organization Four Paws did to try to gather firmer numbers about the prevalence of captive tigers in Europe, offer only partial portraits because of how unregulated and unmonitored this form of animal keeping is. But based on conservative estimates, the claim that there are more tigers in captivity than in the wild seems to be accurate. The World Wildlife Federation deems it true. Most estimates place the number of wild tigers at below four thousand individuals.

Virtually everywhere, the keeping of captive animals is another animal protection patchwork. Many areas' laws are silent about the matter, meaning it's not explicitly legal, but it's not illegal either. Others prohibit or limit some types of animals, or require approvals or licenses. Those restrictions could vary half an hour away in the next town. On the other hand, some regions have all-out bans on captive wild animals other than in zoos. Even when stronger regulations exist prohibiting, limiting, or requiring approval for the importation and transfer of wild species, whether there is sufficient enforcement of the rules is an open question, and one that frequently is answered with no, there are not enough investigators.

"Enforcement is only a small piece of the puzzle," says Elizabeth Cabrera Holtz, wildlife campaign manager for World Animal Protection US.

> Wildlife trafficking can have negative, potentially deadly, consequences for humans. But the United States is one of the biggest consumers of wildlife in the world, both illegal and legal. We are the ones driving the problem. If we look at enforcement from the perspective of whether it's reducing consumer demand, it's not effective at all. We can increase the capacity of Fish and

Wildlife Service inspectors through funding and resources, but that's not the ultimate solution, just like increased policing and incarceration has failed to solve opioid use or any other number of societal problems.

The matter of a legal versus illegal trade is relevant as well. "It's often not easy to distinguish between the two," Cabrera Holtz argues. "Trade can also shift between legal or illegal depending on how the animal is classified as they move through the process. Similar to the patchwork of laws in the United States surrounding wild animal possession, there's no framework guiding why some transactions are legal and others illegal. We need as little legal trade as possible and to work toward a world where the sanctioned wildlife trade is a thing of the past."

So is it possible to work both downstream and upstream when thinking about the trade in wild animals? For World Animal Protection, the answer is yes. "Instead of focusing on the distinction between illegal and legal trade, we are working to end the commercial exploitation of wildlife. Underpinning our strategies is the belief that every wild animal deserves a wild life," says Cabrera Holtz. The organization has a deliberately crafted strategy.

Instead of funding enforcement or increasing resources to stop trafficking, we focus on ending commercial exploitation by pushing companies to adopt wildlife-friendly policies, such as ending the sale of wild animals in pet stores or travel companies banning venues that allow visitors to interact with wild animals. We also work for behavior change, such as shifting demand away from wildlife-based medicines or creating more opportunities for ethical wildlife tourism experiences (such as viewing whales from a distance at a whale heritage site). Finally, we push policy makers to adopt laws and regulations that are protective of wild animals and their habitats.

This issue illuminates deeper questions about the ethics of keeping animals, period. Which animals are loved and kept as "pets" or companions varies, and is always a product of cultural decisions that have evolved over time. Some animal advocates contend that true animal protection—animal liberation, in fact—would be freeing all animals, including cats and dogs, from their subservient places in human-led societies, allowing them to return to their free-roaming statuses.

Blanket statements about animals or people are rarely, if ever persuasive, and that is the case for this one too. As this book illustrates, I see many shades of gray when it comes to human and animal relationships. Ending all human relationships with animals is not a compelling and just solution, let alone a practical, ethical, or environmentally sound one. But it is nevertheless prudent to at least recognize that the animals who have been deemed suitable as companions and family members were also once wild. Evolutionary research suggests that dogs and people may have chosen each other, rather than our ancestors simply trapping and forcing canines to join us. Whether the same was true for other species, from cats to horses to pigs, all of whom were wild animals, is unclear but less likely.[1]

Yet in addition to social ideas about which animals we want to love and live with, other factors have influenced which animals we keep inside or near our homes, including safety and health factors. The logic of not trying to make fatally venomous snakes into pets is obvious, but certain people still have captive animals with highly lethal capabilities on their properties. In some cases, initially cute and gentle youngsters become dangerous as they mature.

"So many wildlife laws are upside down; the burden is on conservationists to prove trade is negatively affecting a species before protections are put in place," Cabrera Holtz points out.

> Beyond intentional abuse, zoonotic disease is being legally imported into the United States without any regulatory mechanisms to stop it. There's no agency in charge of making sure all wildlife coming into the country isn't a public health threat, for example. And severe exploitation can occur long before any regulations might be effective. Overall, there's no coherent policy that's rooted in public health and safety or potential impact on biodiversity, or that recognizes wild animals' capacity to suffer in the commercial trade.[2]

In Belgium, a different approach has been developed called the positive list, which proactively establishes whether a particular kind of animal can be safely and appropriately kept by people in a way that meets the animals' needs and respects people's safety too. In 2009, forty-two animal species were placed on Belgium's list, although there is some variance in different areas of the country. Certain other nations are beginning to employ the same or a similar strategy, including Norway, the Netherlands, and Malta, and cities around the world, including in North America, have put the spirit of the positive list or at least parts of it into practice in different ways.[3]

Human demand is a challenge, for both live animals and parts of animals who are killed and then consumed or used to create new products for personal use or sale. A lot of the "marketing" of wild animals and trade, both legal and illegal, is coordinated online. Entire websites exist from which you can order turtles. Those turtles arrive like mail, and some companies have "guarantees." If the turtle or tortoise arrives dead, the purchaser can obtain a store credit. Some companies have two- or seven-day guarantees—meaning the company "backs" the health of the animal for only two or seven days after delivery.

The reasons people want to consume parts of wild animals vary and can be cultural or religious. The reasons people want to own wild animals also vary: intrigue and fascination, or to obtain status or power. Possession can be about money, especially if someone has commercial aspirations. Sometimes it's because the animals seem adorably humanlike, as is the case for monkeys and apes. How this affects the other primates of this world is rarely positive, as I saw firsthand.

"They will be really loud when they see you," the caretaker explained. *They* are chimpanzees.

The door of the indoor enclosure was opened, and the sound was extraordinary. I have had the pleasure of hearing the renowned Dr. Jane Goodall perform the pant hoot, a now well-studied chimp vocalization that starts with a sequence of low, breathy sounds and then progressively gets louder until it becomes a series of, well, hoots (a short video of Goodall teaching TV host John Oliver various chimp ways of communicating is also one of the internet's gems). These chimps had no interest in any quiet sounds, though, and crashed through their outdoor space like boisterous running backs propelled by tornadoes. They made such a racket, hollering and banging things, grabbing large balls and tossing them around. Then the chimps settled down and began studying these other great apes—about two dozen humans—who were standing there in awe.

This was not a zoo. These were not animals accustomed to being stared at by people. This was the Primate Rescue Center in rural Kentucky, a sanctuary dedicated to providing rescued monkeys and apes a peaceful home, free from the pressures, expectations, and stress of human demands. I had read about a facility like this, the Fauna Foundation outside Montreal in Canada, in Andrew Westoll's award-winning book *The Chimps of Fauna Sanctuary*.[4] I gleefully binged *Meet the Chimps* on National Geographic, a TV series that highlights many of the three hundred animals and their caretakers at Chimp Haven in Louisiana, the world's largest chimp sanctuary. But I did not think I would ever see a primate sanctuary in real life. I got chills from the sheer exhilaration of being in their presence.

The close to fifty monkeys (easily identifiable by their tails) and apes (no tails and larger in size) at the Primate Rescue Center had previously been used in medical research, kept as pets, or used for various kinds of performances and displays. Now the animals enjoy their days and try to move on from whatever their former lives involved. They groom other primates, a seemingly small act, yet one that not only serves a physical function of removing bugs and dirt but also establishes and reaffirms social connections. They play. They sit quietly alone if that's what they feel like doing. Most significantly, they can make choices. There are still practical constraints on their lives—they need to be kept in a confined space for their own well-being and the safety of the human caretakers—but the animals have room to move. They get to explore and be curious. They can feel joy.

Since these are animals who normally live in the wild, usually rich jungles, why not return them to their ancestral lands now? This can be possible, but only rarely. When animals are intercepted early in the trafficking chain, they can sometimes be released or retaught to avoid people and then released.[5] The latter is undoubtedly extremely emotionally daunting work. Even if you know it's best for the monkey in the long term, chasing them away when they approach is difficult.

Often even if the animals are in their homelands, they cannot be rehabilitated. Wild mammals normally grow up with their parents, and often with extended families and social groups. Young animals learn from others how to find food and water, and how that life-sustaining work must change depending on the season. They learn how to (try to) avoid predators, including humans, and how to properly interact and respect the group's customs and other animals. They learn when it's okay to sleep or play, and when it's not. This intergenerational work is essential for wild animals to survive and thrive.[6] When you've been kept in a cage and only seen your kind through bars—or not seen your kind at all—you do not have the necessary skills for navigating life in the wild and are vulnerable as a result.

The nonprofit Comunidad Inti Wara Yassi is busy at work in Bolivia, where the rights of "Mother Earth" to exist and replenish are enshrined in law, and government has the legal duty to invest in the protection of nature. The organization's "name reflects the ethnic diversity of Bolivia and [its peoples'] link with nature, by using words from the indigenous languages of the three main ethnic groups in Bolivia. 'Inti' means 'sun' in Quechua, 'Wara' means 'star' in Aymara, and 'Yassi' means 'moon' in Chiriguano-Guaraní. Bringing these languages together symbolises unity."[7] The organization's history is fascinating and extends back to a happenstance encounter with a monkey being forced to drink alcohol and perform in a bar. Later, one of the cofounders, Tania "Nena" Baltazar Lugones, resolved to create a wildlife refuge after rescuing a spider monkey who was being poorly treated. In 1996, Comunidad Inti Wara Yassi created the first wildlife sanctuary in Bolivia after the municipal government of Villa Tunari signed an agreement for use of the land.

Today there are three sanctuaries, over a dozen staff, and Baltazar Lugones is the president. The organization's team assesses the animals

> to develop an individual care plan that addresses their physical health and their psychological wellbeing. Many of the animals arrive suffering malnourishment, parasites, broken bones, digestive issues and psychological trauma.

Unfortunately, most of these animals cannot be released into the wild because humans have deprived them from learning survival skills from members of their own species. When this is the case, we provide the best quality of life possible, including a personalised diet, an adequate space in accordance with their individual needs and the specific needs of their species, exercise, and daily environmental enrichment to promote natural behaviors.[8]

As a testament to its expertise honed over decades of work, Comunidad Inti Wara Yassi is often asked to advise other NGOs and government agencies about proper care.

There are only marginal genetic differences among humans and all the other great ape species. But only one of these groups of great apes has decided to put the others on display for entertainment. Only one kind has destroyed the habitats of others in pursuit of profit. Thankfully, some members of that atypical kind of great ape have also decided that other primates deserve better.

No sanctuary is perfect, but these kinds of spaces are normally far superior to all-but-certain death in the wild and wherever in captivity the animals came from. The primates at this Kentucky sanctuary almost never see strangers either. They get to know their human caretakers, but there is no endless stream of *Homo sapien* observers passing through. This special and unusual visit was arranged for the scholars attending an animal studies conference being held at Eastern Kentucky University. It was really an honor.

"The chimps love music, and they have different tastes," the caretaker explained. Some will watch television and movies too, and have strong reactions to people, other animals, and action on the screen.

One chimp was pressed against the edge, staring at a specific woman. The caretaker noticed. "She likes your shoes. She's obsessed with shoes." In fact, three of the females are: Noelle, Martina, and Jenny.

Some chimps were dressed up, and this interest in shoes may be a residual reflection of what had been their "normal." Or maybe these chimps just like shoes. Some were born in captivity, while others were taken from the wild as babies. That happened into the 1970s. Michael, a gorilla who lived at the Gorilla Foundation in California along with the late Koko and Ndume, all of whom learned American Sign Language, was taken from his family in the wild. Because he had a language humans could understand, he spoke of those experiences. He shared what he remembered about loud noises, chaos, and his mother.

Donald the chimp was rescued in 1998, but his precise age is unknown. The center notes, "Unlike some primate leaders, Donald has never been brutal; instead, he has exerted his authority by intervening during fights or by pairing with the most desirable females. Still, he becomes upset with unnecessary violence in his group and always accepts submissive gestures from his troop members to resolve the issues. He is always willing to work with his human caregivers, and seems to understand that we truly have his troop's best interests in mind." Donald likes to stay outside, even into the night. "Perhaps he feels better able to protect his troop while outdoors, or maybe he just likes the view of the moon and stars."[9]

Jenny was born in a research laboratory on May 19, 1995. Like other lab-born chimps, she was separated from her mother at an early age. When she arrived at the center in 1996, she and another young female, Pozna, clung to each other, both literally and figuratively. Pozna died suddenly in 2016, and she is survived by her friend. "Jenny has always enjoyed playing pranks on humans (one of her favorites is to get a mouthful of water and wait for an unsuspecting caretaker to walk close by), so we work hard to give her opportunities for silliness and play, without putting ourselves in jeopardy," the center explains. "Playing 'chase' alongside the outdoor enclosure is a longtime favorite game for Jenny, and an easy way for volunteers to safely interact with her."[10]

The center is also home to monkeys who have a similarly diverse set of life stories, but more often were kept as pets or by hoarders: siamangs, spider monkeys, many kinds of macaques, vervets, and capuchins. Some were seized by law enforcement, and others were surrendered by people who realized the animals needed a better life, such as Bob, Vernon, and Maddie. Some of them relish the social interaction with other monkeys and have formed close-knit groups and bonds. Others are too afraid and illustrate symptoms of post-traumatic stress, preferring to keep to themselves. The center shares that Nikki, a vervet monkey who was taken early from her own mother to be sold as a pet, has found surrogate parental figures in Dewey, a rhesus macaque, and Bubbles, a long-tailed macaque. Dewey and Bubbles promptly began grooming Nikki and cuddling with her, and now she enjoys monkey companionship, naps wrapped up in blankets, playing with toys that rattle, and mangoes. Here their individuality is recognized, even as they live together in a group. Both of these dimensions matter—their uniqueness and their right to have relationships. They are no longer defined by their utility or what they provide for humans. They matter in their own right.

These kinds of places teach us a lot about care and compassion.[11] Sanctuary leaders and staff know they cannot heal all the physical and psychological wounds of what has happened to the residents. Their natural social groups and habitats cannot be perfectly replicated. Still, sanctuaries do their best for these animals who are trapped in between the wild and captive spaces that do them harm. Sanctuaries provide animals with peace. They help our species begin to make amends for the physical, emotional, and intergenerational damage we have done.

Sanctuaries are not enough on their own. Much like wildlife rehabilitators and other animal rescues, sanctuaries vary, and many are not regulated. Some well-intentioned efforts result in people becoming overwhelmed and with animals in unacceptable conditions. Others set a high standard for animal care and ethics, trying to cultivate the most positive experiences for the animals as possible.

When it comes to primates, networks and alliances have been formed to provide mutual support and establish standards, both on the continents that are these animals' natural homes and in places like North America. Members of the North American Primate Sanctuary Alliance care for more than eight hundred animals including orangutans, monkeys, and of course, chimpanzees. April Truitt, cofounder of the Primate Rescue Center, "looks forward to the day when keeping primates as pets is unthinkable, and primate sanctuaries are no longer needed."[12] There are food bank and homeless shelter leaders who say the same thing about their organizations. You respond to the need as well as the symptoms of a deeper problem. You do the best you can. But the real solutions would make you obsolete.

The European Union recognized animals' sentience in 1997. Some countries, including Sweden, Britain, France, Spain, and most recently New Zealand (in 2015), now legally recognize animals as sentient beings—as capable of thinking and feeling, and having an awareness of self and others. In 2018, the parliament of Brussels unanimously voted to recognize an animal as "a living being endowed with sensitivity, interests of its own and dignity, that benefits from special protection."[13] Some places' laws have not used the term *sentience* explicitly, but do recognize animals' capacity to feel both physical and psychological pain, and that is progress.

Animals are simultaneously still legally defined as property, however, and not even some potentially linked category like living property. They are simply defined as property, like a car or cell phone. To confront this foundational issue, some lawyers and legal researchers want to see animals recognized as legal persons. In the plainest possible terms, this is not the same as literally being a person, but it is about being a legal subject. Historically, entire groups of people were not recognized as legal persons in the United States, Canada, and elsewhere, namely women, Black people, Indigenous peoples, and children. The US-based Nonhuman Rights Project notes that "around the world, ships, religious idols, [and] holy books have been recognized as legal persons. New Zealand has recognized a river, a national park, and a mountain as legal persons. . . . In 2018, the Colombian Amazon became a legal person."[14] Today in most countries, corporations are recognized as legal "persons."

Lawyers and animal organizations are chipping away at the formidable challenge of animals' legal position in different ways, with varying degrees of success. Legal scholars, like Maneesha Deckha, are proposing fundamentally different ways to conceptualize and organize the law.[15] Angela Fernandez proposes moving beyond the binary of property and person to recognize "quasi" statuses.[16] Some argue for a term like *sentient property*. Notably, many Indigenous systems of knowledge and cultures around the world, including in the western hemisphere, have always understood humans and other animals in relation to each other, and not positioned humans above other species. It is the legal systems rooted in non-Indigenous worldviews that have enshrined human dominance.

The term *abolitionism* has meant different things at various stages of history (abolishing slavery being the dominant example). Today in the animal landscape, it can refer to those who want to abolish prisons and police, and/or those who think animals need one central right—as Gary Francione puts it, the right not to be human property.[17] Philosophers, legal scholars, and political theorists in particular have developed a range of other ways to think about how we could afford animals more protections and entitlements, including through citizenship rights, labor rights, and wild animals' own rights to property.[18] There are many robust debates, and whether or how these theoretical or speculative proposals affect the frontline work of animal defenders varies.

Efforts to change public policy along with legal principles and practice have had varying degrees of success. The Great Ape Project has been working for nearly three decades to secure basic legal rights for nonhuman great apes: the right to life, protection from torture, and the right to individual freedom, including "the right to live in their habitat. Great primates who live in captivity have the right to live with dignity, in large rooms, to have contact with others of their species to form families and must be protected from commercial exploitation."[19]

The Nonhuman Rights Project identifies as a civil rights organization—one seeking to have animals' inherent rights and interests recognized in law. The organization argues that "courts must recognize our nonhuman animal clients as legal persons with the fundamental right to bodily liberty protected by the writ of habeas corpus and then order their release to a sanctuary where this right will be respected."[20] The organization secured the world's first habeas corpus order for an animal in 2015. In nonlegal speak, habeas corpus orders allow courts to assess whether the confinement or detention of someone is lawful or not. As part of the process, the detainer must testify. In the case of animals, the detainer could be a laboratory or a zoo, for example.

As a result, the judge can deem the animals' current situation acceptable or mandate a transfer of guardianship for that animal. This historic habeas corpus order applied to two chimpanzees, Hercules and Leo, who were being kept at New Iberia Research Center at the University of Louisiana at Lafayette, and who now reside at the Project Chimps sanctuary. In 2017, a judge in Argentina recognized a chimpanzee named Cecilia as a legal person. She now resides at the Great Ape Project Brazil's Sanctuário de Sorocaba.

Other cases of this kind are proceeding and being initiated. In 2022, a New York Court of Appeals ruled against the Nonhuman Rights Project's case on behalf of Happy, an Asian elephant taken from the wild in 1971 and moved in 1977 to the Bronx Zoo, where she remains. But even this 5–2 decision, with two judges dissenting, is indicative of changing legal perspectives.

Happy's case also exposes significant divisions within the animal protection landscape about what it means to care for animals and what rights they should have. A number of veterinary associations filed briefs opposing the Nonhuman Rights Project's petition, and in its May–June 2022 newsletter to its members, the American Veterinary Medical Association said the ruling was "a great decision for the profession." The Bronx Zoo is the "flagship park" of the Wildlife Conservation Society, which, aware of the power of job creation, boasts that it is the largest employer of youths in the borough, "providing opportunity and helping to transform lives in one of the most under-served communities in the nation."[21] Even better would be humane jobs that don't depend on anyone being held captive.

Dr. Jackie Gai is the director of veterinary services for the Performing Animal Wildlife Society (PAWS). Its sanctuary, ARK2000 in San Andreas, "covers twenty-three hundred acres of unspoiled California foothills landscape." She paints a beautiful picture of her cherished workplace.

There are gently rolling hills covered with native grasses, golden in the summer, lush and green in the winter and spring. The entire area is dotted with mature oak trees, providing shade as well as acorns for the bears to forage for. There are many days with clear blue sky, sunshine, and gentle breezes. We are located far enough from cities that at night you can see the stars, and the only sounds you hear are those of nature. The resident elephants, big cats, and bears live in large enclosures, with the relative freedom to choose how they spend their days. Elephants often dig in the soft earth, creating their own mud wallows. Tigers lie on their backs in the shade of a tree or swim in their pools. Bears forage to their hearts' content on insects, leaves, tender shoots, and acorns as well as on special treats hidden throughout their enclosures by caregivers.

Gai's journey from a kid obsessed with wild animals in Hawaii to zookeeper to lead veterinarian at a celebrated and special sanctuary is noteworthy.

I gradually realized that keeping wild animals in captivity didn't sit right with me. I learned that 90 percent of the medical and behavioral problems of wild animals in captivity are caused by some aspect of captivity itself, and that bothered me. I began to reexamine my lifelong fascination with wild animals in cages and realized that it was based on a love of animals, but never took into consideration the well-being of the animals themselves. I began to see captivity as selfish and archaic. I gradually left both of my zoo jobs and dedicated myself to PAWS because the mission of a true sanctuary is what resonated best with my soul.

PAWS itself was cofounded in 1984 by a woman who also had a dramatic change in her view of animals, the late Pat Derby, a former animal trainer who worked on prominent television shows, movies, and commercials. After becoming increasingly concerned about the treatment of animals in entertainment, Derby, along with Ed Stewart, created PAWS. Today the organization's three sanctuaries are home to animals primarily retired from films, zoos, and roadside or mobile animal attractions. Some are in a kind of "witness protection" as criminal investigations and prosecutions progress. "Every animal who lives at a PAWS sanctuary has a story to tell," Gai says.

Some are confiscated illegal pets, like Boo Boo the bear, whose "owners" chained him in their backyard as a youngster. Because he was still growing, the chain became tighter and tighter, eventually embedding itself in his neck, requiring surgical removal. Other animals are nonreleasable native wildlife, like Mack the bear. Mack was found as a very small cub, missing one rear leg. He was approaching people and begging for food. No one knows if he lost his leg from an injury or if he was born that way, but it was clear that he had lost his mother and was seeking help from people.

Large animals like elephants, bears, and big cats have physical and psychological needs—and desires—that are particularly challenging to replicate in captivity, but PAWS sets a high standard. "Some of the elephants are retired from AZA-accredited [American Zoological Association] zoos that have decided to close their elephant exhibits. Zoos are increasingly realizing that they simply cannot provide what elephants need physically and emotionally." This clearly is not the case for the Bronx Zoo, however.

But other facilities have taken a different approach. "Zoos face the decision of whether to spend millions of dollars to enlarge an exhibit just a little, or to close their elephant exhibits altogether and place their elephants elsewhere. Lulu, Toka, Thika, and Mara all came from zoos. Many animals come from 'roadside zoos,' where animals are usually kept in small cages with questionable care. Most of the tigers came from these places." These sorts of dynamics are familiar to everyone who watched *The Tiger King*: Cubs taken from their mothers and hand raised to be used for photo ops and petting sessions. Adults being fed processed and expired meat.

"We also care for elephants who are retired from the circus," Gai explains. She highlights Gypsy, a fifty-three-year-old female Asian elephant who was captured from the wild as a baby and "forced to travel from town to town performing in the circus for almost forty years. While traveling, she spent most of her life chained by her legs inside railroad cars, circus tents, or small barns. Asian elephant bulls Nicholas and Prince were born in captivity and were also forced to perform in circuses when they were young." Some PAWS residents have been accepted after roadside or mobile zoos were shut down by authorities, went out of business, or closed for another reason. Gai personally oversaw the transportation of thirty-nine tigers from a defunct roadside zoo in 2003. Dozens more were found too late and were already dead.

Gai shares another powerful story about Lulu, a fifty-six-year-old female African elephant, the oldest African elephant in North America. "She, too, was born in the wild, in Africa, and was captured as a baby and brought to the United States to live in a zoo," Gai says of the all-too-common pattern.

In nature, baby elephants stay close to their mothers and female relatives for many years; females stay with their maternal herds for life. Elephant families are loving, supportive, and protective, and babies are treasured. Babies learn over many years the culture of their herd, and all of its associated survival skills, all the while surrounded by loving family members. Lulu was taken from her family at an age where she should have still been nursing from her mother, and nurtured and taught by her extended family.

But Lulu's life at a zoo caused her to fear other elephants because of a dominant female with whom she shared a barn and small enclosure. "When she first saw another elephant at PAWS, she dropped down onto her elbows and knees and crawled along the ground in a submissive position that is wholly unnatural in a healthy, well-adjusted elephant. At PAWS, we take great care to introduce new elephants to our facility, staff, and other elephants safely, with great patience, and at whatever pace each elephant needs to feel comfortable with their new home." It took months, but Lulu gradually learned to trust and feel safe, including around other elephants.

It was deeply moving to watch her transformation from being timid and fearful to being strong and confident. Today Lulu roams the rolling, grassy hills of the sanctuary with her elephant companions close by. She shows none of the fear or apprehension that she had when she first arrived. She is confident and outgoing, and other elephants look to her for leadership. Lulu has a beautiful face with expressive eyes and an impish sense of humor.

Gai considered the animals and the evidence, reflecting on both the science and ethics, and then made the decision that shaped her career.

I approach my work with the intention of being of service to each animal in my care. With each animal, I ask, "What can I do for you today? What do you need?" This is my guiding and essential principle. It is both an honor and a great privilege to care for animals, many of whom have suffered at the hands of people before their rescue. It is deeply rewarding to be a part of their healing process, to see them learn to trust, and to see their true personalities emerge.

Gai has also identified something that many who work at sanctuaries recognize: other animals seem to recognize that these are spaces of peace. "The sanctuary also preserves large areas of land for native wildlife to thrive, including foxes, bobcats, turkeys, bears, mountain lions, and a huge variety of songbirds, raptors, and other animals native to our area. The sanctuary has a special energy to it—healing, safe, and full of life."

Her daily veterinary work is both responsive and preventative, and can involve performing surgeries on these massive animals. She collaborates with veterinary technicians and other veterinary specialists (such as dentists, ophthalmologists, and oncologists), and as is always the case, some of the essential work is done away from the animals like record keeping, research, and regulatory paperwork. Gai emphasizes that direct care is "only part of what we do to help wild animals." There is also crucial legal and political work like providing testimony, educating people about wild animals in captivity, and supporting and helping to draft legislation so as to go upstream. Sanctuaries rarely receive financial support when they house animals confiscated during criminal investigations. This is another example of nonprofit organizations subsidizing law enforcement work and the public sector. Gai would like to see more convicted animal abusers being required to pay for the care of the animals after their rescue. This is done in certain trials, but not uniformly.

The keeping of wild animals in captivity for any reason is a source of division among those committed to animals. Animal action on film and television sets in the United States at least is monitored by the nonprofit American Humane, including when companion animals like dogs are involved. There are also calls to end the use of wild animals in entertainment, and advances in computer-generated imaging make this increasingly possible. More broadly, questions are raised about whether even accredited zoos that seek to provide quality care can really meet the needs of wild animals. Accredited zoos often support and some fund conservation work for animals in the wild, but the place of wild animals in cities and towns, normally far away from the natural habitats of those animals, is a source of much debate. This is true for both land and aquatic animals overall, including whales and dolphins, who have gained particular attention in recent years. Many of these large marine mammals were wild caught and would normally swim through massive oceanic territories with their family groups, communicating in extraordinary ways humans are just beginning to understand. Yet in captivity, their tanks are smaller than parking lots.

Multifaceted work is being undertaken for these animals too. Former employees like Phil Demers have become whistleblowers, and criminal investigations are taking place, as is the case with Marineland in Canada. Documentarians like Gabriela Cowperthwaite have highlighted aquatic animals in captivity in places like SeaWorld for mass audiences. More consumers are choosing not to visit these facilities and instead donate to solutions-oriented work such as the creation of an ocean-based sanctuary. The Whale Sanctuary Project, founded by Dr. Lori Marino, has secured land off the east coast of Nova Scotia in Canada that will allow cetaceans (whales and dolphins) formerly kept in captivity to live safely in the ocean.

Lesson #11: just because something is legal doesn't mean it's right or good for animals.

This is a significant time. Maybe we are on the precipice of major changes, as we question historical assumptions as well as ask serious questions about many practices currently deemed acceptable and normal like keeping wild animals in zoos and aquariums. As people increasingly question the ethics of captivity and animal use, and make changes to their individual purchasing decisions as a result, and lawmakers modernize laws and what is legally permitted, the practical matters of what to do with the animals in between who are held in human-controlled spaces become paramount. That is why sanctuaries like PAWS are essential. Perhaps one day, PAWS will become obsolete too.

Picture a rabbit. There's a good chance you imagined a furry hopper with long ears and a wiggly nose, most likely in the wild. Maybe you pictured a fictional rabbit who has graced your life like Peter Rabbit, Thumper from

Bambi, the White Rabbit in the *Alice in Wonderland* books, or one of the memorable characters from *Watership Down*. Perhaps you know a rabbit in someone's house who is considered a pet or family member. You probably didn't picture a rabbit waiting for a butcher's knife or at an abattoir. You most certainly didn't picture a rabbit caged in a research lab.

I picture a rabbit neighbor who I affectionately named Bébé when he was indeed a baby, in tribute to the illustrious Moira Rose on *Schitt's Creek*. Bébé was born under a row of cedars. As I write this book, Bébé is a year old, and I hope he will live to see its publication. It's tough out there for rabbits who must avoid vehicles and are hunted for food by other animal neighbors like the foxes and coyotes whose howls fill the night air. We know he is a he because he would have had his own *bébés* by now if he were female. In the summer, he forages among the birds and squirrels in a peaceful multispecies community, and dozes in a rewilded space we created in honor of our beloved dog, the Buster memorial garden. For one of the Indigenous nations on whose traditional territories we live, the Anishinaabe, cedar is a sacred medicine. I like to think Bébé has benefited from being born and raised in a cradle of healing. A second rabbit has joined our community. I named this one Uncle Baby Billy as a lighthearted tribute to one of my favorite character actors, Walton Goggins, and his memorable performance on *Righteous Gemstones*, and so I can delightfully narrate the rabbit's activities. "Uncle Baby Billy is eating clover." "Uncle Baby Billy is napping in the Buster memorial garden." "Uncle Baby Billy did a *binky!*" (the technical term for a rabbit's happy jump).

The rabbits who live outside the pages of our cherished tales, cartoons, and chocolate creations are differently defined, and as a result, differently protected. Rabbits can be part of rewilding plans and thus benefit when land is conserved. More than twenty types of wild rabbit are on the International Union for the Conservation of Nature's list of species at risk. Some are critically endangered like the riverine rabbit in South Africa and Columbia basin pygmy rabbit, the smallest in North America, whose numbers plummeted to fifty individuals at the turn of the millennium. After twenty years of intensive, collaborative protection efforts led by the Nature Conservancy, it is estimated that today there are a hundred.

Rabbits who are members of species not at risk are still injured by our vehicles and companion animals, so become patients of wildlife rehabilitators. Rabbits are farmed for meat and fur, and commonly used in laboratories as models for diseases, treatments, and the toxicity testing of products, including cleaning products and cosmetics. Animals used as part of postsecondary educational programs like in biology labs as well as university and college-based research are normally euthanized afterward due to organizational policy and/or the governing law of the land. Along with guinea pigs, chinchillas, fish, primates, mice, rats, and dogs, animals used in laboratory research are normally legally sectioned off from their counterparts in the wild or homes, and their lives and deaths are governed by specific pieces of legislation determining the realities for "animals in research." Many things that would be illegal if done to a pet rabbit due to the level of pain they cause are permitted when the rabbits are part of a research lab.

These facilities are highly protected, and are places many people never think about or may like to forget exist. Certain animal activists have removed animals from labs and taken them to sanctuaries or released them into the wild, although the animals' chance of survival in the latter is low. Some animal defenders have taken jobs inside these facilities in order to covertly document crimes that would otherwise go unseen or acts that aren't yet illegal but that are nevertheless painful for the animals.[22] These strategies are used to expose and outrage, and ideally, ignite policy changes or testing bans. Some workers who were not opposed to the principle of animal testing become too distraught by what they must witness, and the nightmares, guilt, and stress linger long after their last shifts.

Yet the rabbit has also become the symbol of alternatives to this kind of animal use. The global Leaping Bunny program provides a literal rabbit marker on products that have not been tested on animals. This certification program is not the only possible indicator of an organization's cruelty-free status but it is a prominent one, and more than two thousand cosmetics, personal care, and household products companies have earned the Leaping Bunny designation specifically. Certification is a rigorous process, and animals may not be test subjects during the creation or development of any of the products, nor any of the ingredients used. Some companies do not make the grade because they permit their products to be tested on animals in countries where that is required before importation and sale, such as is currently the case in China.

Animal defenders have a long history of advocating for animals in labs in different ways, with early antivivisection (conducting operations and testing on living animals) efforts stemming back to the late 1800s.[23] In 1876, Britain passed an antivivisection law to provide some regulation of the practice after a public groundswell of concern led by Irish author and suffragist Frances Power Cobbe. Her organization, the British Union for the Abolition of Vivisection, was at work for more than a century before it joined with the New England Anti-Vivisection Society to form a global organization, Cruelty Free International. The precise number of animals used in research is unknown around the world, although Cruelty Free International estimates it is nearly 200 million.

The term *cruelty free* is both an engine and goal, and the work has been multipronged: encouraging consumers to choose cruelty-free products and brands, promoting company-level change, and buttressing nationwide legislation. The logic informing the last strategy means people could walk into any cosmetics aisle, department, or store and know that every product was cruelty-free—a highly worthy goal. Some companies have long refused to test products on animals, while others are now declaring the practice unnecessary and unethical, and making the required organizational changes. More than forty countries have banned cosmetics testing on animals so far, and that number continues to grow. Some US states have banned or limited the practice, but Mexico became the first country in North America to ban cosmetics testing on animals after a unanimous senate vote in fall 2021.

Certain animals who have spent their lives in labs are being adopted in homes, and programs for a small number of rabbits exist. The Beagle Freedom Project had already been at work rescuing animals when, in 2010, a research lab asked if it would take two "experimentally spent" beagles. That helped expand the organization's work, and today it works globally to rescue, rehabilitate, and rehome beagles who are widely used in labs, including for chemical toxicity testing.

People may see a difference between testing on animals for cosmetics and medical research. Every one of us has benefited from health-related products that were created from animal parts and/or animal suffering. Yet the large majority of drugs that have passed and been deemed effective at animal testing phases, fail in clinical trials involving humans. A growing body of research questions the effectiveness of the dominant approach to medical education, testing, and development that sees animals as analogues to humans. More scientists are asking questions about both the effectiveness and ethics of business as usual, and whether there are safer and smarter options for the future. In addition to asking questions, some are actively working for changes. The nonprofit health research and advocacy organization Physicians Committee for Responsible Medicine has worked since 1985 to end the use of animals in medical education. It has nearly two hundred thousand members globally and emphasizes a range of proactive approaches to health care and nutrition as well as the development of scientifically sound alternatives to animal use.

The 3Rs may be promoted: replacing (primarily by instead using computer models, biochemical, invitro, or other cell-based methods), reducing (the number of animals used), and/or refining (minimizing the pain caused to the animal, and/or enhancing living conditions through better housing or nutrition, enrichment, and maybe social contact). In 1986, the Council of Europe signed a convention "designed to reduce both the number of experiments and the number of animals used for such purposes and it encourages not to experiment on animals except where there is no alternative and it promotes research into alternative methods."[24]

Scientists doing this kind of work may or may not see themselves as defending animals. Some do, while others are motivated not by the ethics but rather by the science and desire for better results than those emerging from the status quo. For some, this work is seen as better for both people and animals.

The Canadian Centre for Alternatives to Animal Methods and the Canadian Centre for the Validation of Alternative Methods at the University of Windsor led by Dr. Charu Chandrasekera aim to "develop, validate, and promote non-animal, human biology-based platforms in biomedical research, education, and chemical safety testing." The centers state that "it is not possible to accurately recapitulate complex, multifactorial human diseases in other animals," which in simpler terms means it's not great science.[25] "If the ultimate goal is to advance human medicine and safety testing, then our species must serve as the quintessential animal model, with human biology as the gold standard," Chandrasekera says. The Johns Hopkins Bloomberg School of Public Health's Center for Alternatives to Animal Testing argues that the "best science is humane science" and has partnered with the University of Konstanz to establish a European center. Director Dr. Thomas Hartung says, "Sound science is the bridge, not only across the Atlantic, but also for a future with safer products using fewer animals."[26] In order to go upstream in the service of animals to prevent harm by finding alternatives, bridges of different scales and types often need to be built.

10 HORSEPOWER

Horses are also in between legally, geographically, and culturally. Who are horses? Are they people's companions and friends? Undoubtedly. Are they coworkers? Yes, and for some people they are seen as employees. Are they commodities who are bought and sold? Frequently. Are they athletes? Often. Are they wild animals? Yes. Are they livestock? Legally, most horses are. They are many other identities simultaneously that have nothing or little to do with people—friends, mothers, herd members, and protectors in their own right. Horses and horse protection exemplify every facet and theme of this book.

Few animals have danced through human imagination for as long or as much as horses.[1] From the Queen of England strolling through rural manors on horseback to a young Black man riding proudly through the streets of Philadelphia, horses undoubtedly hold a special place in diverse people's hearts. Horses are still part of cities, including in inner-city riding communities in Philadelphia and Los Angeles. Black-led riding communities have been part of the fabric of US urban life for decades, and offer important work, solidarity, mentorship, and life-changing opportunities, particularly for young people in communities struggling with the effects of poverty, racism, and violent crime. The nonprofit Detroit Horse Power is planning to build a new urban equestrian stable on repurposed, vacant land to engage young people in the city who otherwise would not have access to horses.

Across the Atlantic, the nonprofit Ebony Horse Club and the social enterprise Urban Equestrian Academy prioritize the inclusion of ethnically and religiously diverse young people with "the least experience in the Equestrian world and also individuals/communities with the least access to it."[2] Nonprofit and publicly funded Swedish programs engage the children of refugees with and through horses to interweave sport and learning Swedish as a second (or third) language. Horses don't care about people's racial identity or income. Horses prioritize kindness. They will collaborate with us. They will teach us. They also want room to move around, and time to just be horses and relax, eat, and play. Horses want their bodies and minds to be respected, and to have freedom from fear.

Many Indigenous communities long valued horses and partnered with them for hunting and travel. When European settlers arrived in North America, horses were always part of their communities and were essential. Horses have provided the speed, power, and energy that moved people, and the literal horsepower for everything from construction to mail delivery to fire departments. The work-lives of horses in early towns and cities were not easy anywhere. Anna Sewell made waves with the publication of *Black Beauty*, a moving life story written from the viewpoint of a horse who pulled carts and carriages for compassionate and callous people alike. Although fictional, the book reflected reality, and succeeded in raising the issue of horse welfare to new heights. The book invites readers to experience the world from horses' perspectives, and asks us to care about their friendships, bodies, and fates. Visible cruelty to cart horses in the streets was a key catalyst for the creation of the first animal protection organizations in England, the United States, Canada, and other countries as people moved from empathy to compassion and action.[3] Henry Bergh founded the ASPCA after he witnessed a driver beating a fallen horse in Russia.

Of course, a lot has changed since horses were the primary mode of transportation in the Global North. Today horses are used and involved in a broad range of human pursuits, from racing of different kinds, jumping, dressage (basically horse ballet), and breed-specific competitions, to driving, herding, law enforcement, and therapy. Some horses are kept solely as companions, while others are used by people in competitions in pursuit of money, fun, status, or all three. How horses are viewed, valued, and treated by people varies within and across the different spheres, and affects how people defend these extraordinary animals, whose labor and cooperation helped build societies, and who continue to do so much for our species.

There are wild-roaming horses around the world whose histories and stories are as diverse as the humans around whom they live. Photos of the protected wild horses on Sable Island in eastern Canada grazing alongside napping sea lions are a delight. Conversely, devastating images of horse corpses and skeletons in places like Kazakhstan drive home the lethal effects of droughts. The mustangs who color the US landscape are legally protected from slaughter, but whether they truly have the right to exist and move freely as well as reproduce is a source of significant ongoing debate often pitting animal defenders against cattle ranchers.[4] Wild horses in New Mexico, including within Navajo territories, are at risk of being gathered for slaughter, but also are affected by partnerships that provide veterinary care, including the gelding (castration) of males. Free-roaming horses in the Rocky Mountains of Alberta are currently protected and receive emergency care when needed from dedicated local people as well.

Some of the most controversial horses are those who pull carriages around New York City's Central Park and in other tourist venues to this day. Their lives illuminate fierce debates about what it really means to love and protect horses. On the one side are carriage drivers. While the Teamsters organization gained fame (or notoriety) thanks to Jimmy Hoffa, the labor union was actually created by small *t* teamsters—the people who literally drove teams of horses through US streets more than a century ago. The union still has a horse's head as its logo and represented the three hundred carriage drivers who work in Central Park until 2020 when they joined the Transport Workers Union. These workers and other nonunionized, urban carriage drivers around North America from New Orleans to Niagara-on-the-Lake assert their right to make a living, and say that they love the horses and supply them with quality care, fair working conditions, and good lives.

On the other hand, some animal advocates argue that forcing even a small number of horses to work on concrete, in and around traffic, in all kinds of weather, is too dangerous. Carriage horses do fall at times, and upsetting footage of them splayed out on the road adds fuel to activists' fire. As for equine veterinarians, most do not object to horses continuing to work pulling tourists around towns and cities or the conditions of these animals' lives.

There are often local ordinances governing aspects of carriage horses' working conditions and work-lives beyond the job. It's not exactly labor law, but regulations establishing things like temperature ceilings and floors (meaning the horses cannot be put to work when the temperature is above or below the established standards) offer these animals some additional protections, when enforced.

Certain political leaders have taken an ethical stand against the practice as a whole, including in Santo Domingo in the Dominican Republic. In 2020, Carolina Mejía, the city's first female mayor, announced plans to replace eleven horse-drawn carriages with electric alternatives, keeping the drivers employed and allowing tourists to still view the city, but eliminating the need for living horsepower. A ban on tourist horse carriages or *calèches* in Montreal, Canada, took effect on New Year's Day in 2020. The Montreal SPCA and city government wanted to make sure the approximately fifty horses received a suitable retirement rather than being sold or auctioned into an unknown fate and so partnered to create a placement program for the city's carriage horses. Former owners would be paid a thousand dollars for each horse. Unfortunately, only two drivers took advantage of this program, one of whom was responsible for Sissi, a gentle mare who worked for a staggering seventeen years pulling carriages. She is now enjoying a life of leisure and plenty of time outdoors with horsey friends. Some other horses were retired to A Horse Tale Rescue before the ban took effect.

Anticipating that there would be a need to find homes for the horses and acting accordingly, with financial incentive, is prudent. So why didn't more owners and drivers take advantage of the program? Sophie Gaillard, a lawyer as well as the director of animal advocacy and legal affairs at the Montreal SPCA, says,

> There was a lot of resentment toward the city of Montreal for enacting a ban, and the Montreal SPCA for being historically extremely critical of the industry and instrumental in securing the ban, so my impression is that many owners and drivers refused to participate out of spite. Others used their horses

outside city limits as well, such as for weddings, so wanted to keep their animals for those purposes.

One of the biggest players launched a lawsuit challenging the ban as well, so Gaillard suspects some drivers may be waiting to see what happens with that case. A small number of the horses are still being kept within city limits, despite the city having a kind of "positive list" for permitted animals that does not include horses. Certain drivers have said the amount offered may provide compensation for the horse, but not for the lost future income. Whether and/or how those affected by legal changes designed to protect animals should be compensated is a recurring question—one differently answered around the world when particular industries are outlawed or the welfare standards are raised to levels operators cannot afford.

Thinking downstream even further to potential future harm—by recognizing that when we change laws and standards and outlaw particular practices, the animals currently involved will be affected—is laudable. Gaillard encourages other places considering bans to move forward and include a "buyback" program akin to what was used in Montreal, even if that attempt wasn't overly successful. Perhaps emphasizing conciliatory language would help, although those whose livelihoods are endangered may or may not be open to any alternatives or changes, even those proposed with the spirit of collaboration. This is a powerful reminder that good intentions may not be enough when working with the most complicated species of all—our own.

Many horses and other equids like donkeys and mules, at least 110 million of them, still work every day doing manual labor with and for people in low- and middle-income countries, especially in Latin America, Africa, and Asia. The animals pull plows in fields and carts carrying products to market, and help people, especially women, with essential labor like fetching water. People cannot survive without these animals, and protection efforts look different in these contexts.

Martha Geiger has studied equine protection, particularly involving donkeys, their human coworkers, and their intertwined well-being in Ethiopia and Botswana for over ten years, and is now completing doctoral studies at the University of Warwick. She explains that despite their importance, the animals suffer, both physically and emotionally. They are required to work in extreme heat with inadequate breaks and feed, often in equipment that fits poorly and causes pain. "Equid labor is heavily depended on to complete essential, often daily, tasks for their human caretakers, who are also struggling to meet their own needs and those of their families." In other words, life is tough for everyone. "Human caretakers normally have little or no access to education and training in humane husbandry and handling. . . . In many countries, adequate veterinary and farrier services are in short supply, which means infections, lameness, or wounds."

A report titled *Invisible Helpers* written by the nonprofit the Brooke amplified the voices of women in poor communities who work with equids in Ethiopia, India, Kenya, and Pakistan, and makes it unequivocally clear how significant these animals and the challenges really are. "Having a donkey feels like having a tap in my home. I am confident that I won't run out of water," says Sefiya Hebiso in Ethiopia. Faith Wamalwa Kinyua from Kenya says, "I am lacking words to fully explain how grateful I am and how really my life depends on donkeys." "When my horse was sick I walked 25 kms to buy medicine," shares Ramshri, a forty-five-year-old widow from India.[5]

Having uneven access to knowledge compounded by a lack of access to essential veterinary and other animal care services is a recurring pattern in low-income communities the world over. As is the case within countries, NGOs—especially the Brooke, World Horse Welfare, Society for the Protection of Animals Abroad, and Donkey Sanctuary (United Kingdom)—are working across borders to improve the lives of both animals and people, separately and in coalition. "These NGOs focus on community-based and community-driven programs on the front lines, but they also campaign at the highest levels of international decision-making to draw attention to and garner support for the important work equids do," Geiger explains. The organizations deliver locally relevant health and welfare education as well as work with veterinary schools and primary schools.

> [They] provide training to make cost-effective and humane harness and saddlery equipment and to provide farrier [hoof care] training. They also teach essential health care to owners and local animal health professionals. Through mobile and locally based clinics, these NGOs deliver free urgent medical care

to equids who suffer from various diseases, viruses, injuries, and infections. The NGOs are also equipped to respond to humanitarian emergencies such as extreme weather events like droughts and hurricanes by providing essential feed, fresh water, shelter and veterinary care to equids.

In addition, the Brooke founded what is believed to be the first school for farriers outside North America and Europe in Senegal.

International trade has added another layer of challenge. The traditional Chinese medicine *ejiao* is made from gelatin found in donkey skin "and retails at a very high price in China," Geiger says.

> The increasing popularity of ejiao has resulted in the illegal and legal sale and slaughter of donkeys, with the skins then shipped to China. Unfortunately, as a result of the high demand and price of ejiao in China, there has been a reported increased in theft of donkeys from owners who rely on them for their livelihoods. And donkeys are reportedly kept in terrible, inhumane conditions before being slaughtered for their skin.

NGOs are lobbying for bans on the sale of donkey hides as a result. This involves domesticated animals but mirrors the challenge of the wild animal trade.

Please pardon the pun, but it is a wild west when it comes to horse welfare standards in the Global North. Some countries have national codes that outline the minimum standards horse owners and caretakers should follow to afford these animals a basic level of physical well-being. These are voluntary provisions and not legally enforceable—recommendations not requirements.

In contrast, in some countries there are specialized and more detailed provisions in addition to general animal protection laws. In Sweden, for example, there are species-specific regulations that are legally enforceable for many kinds of animals, including horses—and publicly funded welfare inspectors who do both responsive and proactive work. The regulations establish standards rooted in evidence rather than individual opinion or habit. Barbed wire fencing is prohibited. Horses are not to be kept inside in a stall/box for more than sixteen hours each day. Stalls must be properly bedded to allow horses to lay down comfortably, and minimum dimensions are established based on the size of the horse or pony (smaller equines). Outdoor shelters are mandatory for horses who live outside for more than eight hours a day. Horses must be able to move at all their natural gaits daily.

As is the case in Switzerland and Germany, trimming horses' whiskers is not legal in Sweden either. In some countries where the practice is not yet legally prohibited, some sport and equine associations have established their own rules, preventing participation in competition if whiskers are shaved, such as in France and parts of Australia. This is because horses' whiskers—vibrissae—are sensory organs with their own nerves. Horses use them to feel and navigate their environments, yet many people shave them with clippers for purely aesthetic reasons.

Some sectors, like the growing field of animal-assisted interventions or activities (i.e., animal-assisted therapy, psychotherapy, or learning), that are driven by an ethic of care are more likely to have developed guidelines establishing acceptable standards for horses who are employed in such programs. Again, not exactly labor rights, but guiding policies that can recognize protections and entitlements for the horses along with what I call their work-lives to highlight the importance of their well-being during and after work, on a daily basis, and over the course of their lives, including what happens when they are retired.

Most horses are still kept in the country and so not commonly seen by the wider general public. This is not a problem unto itself, and people who don't understand horses, even if well-intentioned, may incorrectly identify perfectly harmless acts as problematic. Fly masks are an example of this. Masks made of see-through mesh are often placed on horses to protect their eyes from bugs, yet those not familiar with horse care have been known to think these are blindfolds.

Horses are involved in violence link cases. A British Columbia woman and mother of three was killed by her estranged husband after she returned to their formerly shared property to check on her horse. A horse was fatally shot in South Carolina by a man, in front of a woman, as part of a series of violent acts. Victims stay in abusive situations, fearing for the safety of the horses if they flee.

In many places, horses are protected by general animal protection laws. Suspected cruelty, if observed, can be reported to the pertinent enforcement agency. Animal protection officers in SPCAs, animal care and control services, and policing agencies can and do investigate complaints about horse neglect and abuse. Sometimes they are too late, but horses have been seized from abusive situations or surrendered by people who became overwhelmed by the cost and labor required to provide even a minimum standard of care. Horses' natural life spans are generally twenty-five to thirty years, and their care is never cheap. Horses kept alone, with minimal food and without sufficient farrier care for their hooves, are rarely seen, so rarely reported, and they suffer in silence. Proactive inspections, an excellent tool for protecting animals, are unfortunately uncommon. They are tools used primarily in countries like Sweden and the Netherlands. Transportation and the subsequent housing of horses in abuse cases is a challenge, but enforcement agencies can develop partnerships proactively, or find appropriate farms and people who can trailer and house horses in need.

Seeing emaciated horses, even just in photos and videos, is difficult. Neglect means animals suffer physically and psychologically for a long period of time. They feel hunger, thirst, fear, anxiety, and pain. They don't understand why they are being deprived and made to suffer. Images of one horse in Oregon who was formerly known as Shadow and is now fittingly called Justice were extra upsetting to me because he is a black quarter horse who looks like my mother's late equine companion Amigo. Not only linked by color and breed, Justice also has the same gentle look in his eyes as Amigo.

But their life journeys differed significantly. Amigo lived a peaceful life in good health until his death at the age of twenty-five. Justice was left outdoors throughout the winter without food, shelter, or any horse companions. Horses only sleep for short periods of time, and their bodies are designed to be slowly foraging for most of the day and night, near other horses. Regular access to hay is especially essential in winter when the ground is covered in snow or mud because forage helps horses keep warm. Justice suffered lasting liver damage, was three hundred pounds underweight and alarmingly weak, and experienced frostbite that permanently damaged his body in painful and shocking ways.

His former owner was charged and pleaded guilty to criminal neglect, and Justice was rehomed to the rescue organization Sound Equine Solutions. The sentence included restitution (only) for the cost of Justice's care prior to the plea agreement. Some horses who are surrendered or seized in cruelty cases can be successfully rehabilitated and adopted into suitable homes, but Justice's future is still unknown. He may need to remain at the rescue given the extent of his injuries and will always have health issues. Sound Equine Solutions explains that Justice is protective of his food and stall, which is neither surprising nor uncommon for horses who have been starved.

Who covers the cost of animal care and funds or subsidizes animal-focused law enforcement has been a recurring question throughout this book. When humans are injured—say, in a car accident by a drunk driver—we have the right to seek compensation to cover the costs of care and treatment that result. Should animals have the same right? The ALDF says yes and has sought to have Justice's standing recognized in civil court so that he may sue to recover the costs of his "ongoing medical care and to compensate him for his pain and suffering."[6]

Is this in the same legal terrain as the habeas corpus orders being pursued on behalf of the chimpanzees and elephants? Sort of, but ALDF senior staff attorney Amanda Howell explains the key differences, including that this is more of a procedural approach and in many ways an affirmation of an already-existing social reality. "For us, this case is about getting the courts to recognize what people already recognize: animals are victims, and anticruelty laws are designed to protect them."

She helpfully unpacks the legalese and planks of the case. Was the statute/law violated? Yes, Justice's former owner pleaded guilty. Was the plaintiff—in this case Justice—injured? Yes, clearly and undeniably so. Is the injury of the type that the statute was meant to address? Yes, animal cruelty laws are designed to stop both abuse and neglect. Is the plaintiff a member of the class of persons the law is meant to protect? Animal cruelty statutes are designed to protect animals, and Justice is an animal. "The case is procedurally and legally sound," Howell argues. "We don't have anticruelty laws for chairs." It's somehow both intriguing and obvious. "Sanctuaries should not have to bear the cost of indefinitely caring for victims of human abuse, nor should victims themselves."

The Oregon legislature and courts have already recognized that animals are sentient beings and victims in other ways, and Justice's case is working its way through the layers of the legal system. At the time of this writing, an appellate court is considering whether to send the case back to the lower court to continue being tried. If successful, essentially this case would establish the right for animals to sue those who have violated animal cruelty laws by abusing or neglecting them, with the help of human allies, and make convicted abusers more responsible for the long-term financial effects of their actions, or lack thereof. All done in the name of a little black horse who fought to survive against crippling conditions. All done in the name of Justice.

Beyond the clear-cut cases of abuse and neglect, people have mixed views about what constitutes cruelty when it comes to horses, regardless of legal definitions. I consistently find that many people are willing to think proactively and beyond the legal status quo when it comes to horses. "That should be illegal," people will say, demonstrating an understanding that our laws are created by people, and that they can be changed by people, as our knowledge and ethical priorities evolve, develop, and deepen. Which acts, practices, and even uses are deemed unacceptable varies significantly, however.

Whether laws and regulations simply seek to protect animals from physical harm or also to recognize their psychological and emotional well-being varies. In Swedish law, horses must also have social contact with other animals, preferably other horses, and caretakers are directed to "pay attention" to the horses and the signs they will show if they are unhappy. Should we simply prohibit the bad or make regulations that compel people to take steps that allow animals to be happier too? Philosophers call it animals' right to flourish—not just survive, but thrive. It is a compelling goal, and one worth pursuing.

To recognize horses' psychological and emotional well-being, whether it's legally mandated or not, people need to pay attention to what horses are saying and feeling. Animals are responsive to their own life's journey and those they meet along the way. They make choices, when allowed to do so. They may repress their true feelings, especially when we ask them to work for and with us, but they don't lie. The science of animal behavior and cognition should be enlisted to correctly understand animals along with a recognition of the individuality of animals. They are also social beings who are not simply biologically programmed.[7]

Horses tolerate a lot. "Learned helplessness" is what equine behaviorists call it. When horses try to communicate and are repeatedly ignored, they eventually stop trying to share their views. My stomach hurts. My back is stiff. I pulled a muscle. I'm ovulating and feel uncomfortable. I'm bored. This makes me nervous. I'm afraid. I don't like you. These are all sentences we would recognize clearly if spoken by a human, but horses don't speak English. They communicate in their own ways. They stop or back up. They pin their ears, the universal sign for "back off, please" or "back off!" Horses are more likely to try to avoid something—or someone—unpleasant than they are to react with anger or cause pain. Yet sometimes people ignore their ways of communicating or simply don't care what horses have to say.[8]

My horse Henry was abused. Both his body and behavior say so. His cheekbone and front leg were fractured at some point, although it's unclear how those injuries occurred. His ears and nose are scarred, and those were definitely nonaccidental injuries, as the forensic veterinarians put it. Those wounds were caused by humans. It took a long time for him to learn to relax and understand that he has a say over his life. Henry is remarkably resilient and a happy-go-lucky guy in many ways, but he is also sensitive to certain experiences and objects in ways that reveal the pains of his past.

People are learning more about the minds of animals of all kinds from varied forms of research (some of which is ethically problematic). This includes rats and mice who laugh, elephants who cooperate, and monkeys who object to their neighbor getting a better food reward than them for completing a task—or what you could call unequal pay.[9] But humans are still barely scratching the surface of understanding other animals' minds, and as a result, should be acting with far more humility and compassion.[10] By interweaving scientific data with an ethical commitment to genuinely respecting horses—and other animals—as individuals, people are best positioned to be attuned to animals' needs and feelings, and then develop more respectful practices that don't simply defend them from harm but also allow them to thrive. Sometimes this process can be painful.

My older horse Kozzie is a gentleman of leisure. A few years ago, one of his friends, Bono, had to be euthanized. In the subsequent days, Kozzie refused to eat large portions of his grain, including his beloved sweet feed, and quickly lost about fifty pounds. His eyes lacked brightness, and as we walked down the stable aisle together, he would try to enter Bono's stall. When outside, Kozzie and his other pasture mate paced the fence line, calling out for their missing friend. The barn became an interspecies loop of sorrow, and there was nothing I could do to help Kozzie feel better. It took time. The brightness finally returned to his eyes a week later, and he became more interested in eating again.

Throughout his life, Kozzie's friends have been sold and taken off the property for competitions for weeks or months at a time. No doubt each of these social ruptures was upsetting. Yet this was the first friend he had lost due to death. He had never reacted so intensely, so viscerally, to a horse's absence. This story is Kozzie's, but the underlying truth is not unique to him. Many horse people have experienced their own versions of it. Barbara J. King, Jeffrey Moussaieff Masson, and others have explored animals' experiences and expressions of grief in depth.[11] It is a difficult subject, but an essential one. Animals experience the world and their relationships in profound ways. They remember individuals they knew months and years later, and this has been repeatedly observed among horses, elephants, dogs, monkeys, big cats, and animals of all kinds. Animals' emotions and inter-connectedness really cannot be overstated when thinking proactively about animal protection—that is, when thinking downstream.

Number 6027 marked "safe."

These words send waves of relief. Whoever this horse was has been reduced to a number at an auction, but she has been rescued from a painful and premature death.

There are about nine million horses in the United States. Susan Kayne, founder of Unbridled Thoroughbred Foundation in Greenville, New York, is contacted about horses in need all the time, which is both fortunate and unfortunate. It's good news for those being saved at least.

Kayne is a lifelong horsewoman who was heavily involved in racing for years. "My earliest childhood memory is of seeing Canonero II win the Kentucky Derby. It felt as if on that day, Thoroughbreds ran right into my heart." She toured the world's racing stables, and bred, studied, rode, sold, and owned horses. She promoted the racing industry on Unbridled TV. But then she began to question her "rose-colored glasses" after one of her horses, Bourbon Bandit, broke his knee in a race. Kayne was furious and contributed to a front-page story in the *New York Times* questioning the use of both permitted and banned drugs in racing.

"The risk is simply being born as a Thoroughbred in the sport of kings," Kayne tells me. The business model means horses are run hard—and early in their lives. "It is $3,000 to $4,000 a month to keep a horse in training at the top tracks. At lower-level tracks, it is about US$1,500 per month. Many horses are forced to run through pain and race with preexisting conditions. They train on drugs to mask their pain and are at the highest risk of breaking down or suffering a heart attack on the track when they are raced." Steeple-chase, also known as jump racing, adds obstacles the horses must leap over into the mix, and is especially common in England, Ireland, and parts of Australia. I see it as the equivalent of firing a gun into a horse stable.

Unbridled was initially intended "to provide Thoroughbreds coming off the racetrack with a safe haven to detox and let down in the hands of caring, educated, and skilled equestrians, and give the horses the best opportunity to fully recover from the demands of racing and injuries, physical and mental." Horses' lives at racetracks are highly regulated. They rarely, if ever, enjoy time grazing and playing in a pasture. Kayne is committed to giving horses the time they need "to recover from racing, withdraw from the drugs, and reacclimate to the joy of being turned out in a paddock and with other horses. The greatest gift that we can offer any equine being is to take the time to understand how the horse is experiencing the transition into their new environment—even though they are in a better place, to the horses it is another huge and scary change with unfamiliar faces." Innate, ancestral behaviors like grazing in an open area—the most natural thing a horse can do—become foreign due to these horses' experiences. This is a powerful reminder that animals are not merely biologically programmed but also affected by the specifics of their life's journeys in both small and significant ways.

Kayne has promoted practical reforms that would benefit active horses such as mandatory prerace X-rays. "I have worked with legislators and Dr. Sheila Lyons [an expert in equine sports medicine] to get state-of-the-art imaging at the racetracks in New York. The funding is available, the will to see the truth is not," Kayne says. "If as many human athletes died on the playing field as do horses on the racetrack, the venue would come to a halt until a remedy stopped the deaths."

Even greater dangers occur away from the tracks. The idea of eating horses revolts many, but they are killed in slaughter plants around the world to be eaten by people or fed to other animals. Some horses are shipped alive by plane to other countries where they will be slaughtered, including from Calgary, Edmonton, and Winnipeg in Canada. It's a national disgrace, and the government of Canada has at least pledged to end live export.

"For horses to be so disregarded is just the most egregious of crimes," Kayne asserts, yet horse slaughter is not legally banned in the United States. Instead, funding for US Department of Agriculture inspectors at slaughter plants was and is withheld, which has the effect of ending domestic horse slaughter for human consumption. This has been the case since 2007, and some states have bans, but many horse advocates would like a clear federal law. "It is not illegal to transport horses throughout the United States to cross the border into Canada or Mexico for slaughter. It is not illegal to transport horses as zoo food to a slaughter plant within the United States," Kayne says. The story is even more complicated on the ground.

> Any individual owner can ship a horse directly into any horsemeat broker's feedlot. That's not illegal. What was made illegal in the latest New York bill, for example, was if a race owner directly sells their horse to someone to slaughter. Pick up any racetrack program, any sales catalog—these horses have a thirty-year life span. Where are they? When horses leave the racetrack, the security agent just waves to you.

National agricultural statistics from Canada and the United States put the number of horses shipped for slaughter from the United States at over 30,000 a year. The numbers have fluctuated significantly and unpredictably over the last thirty years. In 1989, 348,000 horses were killed inside the United States. In 2001, 28,000 were sent to their deaths in Canada, and 59,000 a decade later. And in 2021, 23,000 were exported from Canada. Many of these horses are Thoroughbreds. Horses are supposed to be a cherished species. Yet thousands of horses—and of all ages—are lined up and sent into industrialized slaughter plants. Death by slaughter is not humane euthanasia undertaken as an act of mercy and compassion.

Rescuing animals from premature and painful death at a slaughterhouse involves navigating a series of facilities that bear no resemblance to typical horse stables, and look even less like the circles of fancy hats and mint juleps at major races. Still, these seemingly disparate spaces are connected. Horses are often first taken to crowded corrals called feedlots before being shipped to auctions where meat brokers and buyers can purchase them for a few hundred dollars or directly to slaughterhouses. "The monetary value of the horse is not an indicator of the level of protection," Kayne explains. She has rescued horses who were initially purchased for millions of dollars and had highly successful racing and breeding careers. "Yet as soon as the horses were no longer productive, they were discarded." The issue of enforcement is crucial. "If the racetracks were genuinely interested in preventing the slaughter of Thoroughbreds, they would have investigators tracking horses leaving the grounds, undercover reps at feedlots, and officers stationed at the local livestock auctions."

Kayne focuses on those least likely to be saved by anyone, especially the older mares who have had many babies, whose bodies are sore and tired, and whose hooves and teeth are neglected. "These mares have done all that has been asked of them, and in return they have been dumped into the slaughter pipeline."

In fall 2021, Kayne learned of two senior mares from a video posted online by a meat broker in Texas who uploads footage of available horses before they are shipped to slaughter. Number 5401 was twenty-seven years old. Number 5400 was about nineteen and mostly blind. "The twenty-seven-year-old seems to be the guide horse for the younger one," Kayne said after viewing the video.

The eyes and bodies of horses on the brink speak volumes. For those used to seeing happy and healthy horses, the difference is shocking. We are scared, their eyes say. We are exhausted. We are hungry. We are in pain. We are defeated.

It was an excruciating few days as Kayne worked to raise the initial funds needed to purchase, quarantine, ship, and care for these two old girls, but she succeeded. Kayne secured the funds—and the horses. The twenty-seven-year-old was named Party Wife, but is now called Velvet. Kayne is working to confirm the identity of the nearly blind mare through DNA testing. Reflecting on the transformation that has taken places in even a few months, Kayne says that "they are now tender, friendly, soft, sweet, and welcoming, wonderful ambassadors of the light and love senior mares offer as companions and friends. When you look into their eyes and hear their stories you can't help but fall in love and wonder how anyone could ever throw them away."

Number 6027 marked "safe." The words are accompanied by a windstorm of emotions.

Who was number 6027? Who were her mother and father? Where did she live? Did she have friends? Who was responsible for her? How many people owned and worked with her? How much money did she make them? Research often allows Kayne to answer at least some of these questions, and DNA can help fill in the remaining gaps. At Unbridled, the horses commonly keep their racing names, such as Skye Serenade, Traveling, Desenfrenado, Appomatox, and Miss Ruud. The ironic Generation of Love. The fitting I'm Lucky. These names are part of their stories.

Number 6027 has a gorgeous face and soft, inquisitive eyes. When she first arrived at Unbridled, she voraciously ate in her stall, then she stood with her head reaching out into the aisle and studied those around her, horses and humans. "I don't know if she's looking for someone, but she is fascinated by us all," Kayne remarks. Unbridled allows the horses to thrive physically, their bony, protrusive hips, jail-cell rib cages, and missing fur being replaced with muscle, fat, and lush, shiny coats. Equally as important is that the look in the horses' eyes changes. Their spirits transform. They form friendships. Number 6027 is playing in a pasture with her friends Lucky and Maddie as I write. She will have a name soon. One linked to her past along with the possibilities for her future.

"When I look back at how entrenched I was in the breeding and racing community without the consideration I now have for how the horse experiences his or her own life I am horrified—but it is those decades of involvement that make me a formidable advocate," Kayne says. Thanks to generous donors, Unbridled moved into a larger farm in late 2021 that not only allows horses to live at peace but is a space for learning too. People can meet the horses, help care for them, read to them, and learn their stories. Kayne sees humane education of many kinds as essential to animal protection. "Senior mares at Unbridled are companions, teachers, therapists, and study buddies for students in our programs." Unbridled will also allow permanent adoptions into particular homes if high-quality care is assured. If horses have formed deep friendships with another horse, those will not be broken either, and highly bonded pairs or trios are kept together.

Some former racehorses can have second (or third) careers, and "make-over" programs exist, including friendly competitions showcasing the skills of the rescued horses. The results depend on many factors, particularly the horses' personality and journey, and if they are properly transitioned away from "racetrack normal" to "riding horse normal." The nonprofit Thoroughbred Aftercare Alliance was created by key organizations in the racing industry to accredit and inspect retraining and retirement organizations, and provide grants for horse care and training. It has supplied over $24 million in funding and nearly fourteen thousand horses have been helped since 2012. But Kayne says that to be accredited, organizations must "agree to always shed a positive light on the integrity of horse racing in all communications." She also has concerns about the frequency of premature euthanasia at some of the facilities, especially after the initial funding provided for the horse ends. She has horses rescued from other rescues. "When the owners learned that the horses were going to be euthanized at Thoroughbred Aftercare Alliance–accredited organizations, they reached out to Unbridled for help. To this day, those horses are serviceably sound, happy, and thriving."

Lesson #12: we have obligations to the animals we bring into this world, from cradle to grave and every step in between.

There are rescues that accept slaughter-bound horses of all sizes, breeds, and abilities along with those who are otherwise neglected or abused. From the tiniest miniature and dwarf horses who literally roam around among rescued dogs, tortoises, goats, cows, donkeys (including one named J-Low!), antelopes, and even kangaroos at gorgeous show jumping farms in Florida and Kentucky as part of the Peeps Foundation, to the Gentle Giants Draft Horse Rescue in Maryland that specializes in the largest breeds, those like the Clydesdales made famous by beer commercials, some horses are finding safe havens.

But when so many horses are being produced, year after year, not all or even most will find other homes. There simply isn't the demand or availability. Horses of all kinds can end up in slaughter plants, but horses in other equine sectors generally live much longer lives, often to their natural deaths, males are castrated in almost all cases, and breeding is heavily restricted. The presence of even one stallion on most horse farms is highly unusual.[12]

Most riding horses are only beginning their careers at age four or five when the majority of their bones and joints have finished forming, in contrast to racehorses who are normally started at age two and might race for a year or two, or maybe a few. To really help the horses in racing and beyond, you also need to work upstream.

As Kayne argues,

> If the industry cared, there could be mandated death reporting to ensure accountability. I think there should be strict breeding limits on horses—the number that the industry can financially sustain for their lives. There should be lifelong commitment, including finances, to support the horses through-out their natural lives. These horses are already owned by people who claim to love them. Why are they no longer their responsibility when they can't race or produce foals? Why don't the regulatory bodies mandate a duty of care tied to licensure? These big farms in Kentucky, California, [and] Florida, why aren't there retirement paddocks at all of them?

Countries from Australia to France to Sweden are grappling with these questions, as more people refuse to simply accept the status quo and the disposability of horses.

The emotional rewards of Kayne's work are clear, but there is also heavi-ness, knowing how many individuals are being born year after year and will be dead in the blink of an eye. "Knowing what I know now about the industry, and about who horses are as fellow sentient beings, I find horse racing morally unsupportable," she says.

Racing is dangerous for jockeys as well. Australian studies have found that it is the most dangerous of professional sporting occupations. The racing industry cannot function without the skilled but poorly compensated labor of human workers, especially Black and Hispanic people. They, too, deserve more protections, or employment alternatives, with or beyond horses.

"It's easy to say, 'I hate people,' but it's people who are going to change this," Kayne emphasizes.

11 THE ELEPHANT IN THE ROOM IS A CHICKEN

Outside Springfield, Vermont, a ewe named Karma lays in the barn to escape the wind as a hen snacks on seeds caught in her wool. "The sheep will also let the chickens sit on top of them, to keep their little feetsies warm!" Anna says cheerfully. There are some turkeys nearby but they're dozing, and so is a peacock. A cow named Mooten (Sir Isaac Mooten, in fact) wanders over for a forehead scratch and then strolls off. Some chickens are clustered together inside the "Baa Baa Bistro." Pumpernickle and Marble are goats. Further outside the barn, two other goats, Church and Rosie, are chewing on what was a Christmas tree. "It's after lunch, so everyone is chilling or chewing on their cud or working a project like Church and Rosie," Anna explains.

It may sound like a typical farm, but it's actually a refuge. It's VINE Sanctuary, and Anna Boarini is the coordinator of humane education and community engagement. In 2000, pattrice jones and Miriam Jones found a chicken in a ditch and brought the bird back to their small farm in Maryland. Then they adopted a few more and told the local humane society to call them if there were any other chickens found. "We were a little property of two and a half acres, literally surrounded by factory farms on the Delmarva Peninsula, where the poultry industry was invented and perfected," jones says. "Within a few months of finding the first bird, I ended up ankle-deep in excrement in a broiler house that was being depopulated. I had permission to grab anybody." By anybody, jones means the chickens. "I was there for hours with tears streaming down my face from the ammonia, tripping over dead and dying birds, knowing that anyone I couldn't catch was going to get grabbed bv the chicken catchers and killed."

It's an experience incomprehensible to most people for many reasons, so let me explain. The US poultry industry is dominated by a small number of major corporations that own almost every part of the production process, including the animals. The National Chicken Council states that this is the "business of raising, processing and marketing chickens on a 'vertically integrated' basis—that is, the company is able to ensure quality . . . at each step of the process."[1] Farmers may instead be called "growers" and often sign a contract agreeing to follow the established procedures outlined. They may need to borrow money from the company to create the requisite facility. According to the National Chicken Council, more than 95 percent of US chicken farmers are in an arrangement like this, twenty-five thousand people who "produce" nine billion chickens annually. For comparison, the entire human population of the planet is just under eight billion. Farm folks earn so little from this process that many must get off-farm jobs or do other kinds of farming to scrape by.[2]

Chicks are delivered and then are to be given the type and amount of feed specified by the company. The Union of Concerned Scientists estimates that land twice the size of New Jersey is currently allocated to grow corporate chicken feed in the United States. Chicken catchers are people paid a small amount to get the chickens and put them onto slaughter-bound trucks when it's time for a barn to be "depopulated. The chicken catchers are on the bottom rung of the labor force," jones explains. "They often don't work for the corporation, they work under someone who is contracted by the corporation, so labor laws don't apply. They typically do the chicken catching at night. The barn door is raised, the chicken catchers run in, and they're just grabbing birds by the legs and by the wings and cramming them into the crates. It's horrific work."

Years of genetic alteration means the birds grow abnormally quickly and are ready to be slaughtered after six to seven weeks. They are rarely alive for even two months.

Renee King-Sonnen was a city girl, and her mother wanted her to get a good, secure job with benefits. But King-Sonnen—then King—fell in love with a man named Tommy Sonnen, a cattle rancher. Today the two live on a beautiful stretch of land of nearly a hundred acres between San Antonio and Houston in Texas.

"I question everything," King-Sonnen says. "It's about my head, heart, and spirit space." This became particularly true after King-Sonnen took on the care of an orphaned calf she named Rowdy Girl.

> [This] started me on a journey, because I saw her just like my dogs and cats. She became a very big part of my life. Then I began to see all the other animals in the pasture in a different way. Almost the whole herd was Black Angus, and you can't tell them apart. But then I started noticing everything about them, their feet, their tails, their underbelly, their noses, their wrinkles. I started naming them. That's Curly, that's Lucky. It was me identifying them. When I began to identify them, they became someone.

The popular TV series *Yellowstone* operatically dramatizes a massive and atypically action-packed Montana cattle ranch. It occasionally provides snapshots of the smaller, less successful farms in the area, and the horses are generally treated with admiration. There is even an animal activist depicted who begins to question her assumptions about the ranchers and their cowboy staff after she sees them helping a calf who wandered across a barbed wire fence line get back to their mother. It's not that ranchers and cowboys don't provide veterinary care or help out animals in need, in drama or reality. But when one son interrupts his father's meeting, the show's patriarch, played by Kevin Costner, asks, "Who died?" "Not who," the son replies. "What." The camera scans a field full of dead cattle.

Writer and animal advocate Carol J. Adams has recognized the rhetorical power of mass nouns like *poultry* and even *meat* that blur and de-individualize animals.[3] King-Sonnen's husband said she couldn't keep naming cows, and the trailer kept arriving to take them away to be slaughtered—that's how the ranch earns income. Cows whose sole purpose is to become meat live longer than most animals in industrial farming (often two years), but they still don't want to die. It doesn't matter how big, social, or smart animals are; the desire to avoid pain and survive is innate. The mothers used for breeding would call out for their calves for hours or days after the trucks had pulled away, which was devastating for King-Sonnen.

She kept questioning the taken-for-granted elements of her life, reading research papers, and watching videos from slaughterhouses. It nearly ended her marriage. But five years later, Sonnen Ranch became Rowdy Girl Sanctuary, named in honor of the calf who had been a catalyst in King-Sonnen's transformative journey. She fundamentally changed her perspective by "undoing all the conditioning. It's better being on the other side of what people call normal. Because normal is relative. You know we have normalized large-scale violence in our culture, and when you normalize violence, you think that's normal."

The word *violence* is noteworthy. The dictionary definition is to use physical force to hurt, damage, destroy, or kill. We outlaw almost all kinds of violence against people. We condemn and are repulsed by violence against many kinds of animals, and have created laws to prohibit it as well as prosecute those who beat and kill animals. Yet at slaughterhouses the world over, we line animals up and then use physical force to kill them, and it's legal. It's legal and considered normal.

Not surprisingly, this seemingly impossible tale of a cattle ranch in Texas becoming a farmed animal sanctuary attracted the attention of many media outlets. As King-Sonnen describes it,

> We were in the paper and on the frickin' evening news across the country, and cattle ranchers who are just common, everyday people like us, saw our story in their living room and started contacting me, especially ranchers' wives. I found myself stopping everything in my life to talk to them. It was like, if you're in AA [Alcoholics Anonymous] and you're recovering from alcoholism and you need to talk to somebody, you want to talk to somebody who has been there, done that, and gotten through it. That's the way it was with me and cattle ranchers and other farmers. They were wanting to talk to me because they couldn't talk

to anybody else. They couldn't talk about the fact that their husband was getting ready to send animals to the kill barn that they had identified as someone.

King-Sonnen created the Rancher Advocacy Program to be a resource, partnership, mentorship, and investment hub to help farmers of all kinds who want to explore how to farm without killing. There are options, depending on the size of the farm, specifics of the land and geography, and interests and skills of the people involved. This can include growing crops of various kinds, or becoming a veganic (organic and vegan) farm and partnering with companies that are developing and creating plant-based foods. It could mean producing solar or wind energy, converting into a feed store or community market, or rewilding land. It could involve becoming a care farm, or ecotourist destination, space of education and training, or nonprofit organization. Or it could involve partnering with Indigenous communities to do any of the above and more. Former garment factories have been turned into housing and office space in major cities all across North America. An abandoned Walmart in McAllen, Texas, was transformed into a library. A former chicken barn in my area is now used as a skating rink. Buildings are repurposed all the time. Farms can be too.

Especially when people depend on the income being earned from harmful actions, a thorough approach rooted in solidarity not only with the animals but also with other humans involves finding, proposing, and implementing alternatives for those people—work that helps, not harms. Humane jobs and humane job transitions are a crucial part of the animal protection story. Jobs and income are not justifications for violence.

"I'm not only an animal advocate, I'm also a ranchers' advocate," King-Sonnen says unequivocally.

Eating other animals is something many humans and our ancestors have long done, but the current situation is a far cry from the days when we mostly moved around in small groups and hunted or fished to supplement the large majority of our diets that came from gathering and foraging.[4] It's also a far cry from early agriculture and the small-scale family farms with twenty or a hundred animals that were more common even fifty years ago.[5] The US Department of Agriculture notes that in 1935, there were 6.8 million farms. In 2020, there were only 2.2 million. The same pattern is true in Canada and much of the Global North.

Legally defined as property and livestock, farmed animals usually have only thin and porous protective nets. Practices "generally accepted" within agriculture are normally exempt from standard definitions of animal cruelty the world over. Kicking a chicken is illegal. Fighting chickens is a felony in all fifty states because it's deemed too violent. But burning chickens' beaks off and killing them at seven weeks old is legal. Not only permitted, it is deemed normal. Chickens are among the most abused animals on the planet.

Lawyer Delcianna Winders has worked in animal protection for fifteen years, including as vice president and deputy general counsel for the PETA Foundation as well as director of Legal Campaigns for Farm Sanctuary, a large and pathbreaking organization founded by Gene Baur, home to more than a thousand rescued animals in New York and California. Now Winders is the animal law and policy institute director at the Vermont Law School. "Most people in America don't realize that there is not a single federal law governing on-farm treatment of the animals we raise for food," she explains. "Most state animal protection laws are interpreted to allow routine abuses of farmed animals that would be considered egregious felonies if inflicted on a cat or dog"—or budgie. Like the millions of individuals used for testing mascara in labs, those in agriculture are among the animals people may prefer to forget about or ignore. Yet the truth is that their lives and deaths raise crucial questions for everyone genuinely interested in animal protection.

Almost incomprehensible numbers of animals are born and killed each year to feed humans, with fishes and chickens being the largest groups. Precise figures can be obfuscated by measurements that calculate pounds or kilograms, not individual animals, but the US Department of Agriculture puts the number at nearly 10 billion animals killed in 2020, not including aquatic species (who are measured by weight). That includes 9 billion chickens, 223 million turkeys, 33 million cows and calves, more than 130 million pigs, 22 million ducks, and more than 2 million sheep and lambs.

The Animal Kill Clock provides a live roll of the numbers by drawing from direct sources like the government agencies in charge of agriculture. The United Kingdom kills over a billion land animals and another 5 billion from the sea each year. In Australia, when land and sea deaths are combined, the number is 5 billion. In Canada, Animal Justice digs into the government number annually. In a country with a population of 38 million people, well over 800 million animals were killed in 2020, not including fishes, rabbits, or horses.

Almost everywhere in the world, the numbers are astounding, and the deaths take place years before the animals would normally die from natural death. Some practices are particularly shocking, such as the routine killing of day-old male chicks born in the egg industry. The process of sexing chicks for this purpose is depicted in the feature film *Minari*. The lead characters provide fictional illustrations of a real job as they pick up chicks, flip them upside down to determine their sex, and then separate the males, who are then incinerated. In real life, male chicks are killed in a range of ways, including by being dropped off conveyor belts onto spinning blades called macerators that chop up their bodies. In an industry dependent on the bodily work of hens laying eggs, male babies who won't grow up to lay eggs are superfluous, and killing them promptly is deemed the most economically efficient way to proceed.

Like all mammals, cows only produce milk in preparation for giving birth and then afterward. On dairy farms, cows are repeatedly impregnated so they will keep lactating. About half of their calves are males, who won't grow up to produce their own babies and therefore milk. Male calves are promptly separated from their mothers (usually the day they're born), isolated and largely immobilized in crates or hutches for four months, and then slaughtered to be served as veal. When their mothers' bodies become tired from years of successive impregnation, they, too, are shipped to slaughter. Footage captured by undercover investigators of "spent" and "downed" cows being sprayed with hoses and dragged by tractors to force them to stand up and walk to slaughter nauseatingly lays bare the violence of disposability. Male and female animals suffer in linked and distinct ways.

Intensive confinement is common because it allows for more animals to be kept simultaneously, thereby increasing economic productivity. Chickens are trapped in battery cages within which they cannot spread their wings, or are cramped into barns. Pigs are kept in individual pens—gestation crates within which they can lie down and stand up, but not turn or otherwise move. Some agricultural lobbyists claim these measures are necessary, yet individual farms and countries around the world disprove that claim. Gestation crates were banned in Sweden in 1994, for example. Terms like *concentrated animal feeding operation* are used neutrally and earnestly. The processes are also called *industrial animal agriculture* and *factory farming*. Although these practices challenge many people's conceptions of real farming, the comparisons to factories are clear—except in these spaces, bodies are taken apart.

The industrialization, corporatization, and intensification of agriculture are why when there's a barn fire or major flood, fifteen hundred pigs can be lost at once, or five thousand turkeys get incinerated. It's also how diseases spread so quickly, including those that endanger both animals and people. Factory farming means manure lagoons that poison ground water, air pollution, and significant greenhouse gas emissions. The industrialization of slaughtering facilities means that hundreds of living animals can be sent through every hour, depending on their size.[6] Few among us want to work in slaughterhouses, and they are disproportionately staffed by local people without other options, and migrant or temporary workers from other countries. In other words, they are staffed by poor people from various countries. The work is exhausting, physically dangerous, especially with larger, terrified animals like cows, pigs, and horses, and fodder for nightmares and worse. The animal welfare officer who had to kill a thousand pigs who were neglected to the point of starvation over the course of a few days said it was the most difficult work of their career. For workers in slaughterhouses, that is their reality, every day.

Jobs or not, few communities want these facilities. "The acronym is NIMBY—not in my backyard. These plants get put in communities that can't fight against them. They impact all rural people, poor white people and people of color," explains Dr. Christopher Carter, a religious scholar at the University of San Diego and a United Methodist reverend. He emphasizes the longer history, upstream, that fundamentally shaped the contemporary landscape. "The systematic removal of land from Indigenous folks and the enslaving of Africans form the beginnings of a plantation system that ultimately lays the framework for industrial agriculture. The way we construct the activities of the food system is built off the backs of people of color."[7]

For more than a decade, the United Nations and other leading scientists have recognized that factory farming is a major contributor to climate change. And as fires, droughts, floods, and extreme weather worsen as a result of the changing climate, it is already disadvantaged people the world over who will suffer the most.

Whether farmed animals and people trapped by the violence of factory farming are included in people's webs of care and compassion varies, including within the animal protection landscape. It is not uncommon for people who say they love animals to put some limits on who exactly is worthy of that love or believe different standards should apply to different kinds of animals. I have sat with animal cruelty investigators in the field while they ate sandwiches made from animals who suffered as much, if not more, than the animals those officers work tirelessly to defend every day. Some animal rescues host fundraisers to generate money to help some animals, such as dogs and cats or even horses, while serving the flesh of others. On the other hand, I have sat with officers, including from police services, who express concern for animals on farms, and as a result, are vegetarians or vegans. There are also people working for companion animal welfare who have broader hopes for animal protection, but whose jobs focus on dogs and cats. These dynamics are far from tidy, even within the spheres of animal protection, and do not break down into neat or rigid camps.

International research led by Dr. Jared Piazza of Lancaster University found that the most commonly used explanations or justifications for eating animals despite the pain and suffering involved are deeming it normal, necessary, natural, and/or nice (as in tasty). For decades, people have been encouraged by marketing campaigns, formal education, and food materials to look in particular directions, avoid others, and think in specific ways about what—and who—they see. Carter also serves as a Faith in Food Fellow with Farm Forward, a thought and advocacy organization focused on combating factory farming. "Those who are fighting to maintain the structure that benefits and profits from the exploitation of animals have organizations. They pay lawyers, consultants, and academics to normalize and moralize the mistreatment of human beings and nonhuman nature."

University of Denver law professor Justin Marceau underscores that

> criminal law is socially constructed to put the cheerleading around prosecutions of discreet acts of abuse or neglect. The public is left with the message that certain acts are criminal, felonious and very bad, and people are distracted from the routine systemic abuse that is going on, often legally right across the street. I don't think it's possible to celebrate the prosecution of certain crimes while ignoring similar harms on factory farms.

Camille Labchuk of Animal Justice has a similar perspective. "Prosecutions for animal cruelty tend to focus almost exclusively on the actions of individuals when high-value victims such as companion animals are involved—even though the vast majority of animal suffering occurs in the commercial context, particularly inside farms. Prosecutions of commercial entities are incredibly rare, despite their far greater moral culpability." Moreover, this raises the question again of what is illegal when it comes to animals. Just because something is currently legal doesn't make it ethically defensible. Legal cruelty is widespread.

"Our laws have been deliberately crafted not merely to give the highly concentrated animal agriculture industry carte blanche to externalize all manner of harms—including to animals, consumers, the environment, and workers—but also to afford it special entitlements, including direct monetary subsidies, to facilitate their profits at the expense of all in their wake," says Winders. Monetary assistance (subsidies, grants, loans, and credits) is provided not only to struggling farmers but also to many kinds of animal agricultural entities automatically, as a normal matter of course. It is a significant reason why the costs to consumers are lower, and, in some cases, are how these industries survive. In addition, animals like foxes and minks are intensively confined in rows of cages on "fur farms," and these farms are often eligible for public agricultural subsidies and bailouts, even as more and more fashion designers remove fur from their lines.

A fraction of the subsidies are provided to nonanimal agricultural products. The policy and advocacy organization Agricultural Fairness Alliance has dug into the 2020 numbers for the United States: more than $50 billion was supplied in subsidies. No more than 11 percent of that amount supported plant crops and plant-based foods destined for human consumption (that is, not for livestock feed), including fruits, vegetables, nuts, seeds, legumes (like lentils, chickpeas, and beans), and grains. The playing field for farmers is highly uneven and stacked against animal life.

Animal defenders who include farmed animals in their spheres of care do so in different ways. This quadrant is where some of the differences between ideas of animal welfare and rights are most clear. If the goal is welfare—succinctly, use but not abuse—people may push for bigger cages for hens, enriched cages, or no cages. They may lobby for laws that shorten the time slaughter-bound animals can be shipped without food, water, or rest.

Commonly known as the twenty-eight-hour law, this federal US statute states that animals cannot be transported across state lines by train or truck for more than twenty-eight consecutive hours. It's undoubtedly a long time to go without water or food. Animal welfare scientists have helped most countries develop these sorts of standards. Many animals can technically survive for that long without food, water, or rest—but should they have to? Is there a place for ethical principles in these decisions? Air and water transportation is not governed by this limit either. There is a busy network of live animal export that flies and moves thousands of animals at a time by ship, where enforcement of even existing standards is far more questionable.

When the Suez Canal was blocked for multiple days in 2021, nearly two dozen ships crammed with sheep were stranded. Whenever borders are blocked, animals who are already en route to certain death go for even longer without food or water.[8]

Is it better to propose a new design for slaughterhouse chutes to try to minimize the fear cows feel before they are stunned with a bolt gun and then bled out, as scientist Temple Grandin did, or work so cows have the right not to be lined up to be slaughtered in the first place? Could it be both, or is one approach inherently superior? Efforts to lower travel time limits, secure commitment from major grocery retailers and restaurant chains to only sell eggs made by cage-free hens, and pursue legal routes that mandate changes to how barns are designed to give pigs more room to move—animal protection organizations are split about whether these kinds of animal welfare strategies are the end goal or not. For some people, the consumption and commodification of farmed animals is acceptable, but changes are needed to reduce the levels of suffering before they are killed to improve their welfare. For others, these steps, if promoted, are seen as imperfect compromises on the path toward more ambitious changes that would dramatically reduce or eliminate industrial animal agriculture.

Leah Garcés, president of Mercy for Animals, says,

> Animals need us to do both. While we work toward a world in which animals are not exploited for food at all, we can't ignore the animals trapped in the system for the foreseeable future and must reduce their suffering. We take a variety of approaches and believe that it is the synergy among them that leads to the greatest impact. This means we work to promote plant-based products and other alternatives, discourage the production and consumption of animal products, and improve animal welfare standards.

Mercy for Animals encourages individual changes because of the power of consumers and emphasizes the importance of "changing the institutions that shape our societies: corporations and governments" in the United States, Canada, Mexico, India, and Brazil, and soon, South and Southeast Asia.

Those on the front lines may engage in direct action for farmed animals, including the kinds of undercover investigations also used in labs.

Some advocates reject the term *animal protection* as too weak and instead argue for animal liberation—animals need to be freed from their subservient positions, legally and literally. The term *animal liberation* itself has different meanings, with some liberationists tracing their roots to the eponymous book by Peter Singer, and others promoting the full abolition of human ownership of animals, and animals' right not to be human property, as noted earlier. As a result, it is helpful to ask how the term *liberation* is being used.

Others may employ the term *animal protection* and see these kinds of exposés as contributing to greater awareness of what goes on beyond closed doors and down gravel roads, or as one part of a larger repertoire of tactics intended to buttress legal and cultural change.[9] What have been dubbed *ag-gag* laws—legislative changes that additionally penalize those who gather undercover footage if convicted—seek to curb these kinds of strategies and are of great concern to many animal advocates, even those who do not personally participate in the tactic, because they consider the footage gathered to be a valuable window into a largely hidden world of animal pain. Those who profit from eating animals not only receive significant subsidies and other forms of governmental support but also invest in public relations campaigns and lobbying efforts to defend the status quo or remove what few regulations exist. The resources of even the most well-funded animal advocacy organizations pale in comparison.

But another cross-section of individuals often has more resources than animal protection nonprofits and may play a significant role in reducing animal suffering and saving animals' lives: businesspeople.

Different cultures and religions around the world have long emphasized alternatives to animal consumption, and in most places, even if meat eating is promoted as the norm, there are always those who object for various reasons, especially moral and/or environmental ones. Businesspeople and chefs have sought to create new products to either replace the animal-rooted equivalent or offer a new way of thinking about food. Early efforts by US companies like Tofurky and Follow Your Heart have been joined by an explosion of small, medium, and large businesses around the world, particularly over the last decade. Some are motivated purely by the quest for financial success and see growing consumer demand, while others merge economic and ethical goals.

Miyoko Schinner, founder of Miyoko's Creamery and of the sanctuary Rancho Compasión, as well as a path-making sector leader, sees her business as a form of animal protection. "Why am I making cheese out of cashews and legumes? Because it's all about the animals," she told the Unbound Project. Businesses like hers use no ingredients made from animals or animals' bodily processes in their products—called vegan or plant-based.

I call this the business of animal protection. It's different than protecting individual animals by investigating cruelty or physically rescuing them. It's about creating alternatives to business practices that cause harm to animals in order to help stop violence before it happens, upstream. Schinner is also developing a program to help dairy farmers move away from animal farming, and there are examples of these kinds of transition programs in Europe as well.

Garcés realized that if "we want to create lasting change, we can't just stand on the sidelines and point out what is wrong. We must roll up our sleeves, build the solutions, and find the win-wins."[10] Under her leadership, Mercy for Animals has created the Transfarmation Project to help farmers repurpose and fill former chicken houses with mushrooms and hemp crops. "Transfarmation is groundbreaking because once sworn enemies—animal rights activists and factory farmers—are joining forces," Garcés explains. "It's a manifestation of the fact that the factory farming system oppresses so many, from rural American farming families to the animals themselves, and only by uniting as one movement will we succeed in creating a food system that is just for all."

Sometimes the impetus for substantial change is internal. Henry Schwartz led Elmhurst Dairy, which had been in his family for ninety years, to become Elmhurst 1925, a maker of plant-based milks. Organizations are being created, changed, expanded, purchased, and revolutionized all the time, from food to fashion to retail to tourism and hospitality. Some operate as social or ecosocial enterprises, while others are profitable, and that is the goal. Many seek to not only sell products or services but also educate. The Swedish-created company Oatly made waves with its international marketing slogan for oat milk: "It's like milk, only made for humans."

The aptly named Nuts for Cheese was founded by Margaret Coons in London, Canada.

"As a vegan business, animal protection is inherent to all that we do. I've been a plant-based consumer for almost twenty years, and I've witnessed a significant change being reflected in mainstream media and behavior as well as in deals with much larger companies acquiring brands in this space." The company's geographic reach has expanded across Canada and into nearly all US states; it has added new varieties and is developing additional product lines. "Since my days working as a vegan chef, the plant-based food sector has exploded as consumers shift toward animal-friendly products for ethical, environmental, and health reasons," Coons says. "It is my mission as a chef and foodie to make that transition one that is of quality, flavor, and indulgence."

Like the terrain of animal law and policy making, the vegan and plant-based economic landscape is consistently diversifying, and it's impossible to keep up with the developments and expansion. Consumer demand and curiosity keep growing, especially among younger and Black people, many of whom are creating and leading businesses that unite economic and social goals. Some advocates are encouraging larger organizational consumers like hospitals, schools, and prisons to commit to plant-based menus one or many days of the week, seeking to leverage the larger power of institutional purchasing (and provide health benefits to those they feed). Politicians are contributing too, and New York mayor Eric Adams is advocating for school dietary policy change in his city.

Many vegan companies are being propelled not only by an ethical commitment to animals but also by a broader set of priorities, including environmental sustainability and human well-being. This translates into local or other kinds of ethical sourcing (such as fair trade and/or organic certified products), providing better quality working conditions for staff, enshrining diversity throughout the company, deliberately hiring from marginalized groups including people with criminal records, and/or promoting equity and justice within their communities. There are still workforce challenges, bad vegan bosses, and trade-offs. But the expansion and deepening of business ethics is noteworthy—the economic equivalent of the one health and one welfare trio. Certain animal defenders believe the pursuit of profit is a fundamental problem for people and animals alike, but most see a place for private economic interests alongside a robust public sector and civil society—a social democratic vision.

Along with an explosion of vegetarian and vegan products, a humane future could involve meat, but not meat made from killing animals. Meat and dairy can be created in labs, and the development of these products is growing around the world. What to call these items is tricky; clean meat, cellular agriculture, and alternative proteins have all been used.[11] Whether for economic, environmental, and/or ethical reasons, significant time, labor, and money are being invested to create replacement products, and expand and refine the production process in order to mass-produce at a competitive price point. These products include burgers, chicken, bacon, fish, milk, and other dairy products. They also include specialized products like foie gras (conventionally made by force-feeding geese) and Wagyu beef steak. The technology differently involves stem cells, 3D printing, and other processes currently confidential as patents are sought. Even elite chefs who sample these products agree that they are indistinguishable—because structurally they are.

Jessica Almy is vice president of policy at the Good Food Institute, an international nonprofit organization working to advance and expand alternative protein innovation. "My work benefits nonhuman animals, but its success does not depend on policy makers affording them more protections or even consumers deciding to take them into consideration when making purchases," she explains. "Lots of people support alternative proteins for reasons having nothing to do with animals too, including biodiversity, climate, global poverty, and national security, to name a few." Alternative proteins mean people would not need to fundamentally change their diets or empathize with farmed animals. Instead, it's the process for creating food products that changes, meaning death-free dairy and meat without factory farms.

For-profit investors and entrepreneurs have been leading the charge, and it's a sector that is moving forward at full throttle. "Public investment in alternative proteins could benefit the entire sector, including companies that don't even exist yet, as well as stimulate economic growth and improve the productivity of our food supply," notes Almy. "The United States took a step in the right direction in 2021 when the Department of Agriculture dedicated $10 million to create the National Institute of Cellular Agriculture to advance cultivated meat—but the kind of investment that's really needed is at least an order of magnitude larger." In 2021, the Danish government announced an investment of 1.25 billion kroner (about US$140 million) for the development of plant-based and cellular agricultural products, but these sorts of public investments remain rare so far.

The Farm System Reform Act was introduced in 2021 by Senator Cory Booker and Congressman Ro Khanna with the goals of using governmental powers and incentives to restrict new factory farm construction, phase out factory farms, and create a robust fund to facilitate farm transitions. This sort of political leadership is fertilizing the terrain and helping to outline a vision of what new agricultural landscapes could look like. Advances in these fields—both plant-based products and cellular agriculture—could help create new humane jobs, in rural and urban communities alike. There is potential to consciously develop the future of food production, distribution, retailing, and serving so that existing inequities are addressed rather than simply reproduced.

This includes taking seriously the well-being of migrant workers, whose labor makes most fruit and vegetable farming possible. Promoting an integrated approach to justice in this way drives the Food Empowerment Project, an organization working for

> a food system free from the exploitation of humans and the environment and with equitable access to healthy, sustaining food for all communities; where non-human animals are not seen as food but as individuals with lives, personalities, friendships, and family and are free from harm and exploitation; and where workers, communities, and the environment are always protected and treated with dignity, respect, and appreciation.[12]

lauren Ornelas created this multifaceted organization because she "believed that I was not the only one who cared about working toward justice for human and nonhuman animals. I felt there were connections, especially when looking at food, that needed to be made. I also wanted there to be an organization that highlighted and focused on those of us vegans who are not white."[13]

Over her career, Ornelas has seen the shift in understanding, as more people who care about animals, recognize the need to care about workers too. "More people seem to get these issues—why they are important and how they are connected. It makes me incredibly hopeful and more determined." It's about promoting justice today and in the future. In some ways, the early, multifaceted emphases of animal protection are being revived and deepened, and environmental concerns are being added, by necessity.

Some of this work is being done in the upper echelons of the economy. The Farm Animal Investment Risk and Return (FAIRR) initiative is a collaborative investor network (its members manage nearly $50 trillion in assets) founded by equities investor Jeremy Coller and the Coller Foundation that focuses on the material risks of intensive animal agriculture. Coller recognized that the main frameworks used to make business more responsible—environmental, social, and governance approaches—were largely silent about factory farming and food. "In 2015, investors were pouring money into agricultural businesses without considering how much of it was being used in ways that cause harm to animals, people, and the planet," explains FAIRR executive director Maria Lettini. "FAIRR set out to change this by producing expert research and tools for institutional investors to be able analyze risk and opportunities." Zoonotic disease risk, antimicrobial resistance, and workers' safety—the one health lens is integrated through FAIRR's work.

FAIRR generates robust and unique research such as the Coller FAIRR Protein Producers Index, which tracks the performance of major meat, fish, and dairy producers on environmental, social, and governance issues. "The index not only provides the data needed to model and integrate these risks for investors but it also drives transparency and disclosure within the animal agriculture industry itself," Lettini says.

In essence, we are harnessing the power of capital to drive positive change in the global food system. When you think about "Big Meat" and the power the industry has, it is difficult to imagine how we might get them to change. What are the levers of change? Obviously, if maximizing profits is front of mind, changing the system will have to make business sense as well. Investors can have a voice in this process as catalytic change agents.

FAIRR facilitates many kinds of investor engagements "including making the business case for large fast-food companies and restaurant chains to reduce the use of antibiotics in their animal supply chains—something that directly contributes to antimicrobial resistance in humans," Lettini explains.

Or engaging in dialogues with food manufacturers and retail chains to think about their overexposure to animal protein in their products and how that presents a strategic risk to their reputation, climate goals, and nutritional product profiles. By moving to nonanimal protein, companies can create business opportunities that improve outcomes for animals, humans, and the planet as well as responding to important consumer trends in the market. It ends up driving change in the right direction and ultimately reducing the number of animals reared intensively in poor conditions.

Activist investor Carl Icahn's efforts to encourage McDonald's to eliminate meat sourced from pigs who are trapped in gestation crates is another example of how this work can promote reform.

"Intensive animal agriculture is the number one contributor to Amazon deforestation," and Lettini lauds major governmental pledges to halt and reverse forest loss and land degradation. "We are also seeing commitments around innovative shifts to more climate-resilient food systems, low carbon farming practices, and a real focus on creating an equitable transition for farmers. But commitments are not enough, and we need the finance and regulatory community to incentivize and scale new technologies to help transition farming and diversify the types of protein produced." FAIRR sees a central role for alternative proteins, both plant-based and cultured meat, to offer consumers healthier, more sustainable, and more ethical food choices. "It is definitely time for food and animal agriculture to be the focus of the conversation as we look to address the welfare of animals, the health of humans, and the very viability of economies and societies. In 2020, the alternative protein industry raised $3.1 billion in investments. We are seeing this opportunity being embraced by companies, investors, and even regulators and policy makers." In other words, FAIRR is promoting many of the same changes consumers and advocates are pushing for "from below" through the highest levels of financial decision-making. It is a powerful example of going upstream to shape how and where money is invested.

Almy has seen a marked change during her career.

> I believe that using markets and innovation in this way can change the world. Five years ago, alternative proteins were a nonissue in policy circles. Now one of the most powerful officials in Congress [Rosa DeLauro, chair of the House Appropriations Committee] is calling for parity in alternative protein research relative to conventional agriculture. Imagine what we will accomplish in the next five years!

I see the development and expansion of alternative proteins as the most significant animal protection strategy available because of the numbers of animals it would help and the depth of suffering those animals experience in their short lives. "It is a good example of how a disruptive technology can change the system as we know it," Lettini says. The most severe forms of cruelty are legal, yet a seismic shift may be underway as power and money are shifted away from normalized patterns of violence.

May the alternative become the norm.

Like dogs and cats, farmed animals have rich emotional layers and personalities.[14] Pigs are as smart as dogs. Cows enjoy music. Chickens can be funny and cuddly. They like shiny items, and will form friendships and remember faces. I've known chickens—Buffy, Cinnamon, Henny Penny, Good Hen, Roger, and Ronald—who recognize and will run at top speed to the specific cars of people who give them tasty blueberries. Regardless of whether they have been given names or not, all animals want lives without pain.

Sanctuaries for farmed animals are growing in number—such as the Gentle Barn, Rancho Compasión, Penny Lane Farm Sanctuary, Cedar Row Farm Sanctuary, Woodstock Farm Sanctuary, Catskill Farm Sanctuary, Piebird Farm Sanctuary, the Little Red Barn, and Lailo Farm Sanctuary—but are still not common. VINE Sanctuary cofounder jones has spent decades working upstream and downstream for animal protection, LGBTQ rights, antiracist action, and environmental preservation. The sanctuary is home to more than seven hundred animals, most of whom are chickens. They are joined by many other kinds of birds, goats, cows, sheep, and alpacas. VINE is deliberately envisioned and maintained as a multispecies community, and labor is expected from human visitors so that they, too, can become part of the fabric of the farm. Sanctuaries save lives, and are places of recovery and possibility, whether they are home to chimpanzees or chickens. Maybe they also provide glimpses of how we could coexist with other species by prioritizing mutual respect and solidarity.

Some fundamental rights are respected every day at VINE, including the animals' right to privacy and freedom of association. It seems unusual because purging farmed animals of their identities has been so normalized and unquestioned. At Happily Ever Esther Farm Sanctuary in southern Ontario, there is a similar respect for animals' own choices. The now-famous Esther the Wonder Pig came through the patio door on her own time after I'd met with the many other animals in safe harbor at the farm named in her honor, including April, who had just given birth to piglets, Captain Dan, and the now-late Lenny, who was nestled in straw napping. Animals die at sanctuaries, sometimes after many joyful years, and sometimes much too early because of what has been done to their bodies. After cooling off in her little pool, Esther devoured watermelon, an offering that cannot even begin to redress what our species does to hers, but a happily received gift nonetheless.

What a fundamental commitment to animals' agency means at VINE is that there are some practical limitations for safety reasons, but many of the animals are able to move around the pastures, barn, and forests as they choose. "We decided that our model would be let birds be birds. Some people don't even think of chickens as birds, but they want to be in trees more than in a mowed yard. Chickens are jungle fowl. Today many are genetically tampered with, but there are others who are genetically indistinguishable from wild birds in the jungles of South Asia. Chickens go feral as readily as cats if the climate and habitat are suitable," jones explains. "We thought that the proper role for us would be to create a refuge here where we would provide, insofar as is possible, something resembling the habitat their bodies want, and that we would get out of the way. Their relationships with each other are probably going to be more important to them than any relationship they might have with people." It's bold yet completely logical.

Hens lay eggs regularly as part of their natural biological processes, but those eggs will produce chicks only if the hen was mounted by a rooster, and if the hen then sits on them at length to provide warmth. Of VINE's approach, jones says,

> We decided that if a hen got broody [meaning she clearly wanted to incubate her eggs], and she did it in a place where she would be safe, then we would not interfere. Everybody was saying, "It'll be overpopulation." We have hundreds of chickens here, and maybe one or two hens a year decide they're going to have chicks. We once had a duck who had ducklings who then rewilded themselves. There are all of these wild ducks around who are the great-great-great-grandchildren of those two. The additions to the population here come from all the roosters.

There's something particularly intriguing about an LGBTQ-led sanctuary caring for so many roosters—animals who are used in violent fighting circles around the world seeped in toxic masculinity. The very first bird jones rescued ended up being a rooster. "This sanctuary wouldn't exist if it weren't for his charms." Shortly after, a humane officer contacted jones about taking in twenty-four roosters. "When the truck pulled in, many of the hens were lined up along the fence line looking to see what was going on. Then these roosters began appearing, these extraordinary birds, Polish ones with the big flippy feathers on their heads, all of these different colors. The hens were just staring at these roosters. I'll never forget that sight. But these were birds, they weren't avatars for masculinity." In fact, VINE has developed a way to rehabilitate roosters and even help people keep roosters who are becoming difficult. "It's a combination of the kinds of treatment that you might use to solve a phobia combined with treatment you use to respond to post-traumatic stress, combined with some social learning that can only be done by the other roosters."

When you really try to see things—time, spaces, relationships, and what's possible—from animals' perspectives, the world looks different. "We feel very strongly about respecting self-determination and freedom. There's an ongoing war against animals, and this is the equivalent of a refugee camp," jones says.

Writer Jonathan Safran Foer sees factory farming as war.[15] Building on the work of French philosopher Jacques Derrida, University of Sydney scholar Dr. Dinesh Wadiwel titled a book *The War against Animals*.[16] Versions of this sentiment circulate in animal protection circles. It's jarring. The process looks different from human-human wars, although animals have been enlisted into and are always damaged by those too. The truth is that the most violent acts against animals are routinized and corporatized. The casualties live short lives of intense misery. Most of the victims are hidden away, and the goal is not to destroy them all but rather to kill each successive generation in a never-ending cycle of death and profit. It's an onslaught of pain the depths of which are hard to fathom yet impossible to condone. All animals fear pain and want to live.

"I would argue this is the challenge of our time," Carter shares. "For me, this is about who I am called to serve. If we are going to be actually living our faith, that means we need to engage in ways that promote the flourishing of life and serving the poor. And so much of that is wrapped up in our environmental policies and the ways in which we think about nature and interact with nature. I think about it as the interconnectedness we have with all life."

"It's real simple, you know, live and let live. Thou shalt not kill," King-Sonnen says. "I can get real philosophical so pardon me, but I really do believe that we have misrepresented so much because of money. We need to redefine what food is—food is grown. We need to redefine what killing is. We need to redefine what it means to be compassionate and to be humane."

When I was three, a roasted chicken was served at the day care I attended. I have a visual memory of the bird's corpse to this day. The staff told my mother that I started to cry and was inconsolable. I had realized that "chicken" is "a chicken." This happened again when the body of a fish was presented as lunch. There are now many videos of this very scenario online showing children asking questions, and some are tearfully begging not to have to eat animals.

Children are taught such contradictory ideas about animals and how to feel about them, whether they live on farms and participate in programs that emotionally prepare kids for sending animals to slaughter, or in towns and cities far away from living, breathing farmed animals who simultaneously appear in children's stories and on their plates.[17] Yet children, in their innocence, also reveal a depth of understanding, untarnished.

In one video, a little boy in Brazil identifies all the food that is, in fact, an animal. "Fish are animals. Octopus are animals. Chickens are animals. Cows are animals. Pigs are animals." He says people are supposed to take care of animals and that he wants them upright and happy. It moves his mother to tears. In another, a girl is asked why she doesn't want to eat meat anymore. She replies, "Because they're animals, and I like animals." She is crying. "I know we like to eat animals that we cook, but that's not nice for them."

Lesson #13: some practices can be reformed to protect animals. Those involving violence should be replaced.

CONCLUSION: THE FUTURE IS HUMANE

Award-winning animal photojournalist Jo-Anne McArthur is not only the cofounder of the Unbound Project, which highlights women's work for animals around the world, but also the founder of We Animals Media, which has developed the concept of animal photojournalism. It is an animal-focused, inclusive approach that "captures, memorializes, and exposes the experiences of animals who live among us, but who we fail to see." The images "document the broader human-animal conflict and its resultant eco-systems of suffering. . . . Animal photojournalism descends from conflict photography in that the photographer is exposing a story that is kept hidden from the public through political and economic agendas." McArthur has said she feels like a war photographer, and she has traveled the globe for decades, documenting a scale and depth of suffering that has affected her deeply, and that few can properly comprehend. She has seen the front lines, not only of the work of protection, but of the many assaults on animals' very being—acts of brutal violence that are difficult to speak about and yet made routine.

In contrast, with genuine joy she shares the story of meeting a chimpanzee named Tatu at the Fauna Foundation near Montreal, Canada, who had been part of a behavioral experiment and learned sign language before being rehomed to the sanctuary. McArthur's colleague was holding a mug, and the chimp signed to the translator, who then explained in English that Tatu had asked if the drink was coffee. Coffee is one of her favorites. "It's important for me to also talk about the animals I meet and how they've expressed themselves because that really illuminates the individuals and who they are," McArthur says. "And that's why you see so much eye contact in my images. Because if they're looking at me, they're looking at all of us, with intelligent eyes full of questions. And unfortunately, often the question is what are you going to do to me? It's a terrible legacy."

McArthur is honest about the impact of what she's seen. "Knowing what I know and seeing what I've seen, and the urgency of it, I don't spend time thinking about how long things will take. I do my best every day. Sometimes that's a little and sometimes that's a lot."

Amanda Arrington of the Humane Society of the United States, senior director of the Pets for Life program, admits that

> some days I don't have hope, if I'm honest. Some days it's hard. We should admit it because if you think you're alone those days are harder to deal with. Some days I feel like nothing is going to change. But what's the alternative? It's to do nothing, and that's not an option. I don't think that most people who have a desire to make the world better for animals will sit with that idea for very long. I can have my self-care time and have moments to wallow, but then I can either accept things as they are and do nothing about it, or I can keep trying.

Almost everyone I've interviewed has seen changes firsthand, in whatever acre of the animal protection landscape they're working in. The fact that it's impossible to properly map all the developments is cause for celebration. From the expansion of programs that work in partnership with low-income people to protect animals, to women changing the face of conservation in their communities, to the abuse victim who is able to escape and find safe haven, to the growing number of countries banning fur farming, to the creation of alternative protein companies and new Black-led plant-based businesses—these are all why I maintain hope.

McArthur highlights the organization Animal Equality, which was created in Spain. "When I started investigations with them, they were three people, they shared an apartment, and they took turns keeping lousy jobs just to make enough money to feed themselves and pay for gas to do investigations." Today the organization has offices in eight countries, and Oscar-winner Joaquin Phoenix—who uses his massive platform to powerfully raise the plight of animals—can regularly be seen wearing an Animal Equality hoodie. "I had a meeting two days ago with a four-person NGO in Zimbabwe, and they're looking at factory farming and investigations," McArthur shares. When compassion, solidarity, and courage are intertwined, the results transcend real and perceived barriers.

"Animal protection work in the United States has matured and professionalized significantly," says Delcianna Winders, director of the Animal Law and Policy Institute at the Vermont Law School. The same is true in Canada and countries around the world. "There are more jobs in the field than ever before, and those of us doing this work are no longer laughed out of the room. Animal protection issues are on the agenda in a way they never have been, and significant strides are being made as a result—though there is still tremendous work to be done." This final thought is key. Animals are still in danger and being hurt and killed every moment of every day, especially those deemed disposable. And as fires, floods, droughts, and other extreme weather crises increase in frequency and severity, the need to properly and more widely integrate the protection of animals becomes dire and urgent, whether the animals are people's companions, kept on farms and other properties, or trying to survive in the increasingly treacherous wild. When droughts and floods decimate crops like hay, our ability to even provide baseline care for animals is endangered.

It would be silly to suggest a humane future is guaranteed, or that people are not polarized, economically and politically. Yet alongside examples of violence and hate, there is remarkable evidence of care and solidarity. Solidarity is rooted in empathy, yet the idea, commitment, and vision go further. Solidarity requires work. Solidarity is a process, and it involves support despite differences. Solidarity challenges us to not only feel empathy and compassion but also act to make interpersonal and political changes.

"I hold steadfast to this: animals can be what brings us together," Arrington argues. "It can look different for different people, and it can vary by culture, but if we can focus on what we have in common, I think animals can be a unifying force. I still think that even with it getting more polarized and when it seems like we are so far apart, more than ever animals are the key."

Even among those who agree about so much, there are debates, and uniformity is not a prerequisite for animal protection. In many ways, the differences and disagreements enrich the work, and ideally, challenge people to listen, learn, and think through their perspectives, and when necessary, evolve to better serve, support, and uplift others.

People harm different animals for different reasons, so animal protection must be multifaceted. Responsive work that focuses on individual victims, including investigations and enforcement, as well as proactive strategies that seek to prevent harm before it happens will both continue to be needed, and neither should be neglected. I do not see a question as to whether to work in enforcement, community-based, legal, political, or economic spheres for animal protection. All are crucial pathways for change and should be thoughtfully, ethically, and strategically used, and ideally, complementary.

Thinking both upstream and downstream will always strengthen the work done today. The animal protection terrain is also part of a larger social landscape.[1] Broader inequalities and debates shape animal protection work and workers, and the opposite can be true too. Animal protection is about how we view and treat each other—the members of other species, and the members of our own; who is cherished and deemed worthy of investment, and who is written off. It requires solidarity with animals and with other people. This means not only looking up and down the stream but also at the broader terrain within which animals and people are living and working.

Money and jobs cause so much harm. But money and jobs—ethical investments and humane jobs—are also essential to defending animals. Creating more humane jobs means increasing the number of people on the front lines to make sure there are enough of them to reach all the animals in need efficiently and more safely. Creating more humane jobs is also about making animal protection positions better for those who do the work. The financial constraints on organizations responsible for cruelty investigations in both the public and nonprofit sectors are real. But investing in the physical and mental well-being of those on the front lines is an investment in the physical and mental well-being of vulnerable animals as well. This applies to cruelty investigators in North American communities and even more so for park rangers tasked with protecting endangered species in places like Central Africa. The effective protection of animals works hand in hand, hand in paw, and hand in hoof with the well-being of frontline workers.

At the same time, whether it's someone struggling to survive by poaching sea turtles or toiling in a slaughterhouse or factory farm to try to make ends meet, the importance of creating humane alternatives to the many kinds of work that harm other species—legally and illegally—is essential for protecting animals. Humane job alternatives can employ those who used to kill or trade animals directly in protection programs, or in other kinds of work that do no harm. From the coastal beaches of Latin America to the heartland of Texas, this crucial work is underway and must be expanded.

Moreover, this foundational recognition of the interconnectedness of human and animal vulnerabilities shapes the work being done to confront the violence link around the world. A commitment to seeing both marginalized people and animals not only survive but also thrive underscores programs like Pets for Life in the United States and the International Anti-Poaching Federation's work in Zimbabwe. Working to defend animals is equally about defending people, especially those who have been marginalized and disadvantaged by the same forces that hurt animals: callousness, indifference, ignorance, insecurity, hatred, arrogance, greed.

This rejection of zero-sum strategies that pit groups against each other was part and parcel of the earliest animal protection efforts when advocates saw connections between animals' welfare and people's rights, including women, children, and enslaved people. Across today's animal protection landscape, there are more and more examples of this core truth being recognized. As Carol J. Adams has argued, gender is and has always been central.[2] Abusive men who—depending on their place, position, and power—harm one or millions of sentient beings are a significant cause of animals' and people's suffering. Women are disproportionately victimized, but are also centrally involved in animal protection, resisting harm, and increasingly, leading humane action from community-based to economic arenas.[3] Given the stakes, people of all genders need to confront abuse and create change.

People working behind-the-scenes in animal protection organizations, including janitorial, maintenance, accounting, office management, communications, design, information technologies, and fundraising staff, are essential too. Organizations do not exist or function, and animals are not protected, without these workers. Staff at the ALDF unionized in 2021, joining animal protection workers of different kinds across Canada and Europe who have recognized the importance of self-advocating and labor rights. Animal defenders are confronting gender-based harassment, white supremacy, and entrenched inequities and exclusions in both the outcomes of their work and their own workplaces.[4] More organizational leaders are beginning to better reflect the diversity of our societies.

Aryenish Birdie founded and led Encompass, an organization that was driven to ensure that the animal protection movement reaches "its fullest potential because it reflects a globally diverse population and embraces a culture of equity." She highlights a powerful statement of enduring and expansive relevance from Audre Lorde, a Black writer, feminist, and civil rights activist: "There is no such thing as a single-issue struggle because we do not live single-issue lives."[5]

"Diverse groups are more creative, insightful, and productive than homogeneous ones," Birdie asserts. "They enjoy lower rates of burnout and stronger feelings of belonging and engagement. And diverse groups better reflect our evolving world—which means they are more adaptable, resilient, and successful." It's also about not losing or failing to benefit from talent. Birdie cautions against superficial efforts, and instead argues for equity and racial representation to become "cornerstone principles." And this essential work is itself a process of ongoing learning, listening, and engagement. Encompass highlighted "the fact that [even though] people of color are still sometimes called 'minorities' in the United States, we are actually the majority of the global population" and the landscape of animal protection is undoubtedly global.

"My journey has shown me that the power of belonging must be central to our work," Birdie says. "We need more representation at all levels, and we also need organizations to understand our desire for equity. This is how we will grow, adapt, and win. It's how we will realize our fullest potential to make the world a better place for animals." Birdie founded Encompass because she knew it was both the right and smart thing to do—for people and animals.

Those who fund animal protection work—individual and organizational donors including foundations in the case of nonprofits, and political representatives and leaders in the public sector—have the potential to propel or hinder a humane future. Animals are not protected without people, solidarity, or money. Donate to the organizations whose approaches and emphases you value. Support political candidates and leaders who will invest in the animal protection projects you deem important and the laws you believe in. Animals will not be protected, and meaningful changes will not happen, without investment and work to transform ethical priorities into immediate and larger changes.

So much animal protection work has been either pushed or left to nonprofits, even as governments use public money to subsidize industries that cause and profit from animal suffering. The scale of animal suffering would be far greater if it weren't for nonprofit organizations taking the lead and doing so much of the labor. But something as significant as animal protection should not be so dependent on donations. The public sector should spend more money protecting animals. Given the link between violence against animals and people, investments in cruelty investigations and preventative programs are particularly strategic and overdue, and likely to be least contentious. Public leadership should aim higher, though, and support humane job creation and transitions across sectors, including in animal care and food production. A truly humane society would eradicate both illegal and legal cruelty.

This is about our species. Yet simultaneously, it can't just be all about humans. Animals are family members and friends as well as neighbors, coworkers, and fellow beings in their own right who deserve to live joyful and peaceful lives on this one planet we all call home. People make choices every single day, and each one affects animals.[6] We make choices when we buy food and clothes, interact with others, make proposals at work, speak up or stay silent, vote, and plan or change careers. We are each positioned differently, but can all make a difference in our acres.

The story of animal protection is still being written, and we are all authors. This book is not simply an exposé of the problems, nor is it entirely a cheerful portrait of successes and struggles overcome. It is a landscape of work and hope ongoing, inextricably intertwined, as we strive not to be merely human but to be truly humane.

Acknowledgments

Writing this book was a genuine pleasure and honor, and I am grateful for so much and so many.

My deep thanks to everyone across the animal protection landscape who spoke with me, shared their experiences and analysis, trucked me around, and opened the doors to protective labor not often seen or properly considered. The breadth of voices I am able to amplify is another testament to the generosity and commitment of people defending animals, even when the pandemic forced changes to some field research plans.

I have long collaborated with and benefited from the knowledge and good humor of Amy Fitzgerald. Research assistants have provided invaluable data through their digging work, including Bridget Nicholls, Brittany Campbell, Curtis Morrison, Alejandra González Jiménez, Erin Jones, Daphne Brouwer, Darren Chang, Kirsten Francescone, Taryn Graham, Alden Eakins, Cogie Cogan, Elizabeth Greene, Angela Zhang, and Madeleine Browne. Susanna Hedenborg and Charlotte Lundgren opened many gateways in Sweden, and Peter Sankoff and Marcelo Rodriguez Ferrere have provided helpful perspective on the ever-changing realities of animal law scholarship. I am thankful for other academic colleagues, many of whose work and names are cited, for their support and own contributions to the expansive challenge of ending suffering and improving lives. Karen Dalke would have adored this book and she is missed and remembered with love. I work in a wonderful academic community propelled by commitments to excellence and social responsibility, Huron University College at Western

University, and am grateful every day. I also am very thankful for funding from the Social Sciences and Humanities Research Council of Canada, which helped make this book possible.

When Chris Bucci of Aevitas Creative Management approached me about becoming my agent and bringing animal protection and ethics to a large, global audience, I was immediately grateful for his vision and foresight, and remain thankful for his humor, insight, and skill. The enthusiasm and detailed plan of the brilliant minds at the MIT Press made it clear that this project, a genuine labor of love, belonged in their capable hands. My editor, Beth Clevenger, an essential part of the "C&C Book Factory," has provided thoughtful guidance and analysis that has helped elucidate the story of animal protection and bring this book to life. I am thankful for the commitment of everyone at the MIT Press, including Anthony Zannino, Jessica Pellien, Nicholas DiSabatino, and Ginny Crossman, among many others. I also appreciate the helpful feedback of the anonymous peer reviewers.

My mother, Rebecca, first recognized and then fertilized my love for animals, the seeds from which so much has grown, and I am thankful for her ongoing support. I am also grateful for Violet, Jorge Emilio, Jennifer, Rick, Riley, Nancy, Daniela, and all the loyal friends who add great joy to life.

My heart overflows with gratitude for my multispecies family and neighbors, past and present, including Sunny, Buster, Zeke, Kozzie, Henry, Zella, Ms. Macey, Trooper, Quinn, Sophie, Aquila, Sarge, Martha, Mighty, Penelope, Bébé, and Uncle Baby Billy. I hope this book does justice to the future they and animals everywhere deserve.

My husband, John, epitomizes love, intelligence, and partnership. If more men were even half the man he is, the world would be assured a humane future.

Notes

INTRODUCTION

1. I do not do justice to the range of work being done in the Global South or countries like China and India. I hope that more will be written, particularly by people from the Global South, about their contexts—and that this work will be read around the world. It is not only the Global North, nor is it any single country, that offers important insights. In fact, those people who include other species in their webs of care in war zones and other contexts of intense social unrest, conflict, and formidable political and social opposition are the most inspiring, and worthy of both attention and support.

2. I first developed the concept of humane jobs in Kendra Coulter, *Animals, Work, and the Promise of Interspecies Solidarity* (New York: Palgrave Macmillan, 2016). I expand on it in Kendra Coulter, "Humane Jobs: A Political Economic Vision for Interspecies Solidarity and Human–Animal Wellbeing," *Politics and Animals* 3 (2017): 31–41; Kendra Coulter, "Towards Humane Jobs: Recognizing Gendered and Multispecies Intersections and Possibilities," in *Climate Change and Gender in Rich Countries: Work, Public Policy and Action*, ed. Marjorie Griffin Cohen (London: Routledge, 2017), 167–182.

3. Some writers and researchers use the term *nonhuman animals* to differentiate between *Homo sapiens* and other animals. As primatologist Frans de Waal says, you could also say nonpenguin animals when talking about animals other than penguins. To avoid both continually referring to other species by what they are not and inadvertently re-centering humans, and for simplicity of language, I use *people*, *humans*, and comparable terms to refer to our species, *animals* to refer to other species as a whole, and then additional details as needed (such as horse, gorilla, etc.).

4. Lauren Corman was among the first scholars to thoroughly confront the issue of animals' "voices" in the animal protection landscape. See, for example, Lauren Corman, "The Ventriloquist's Burden," in *Animal Subjects 2.0*, ed. Jodey Castricano and Lauren Corman (Waterloo, ON: Wilfrid Laurier Press, 2016), 473–512. Communications, art history, literary, and philosophy scholars have also considered the representation of animals' voices, including J. Keri Cronin, *Art for Animals: Visual Culture and Animal Advocacy, 1870–1924* (University

Park: Pennsylvania State University Press, 2018); Eva Meijer, *When Animals Speak* (New York: NYU Press, 2019).

CHAPTER 1

1. Dawn Rault, Stacy Nowicki, Cindy Adams, and Melanie Rock, "To Protect Animals, First We Must Protect Law Enforcement Officers," *Journal of Animal and Natural Resource Law* 14 (2018): 1–32.

2. Arnold Arluke, *Brute Force: Animal Police and the Challenge of Cruelty* (West Lafayette, IN: Purdue University Press, 2004).

3. Katja M. Guenther, *The Lives and Deaths of Shelter Animals* (Redwood City, CA: Stanford University Press, 2020).

CHAPTER 2

1. Kendra Coulter and Amy Fitzgerald, "The Compounding Feminization of Animal Cruelty Investigation Work and Its Multispecies Implications," *Gender, Work and Organization* 26, no. 3 (2019): 288–302. On the gender of those who abuse animals, see, for example, Andrew Linzey, *The Link between Animal Abuse and Human Violence* (Brighton: Sussex Academic Press, 2009); Lisa Emmett, Nina Kasacek, and Birgit Ursula Stetina, "Demographic Characteristics of Individuals Who Abuse Animals: A Systematic Review," *People and Animals: The International Journal of Research and Practice* 4, no. 1 (2021): 1–30; Jade Ford, Emma Alleyne, Emily Blake, and Amanda Somers, "A Descriptive Model of the Offence Process for Animal Abusers: Evidence from a Community Sample," *Psychology, Crime and Law* 27, no. 4 (2021): 324–340; Anton van Wijk, Manon Hardeman, and Nienke Endenburg, "Animal Abuse: Offender and Offence Characteristics: A Descriptive Study," *Journal of Investigative Psychology and Offender Profiling* 15, no. 2 (2018): 175–186.

2. I introduced the concept of the animal harm spectrum in Kendra Coulter, "The Organization of Animal Protection Investigations and the Animal Harm Spectrum: Canadian Data, International Lessons," *Social Sciences* 11, no. 1 (2021): 22–44.

CHAPTER 3

1. For more historical details, see, for example, Diane Beers, *For the Prevention of Cruelty: The History and Legacy of Animal Rights Activism in the United States* (Athens, OH: Swallow Press, 2006); Ernest Freeberg, *A Traitor to His Species: Henry Bergh and the Birth of the Animal Rights Movement* (New York: Basic Books, 2020); Marion S. Lane and Stephen L. Zawistowski, *Heritage of Care: The American Society for the Prevention of Cruelty to Animals* (Santa Barbara: Praeger, 2007).

2. See, for example, Maya Schenwar, Joe Macaré, and Alana Yu-lan Price, eds., *Who Do You Serve? Who Do You Protect? Police Violence and Resistance in the United States* (Chicago: Haymarket Books, 2016); Andrea J. Ritchie, *Invisible No More: Police Violence against Black*

Women and Women of Color (Boston: Beacon Press, 2017); Alex Vitale, *The End of Policing* (Brooklyn: Verso Books, 2021); Robyn Maynard, *Policing Black Lives: State Violence in Canada from Slavery to the Present* (Toronto: Fernwood Publishing, 2017).

3. See, for example, Charles M. Katz and Edward R. Maguire, eds., *Transforming the Police: 13 Key Reforms* (Long Grove, IL: Waveland Press, 2020); Rosa Brooks, *Tangled Up in Blue: Policing the American City* (New York: Penguin Press, 2021).

4. For a synthesis, see Hope Gillette, "What Causes Domestic Violence?," Psych Central, September 30, 2021, https://psychcentral.com/lib/what-causes-domestic-violence.

5. They are also called courthouse dogs in some countries, including the United States.

CHAPTER 4

1. "Animal Cruelty as a Gateway Crime," National Sheriffs' Association, accessed December 12, 2022, https://www.sheriffs.org/animalcrueltygateway.

2. For a comprehensive discussion of coercive control, see, for example, Evan Stark, *Coercive Control: How Men Entrap Women in Personal Life* (Oxford: Oxford University Press, 2007).

3. For a compilation of decades of research, see Phil Arkow, "Bibliography—the LINK," Therapy Animals, September 21, 2022, https://www.animaltherapy.net/animal-abuse-human -violence/bibliography-the-link/. Recent books include Nik Taylor and Heather Fraser, *Companion Animals and Domestic Violence: Rescuing Me, Rescuing You* (Houndsmills, UK: Palgrave Macmillan, 2019); Andrew Campbell, *Not without My Pet: Understanding the Relationship between Domestic Violence Victims and Their Pets* (Warrenton, VA: Freiling Publishing, 2021).

4. Shelby Elaine McDonald, Elizabeth A. Collins, Anna Maternick, Nicole Nicotera, Sandra Graham-Bermann, Frank R. Ascione, and James Herbert Williams, "Intimate Partner Violence Survivors' Reports of Their Children's Exposure to Companion Animal Maltreatment: A Qualitative Study," *Journal of Interpersonal Violence* 34, no. 13 (2019): 2627–2652; Betty Jo Barrett, Amy Fitzgerald, Rochelle Stevenson, and Chi Ho Cheung, "Animal Maltreatment as a Risk Marker of More Frequent and Severe Forms of Intimate Partner Violence," *Journal of Interpersonal Violence* 35, no. 23–24 (2020): 5131–5156.

5. See, for example, Frank R. Ascione, and Phil Arkow, eds., *Child Abuse, Domestic Violence, and Animal Abuse: Linking the Circles of Compassion for Prevention and Intervention* (West Lafayette, IN: Purdue University Press, 1999).

6. National Link Coalition, *The Link between Violence to People and Violence to Animals* (Stratford, NJ: National Link Coalition, 2013), https://nationallinkcoalition.org/wp-content/ uploads/2013/01/LinkSummaryBrochure3-panel.pdf.

7. Julie M. Palais, "Using the National Incident-Based Reporting System (NIBRS) to Study Animal Cruelty: Preliminary Results (2016–2019)," *Social Sciences* 10, no. 10 (2021): 378–405.

8. Stefanie Marsh, "The Link Between Animal Abuse and Murder," *Atlantic*, August 31, 2017, https://www.theatlantic.com/science/archive/2017/08/melinda-merck-veterinary -forensics/538575/.

9. Margaret Atwood, *Second Words: Selected Critical Prose 1960–1982* (Toronto: House of Anansi, 2011).

10. See Laura Bates, *Men Who Hate Women: From Incels to Pickup Artists: The Truth about Extreme Misogyny and How It Affects Us All* (Naperville, IL: Sourcebooks, 2020); Kate Manne, *Down Girl: The Logic of Misogyny* (Oxford: Oxford University Press, 2018).

11. Research on gender-based violence and femicide often recognizes multiple levels of response and prevention. For a synthesis, see "Preventing Femicide," Canadian Femicide Observatory for Justice and Accountability, https://www.femicideincanada.ca/preventing.

CHAPTER 5

1. Jessica Pierce and Marc Bekoff, *A Dog's World: Imagining the Lives of Dogs in a World without Humans* (Princeton, NJ: Princeton University Press, 2021).

2. For more, see Amanda Arrington and Michael Markarian, "Serving Pets in Poverty: A New Frontier for the Animal Welfare Movement," *Sustainable Development Law and Policy* 18, no. 1 (2017): 40–43.

3. See, for example, Arnold Arluke and Andrew Rowan, *Underdogs: Pets, People, and Poverty* (Athens: University of Georgia Press, 2020).

4. See, for example, Monika Pronczuk and Ruth Maclean, "Africans Say Ukrainian Authorities Hindered Them from Fleeing," *New York Times*, March 1, 2022, https://www.nytimes.com/2022/03/01/world/europe/ukraine-refugee-discrimination.html; Amnesty International, "Mozambique: Rescue Efforts Jeopardized by Racial Discrimination following Palma Attack—New Survivors' Testimony," May 14, 2021, https://www.amnesty.org/en/latest/news/2021/05/mozambique-rescue-attempts-jeopardized-by-racial-discrimination-following-palma-attack-2/.

5. "About Homeless Health Care Los Angeles," Skid Rover, accessed December 12, 2022, https://www.skidrover.org/.

6. "Frequently Asked Questions," My Dog Is My Home, accessed December 12, 2022, https://www.mydogismyhome.org/faqs.

7. "What We Do," Feeding Pets of the Homeless, accessed December 12, 2022, https://www.petsofthehomeless.org/about-us/what-we-do/.

8. Leslie Irvine, *My Dog Always Eats First: Homeless People and Their Animals* (Boulder, CO: Lynne Rienner Publishers, 2013).

9. See "Program for Pet Health Equity," https://pphe.utk.edu/aligncare/.

10. Kris Clarke and Michael Yellow Bird, *Decolonizing Pathways: Towards Integrative Healing in Social Work* (London: Routledge, 2021), 163.

11. "Northern Dogs Project—Canada," International Fund for Animal Welfare, accessed December 12, 2022, https://www.ifaw.org/ca-en/projects/northern-dogs-project-canada.

12. Ermineskin Cree Nation Dog and Prohibited Animal Control Law, no. E16-01, Section 81 of the Indian Act, Part II—Enacted First Nations Laws (2016), https://partii-partiii.fng.ca /fng-gpn-ii-iii/pii/fr/item/473364/index.do?q=138+animal+control+by+law+10+03&site _preference=normal.

13. "Volunteering," Geronimo Animal Rescue Team, accessed December 12, 2022, https:// garteam.org/help-animals.

CHAPTER 6

1. For an analysis of the racial and other politics, see Claire Jean Kim, *Dangerous Crossings: Race, Species, and Nature in a Multicultural Age* (New York: Cambridge University Press, 2015).

2. Jim Gorant, *The Lost Dogs: Michael Vick's Dogs and Their Tale of Rescue and Redemption* (New York: Gotham Books, 2011).

3. See, for example, Tracy K. Witte, Elizabeth G. Spitzer, Nicole Edwards, Katherine A. Fowler, and Randall J. Nett, "Suicides and Deaths of Undetermined Intent among Veterinary Professionals from 2003 through 2014," *Journal of the American Veterinary Medical Association* 255, no. 5 (2019): 595–608.

4. "Política pública distrital de protección y bienestar animal 2014–2038" ("District public policy for animal protection and welfare 2014–2038"), District Secretary of Environment, accessed December 20, 2022, https://www.ambientebogota.gov.co/web/sda/politica-de -bienestar-animal; translated by Alejandra González Jiménez.

5. "Position Statement on Animal Abuser Registries," ASPCA, December 12, 2022, https:// www.aspca.org/about-us/aspca-policy-and-position-statements/position-statement-animal -abuser-registries.

6. Angus Nurse, "Masculinities and Animal Harm," *Men and Masculinities* 23, no. 5 (2020): 921. See also Angus Nurse, *Animal Harm: Perspectives on Why People Harm and Kill Animals* (London: Routledge, 2013); Arnold Arluke, *Just a Dog: Understanding Animal Cruelty and Ourselves* (Philadelphia: Temple University Press, 2006).

7. See Justin Marceau, *Beyond Cages: Animal Law and Criminal Punishment* (Cambridge: Cambridge University Press, 2019); Justin Marceau, "Palliative Animal Law: The War on Animal Cruelty," *Harvard Law Review* 134, no. 5 (March 2021): 250–262.

8. For more on this, see Randall Lockwood, "Animal Hoarding: The Challenge for Mental Health, Law Enforcement, and Animal Welfare Professionals," *Behavioral Sciences and the Law* 36, no. 6 (2018): 698–716.

9. "Courtroom Animal Advocate Programs (CAAP)," Animal Legal Defense Fund, accessed December 12, 2022, https://aldf.org/article/courtroom-animal-advocate-programs-caap/.

10. See Jessica Rubin, "Desmond's Law: Early Impressions of Connecticut's Court Advocate Program for Animal Cruelty Cases," *Harvard Law Review* 134, no. 5 (March 2021): 263–275; Jessica Rubin, "Desmond's Law: A Novel Approach to Animal Advocacy," *Animal Law* 24 (2018): 243–275.

11. Rubin, "Desmond's Law."

12. Personal communication.

13. Rubin, "Desmond's Law."

CHAPTER 7

1. See, for example, Michelle Nijhuis, *Beloved Beasts: Fighting for Life in an Age of Extinction* (New York: W. W. Norton and Company, 2021); William Bill Adams, *Against Extinction: The Story of Conservation* (London: Earthscan, 2004).

2. For a more detailed outline of her analysis, see Vanda Felbab-Brown, *The Extinction Market: Wildlife Trafficking and How to Counter It* (Oxford: Oxford University Press, 2017). See also Rachel Love Nuwer, *Poached: Inside the Dark World of Wildlife Trafficking* (New York: Da Capo Press, 2018); Ragnhild Aslaug Sollung, *The Crimes of Wildlife Trafficking: Issues of Justice, Legality, and Morality* (Milton Park, UK: Routledge, 2019).

3. There are many accessible books written by and about these women and ape conservation. See, for example, Sy Montgomery, *Walking with the Great Apes: Jane Goodall, Dian Fossey, Biruté Galdikas* (White River Junction, VT: Chelsea Green Publishing, 2009).

4. Jessica Hatcher, "Meet the First Female Rangers to Guard One of World's Deadliest Parks," *National Geographic*, October 14, 2015, https://www.nationalgeographic.com/adventure /article/151014-virunga-women-rangers-mountain-gorillas-congo.

5. "'New Deal' for Conservation Rangers Signals a Critical Step for the Planet's Health on World Ranger Day, New Alliance Announces Action Plan to Develop Global Welfare Standards and Code of Conduct for Rangers," World Wildlife Fund, July 31, 2020, https://wwf.panda.org /wwf_news/press_releases/?364767/New-Deal-for-Conservation-Rangers-Signals-a -Critical-Step-for-the-Planets-Health.

6. "In Pictures: The Life of Ndakasi, a Gorilla Who Went Viral," BBC News, October 7, 2021, https://www.bbc.com/news/world-africa-58826986.

7. "Black Mambas Anti Poaching Unit," Helping Rhinos, accessed December 12, 2022, https:// www.helpingrhinos.org/black-mambas/.

8. Corinne Benedict and Jo-Anne McArthur, "The Black Mambas," Unbound Project, February 3, 2018, https://unboundproject.org/the-black-mambas/.

CHAPTER 8

1. See, for example, Margaret Robinson, "Veganism and Mi'kmaq Legends," in *Colonialism and Animality*, ed. Kelly Struthers Montford and Chloë Taylor (Milton Park, UK: Routledge, 2020), 107–114.

2. Darren Chang, "Tensions in Contemporary Indigenous and Animal Advocacy Struggles: The Commercial Seal Hunt as a Case Study," in *Colonialism and Animality*, ed. Kelly Struthers Montford and Chloë Taylor (Milton Park, UK: Routledge, 2020), 29–49; Sue Donaldson

and Will Kymlicka, "Animal Rights and Aboriginal Rights," in *Canadian Perspectives on Animals and the Law*, ed. Peter Sankoff, Vaughan Black, and Katie Sykes (Toronto: Irwin Law, 2015), 159–186.

3. See, for example, Jane Goodall with Thane Maynard and Ruth Hudson, *Hope for Animals and Their World: How Endangered Species Are Being Rescued from the Brink* (New York: Grand Central Publishing, 2007); Christopher J. Preston, *Tenacious Beasts: Wildlife Recoveries That Change How We Think about Animals* (Cambridge, MA: MIT Press, 2023).

4. See, for example, Paul Jepson and Cain Blythe, *Rewilding: The Radical New Science of Ecological Recovery, the Illustrated Edition* (Cambridge, MA: MIT Press, 2022); Dolly Jørgensen, *Recovering Lost Species in the Modern Age: Histories of Longing and Belonging* (Cambridge, MA: MIT Press, 2019); George Monbiot, *Feral: Searching for Enchantment on the Frontiers of Rewilding* (London: Allen Lane, 2013).

5. Henry Nicholls, *Lonesome George: The Life and Loves of a Conservation Icon* (Houndmills, UK: Palgrave Macmillan, 2006).

6. See, for example, Costanza Manes, Daniele Pinton, Alberto Canestrelli, and Ilaria Capua, "Occurrence of Fibropapillomatosis in Green Turtles (Chelonia Mydas) in Relation to Environmental Changes in Coastal Ecosystems in Texas and Florida: A Retrospective Study," *Animals* 12, no. 10 (2022): 1236–1260.

7. "Giant Tortoise Restoration in the Galápagos Islands," Galápagos Conservancy, accessed February 1, 2022, https://www.galapagos.org/conservation/giant-tortoise-restoration/.

8. "Purpose and Mission," Paso Pacífico, accessed December 12, 2022, https://pasopacifico .org/our-purpose/.

9. "Saving Sea Turtles," Paso Pacífico, accessed December 12, 2022, https://pasopacifico.org /project/saving-sea-turtles/.

10. "Amphibians," National Wildlife Federation, accessed December 12, 2022, https://www .nwf.org/Educational-Resources/Wildlife-Guide/Amphibians.

11. David B. Wake and Michelle S. Koo, "Amphibians," *Current Biology* 28, no. 21 (2018): R1237–R1241.

CHAPTER 9

1. See, for example, Pat Shipman, *Our Oldest Companions: The Story of the First Dogs* (Cambridge, MA: Harvard University Press, 2021).

2. See also Aysha Akhtar, *Animals and Public Health: Why Treating Animals Better Is Critical to Human Welfare* (Houndmills, UK: Palgrave Macmillan, 2012).

3. Elaine Toland, Monica Bando, Michèle Hamers, Vanessa Cadenas, Rob Laidlaw, Albert Martínez-Silvestre, and Paul van der Wielen, "Turning Negatives into Positives for Pet Trading and Keeping: A Review of Positive Lists," *Animals* 10, no. 12 (2020): 2371–2409.

4. Andrew Westoll, *The Chimps of Fauna Sanctuary: A Canadian Story of Resilience and Recovery* (Toronto: Harper Perennial, 2011).

5. Rosemary-Claire Collard, *Animal Traffic: Lively Capital in the Global Exotic Pet Trade* (Durham, NC: Duke University Press, 2020). For a consideration of the complicated place of reproduction in some sanctuaries and conservation efforts, see Juno Salazar Parreñas, *Decolonizing Extinction: The Work of Care in Orangutan Conservation* (Durham, NC: Duke University Press, 2018); Thom van Dooren, *Flight Ways: Life and Loss at the Edge of Extinction* (New York: Columbia University Press).

6. I first proposed using the term *social reproduction* to understand this dynamic, and developed the term *ecosocial reproduction* to recognize the impacts of wild animals' subsistence and care work on ecosystems, in Kendra Coulter, *Animals, Work, and the Promise of Interspecies Solidarity* (Houndmills, UK: Palgrave Macmillan, 2016). Ecosocial reproduction complements ideas of ecoservices and bioservices, but foregrounds animals' labor. See also Kendra Coulter, "Beyond Human to Humane: A Multispecies Analysis of Care Work, Its Repression, and Its Potential," *Studies in Social Justice* 10, no. 2 (2016): 199–219.

7. "Our Story," Comunidad Inti Wara Yassi, accessed December 12, 2022, https://www.intiwarayassi.org/our-story/.

8. "Animal Care," Comunidad Inti Wara Yassi, accessed December 12, 2022, https://www.intiwarayassi.org/our-work/animal-rescue-care-rehabilitation/.

9. "Donald," Primate Rescue Center, accessed December 12, 2022, https://www.primaterescue.org/staff-primate/donald/.

10. "Jenny," Primate Rescue Center, accessed December 12, 2022, https://www.primaterescue.org/staff-primate/jenny-2/.

11. Elan Abrell, *Saving Animals: Multispecies Ecologies of Rescue and Care* (Minneapolis: University of Minnesota Press, 2021).

12. "April D. Truitt," Primate Rescue Center, accessed December 12, 2022, https://www.primaterescue.org/staff-primate/april-d-truitt/.

13. Nicole Pallotta, "Brussels Recognizes Animals as Sentient Beings Distinct from Objects," Animal Legal Defense Fund, December 8, 2018, https://aldf.org/article/brussels-recognizes-animals-as-sentient-beings-distinct-from-objects/.

14. "Frequently Asked Questions," Nonhuman Rights Project, accessed December 12, 2022, https://www.nonhumanrights.org/frequently-asked-questions/.

15. Maneesha Deckha, *Animals as Legal Beings: Contesting Anthropocentric Legal Orders* (Toronto: University of Toronto Press, 2021).

16. Angela Fernandez, "Not Quite Property, Not Quite Persons: A Quasi Approach for Nonhuman Animals," *Canadian Journal of Comparative and Contemporary Law* 5 (2019): 1–77.

17. See, for example, Gary L. Francione, *Animals as Persons: Essays on the Abolition of Animal Exploitation* (New York: Columbia University Press, 2008).

18. See, for example, Sue Donaldson and Will Kymlicka, *Zoopolis: A Political Theory of Animal Rights* (Oxford: Oxford University Press, 2011); Charlotte E. Blattner, Kendra Coulter, and Will Kymlicka, eds., *Animal Labour: A New Frontier of Animal Justice?* (Oxford: Oxford University Press, 2020); Karen Bradshaw, *Wildlife as Property Owners: A New Conception of Animal Rights* (Chicago: University of Chicago Press, 2020); Alasdair Cochrane, *Animal Rights without Liberation* (New York: Columbia University Press, 2012).

19. "World Declaration on Great Primates," Great Ape Project, accessed December 12, 2022, http://www.greatapeproject.uk/worlddeclaration.html. See also Paola Cavalieri and Peter Singer, eds., *The Great Ape Project: Equality beyond Humanity* (New York: St. Martin's Griffin, 1993).

20. "Frequently Asked Questions," Nonhuman Rights Project.

21. "NRP Continues to Misuse the Writ of Habeas Corpus, Potentially Risking the Health and Welfare of Happy, an Elephant at the Bronx Zoo," WCS Newsroom, May 18, 2022, https://newsroom.wcs.org/News-Releases/articleType/ArticleView/articleId/17549/NRP-Continues-to-Misuse-the-Writ-of-Habeas-Corpus-Potentially-Risking-the-Health-and-Welfare-of-Happy-An-Elephant-at-the-Bronx-Zoo.aspx.

22. See, for example, Lori B. Girshick, *Advocates for Animals: An Inside Look at Some of the Extraordinary Efforts to End Animal Suffering* (Lanham, MD: Rowman and Littlefield, 2017).

23. Coral Lansbury, *The Old Brown Dog: Women, Workers, and Vivisection in Edwardian England* (Madison: University of Wisconsin Press, 1985).

24. "Alternatives to Animal Testing," European Directorate for the Quality of Medicines & HealthCare, Council of Europe, accessed December 12, 2022, https://www.edqm.eu/en/alternatives-to-animal-testing.

25. Canadian Centre for Alternatives to Animal Methods, "Welcome to CCAAM/CaCVAM," University of Windsor, accessed December 12, 2022, https://www.uwindsor.ca/ccaam/; Canadian Centre for Alternatives to Animal Methods, "Current Paradigm," University of Windsor, accessed December 12, 2022, https://www.uwindsor.ca/ccaam/299/current-paradigm.

26. "Center for Alternatives to Animal Testing—Europe Established," Johns Hopkins Bloomberg School of Public Health, accessed December 12, 2022, https://publichealth.jhu.edu/2010/caat-eu.

CHAPTER 10

1. See, for example, Sarah Maslin Nir, *Horse Crazy: The Story of a Woman and a World in Love with an Animal* (New York: Simon and Schuster Paperbacks, 2020); Halimah Marcus, ed., *Horse Girls: Recovering, Aspiring, and Devoted Riders Redefine the Iconic Bond* (New York: Harper Perennial, 2021); Susanna Forrest, *The Age of the Horse: An Equine Journey through Human History* (New York: Atlantic, 2017).

2. "We Ride Too," Urban Equestrian Academy, accessed December 12, 2022, http://www .urbanequestrian.co.uk/we-ride-too.html.

3. For more comprehensive histories, see Harriet Ritvo, *The Animal Estate: The English and Other Creatures in Victorian England* (Cambridge, MA: Harvard University Press, 1987); J. Keri Cronin, *Art for Animals: Visual Culture and Animal Advocacy, 1870–1924* (University Park: Pennsylvania State University Press, 2018); Clay McShane and Joel Tarr, *The Horse in the City: Living Machines in the Nineteenth Century* (Baltimore: Johns Hopkins University Press, 2007); Emily Patterson-Kane, Michael P. Allen, and Jennifer Eadie, *Rethinking the American Animal Rights Movement* (New York: Routledge, 2022). See also Darcy Ingram's research, https://www.darcyingram.com/.

4. David Philipps, *Wild Horse Country: The History, Myth, and Future of the Mustang* (New York: W. W. Norton and Company, 2017).

5. Delphine Valette, *Invisible Helpers: Voices from Women International Report* (London: Brooke, 2014), 35, 33, 25, https://www.thebrooke.org/research-evidence/invisible-helpers -voices-women.

6. "Justice the Horse Sues Abuser," Animal Legal Defense Fund, last updated August 31, 2022, https://aldf.org/case/justice-the-horse-sues-abuser/.

7. For accessible explanations of cognitive ethnology in particular, see, for example, Marc Bekoff and Jessica Pierce, *Wild Justice: The Moral Lives of Animals* (Chicago: University of Chicago Press, 2009). See also Marc Bekoff and Jessica Pierce, *The Animals' Agenda: Freedom, Compassion, and Coexistence in the Human Age* (Boston: Beacon Press, 2017); Carl Safina, *Beyond Words: What Animals Think and Feel* (New York: Routledge, 2018).

8. Science researchers like Cecilie M. Mejdell and team, Leanne Proops and team, and Jen Wathan and team as well as social science researchers like Gala Argent, Lynda Birke, Keri Brandt, Kate Dashper, Charlotte Lundgren, Andrea Pettit, and Kirrilly Thompson, among others, have studied horses' ways of communicating and understanding the communications of others (both horses and humans).

9. Sarah F. Brosnan and Frans de Waal, "Monkeys Reject Unequal Pay," *Nature* 425, no. 6955 (2003): 297–299.

10. Frans de Waal, *Are We Smart Enough to Know How Smart Animals Are?* (New York: W. W. Norton and Company, 2016); Jennifer Ackerman, *The Genius of Birds* (New York: Penguin Press, 2016).

11. Barbara J. King, *How Animals Grieve* (Chicago: University of Chicago Press, 2013); Jeffrey Moussaieff Masson and Susan McCarthy, *When Elephants Weep: The Emotional Lives of Elephants* (New York: Dell Publishing, 1995). See also Lawrence Scanlan, *The Horse God Built: The Untold Story of Secretariat, the World's Greatest Racehorse* (Toronto: Harper Perennial, 2006).

12. The place of reproduction in many animal protection circles is complicated. Especially in companion animal welfare, medically removing animals' abilities to reproduce is considered

essential in order to reduce the number needing care and homes. The castration of males is widely promoted for horses to manage breeding and make stables safer. Most sanctuaries sterilize animals as well. There are fundamental questions about bodily autonomy to consider, but at this point, controlling the reproduction of domesticated animals is generally seen as necessary, even though animals might like to reproduce.

CHAPTER 11

1. "Broiler Chicken Industry Key Facts 2021," National Chicken Council, accessed December 12, 2022, https://www.nationalchickencouncil.org/chicken-processors-redoubling-efforts -to-keep-essential-workers-safe-and-healthy/.

2. Christopher Leonard, *The Meat Racket: The Secret Takeover of America's Food Business* (New York: Simon and Schuster, 2014); Maryn McKenna, *Big Chicken: The Incredible Story of How Antibiotics Created Modern Agriculture and Changed the Way the World Eats* (Washington, DC: National Geographic Books, 2017).

3. Carol J. Adams, *The Sexual Politics of Meat: A Feminist-Vegetarian Critical Theory*, 20th anniversary ed. (New York: Bloomsbury, 2010).

4. People in colder climates relied more heavily on hunting and fishing.

5. Bill Winders and Elizabeth Ransom, eds., *Global Meat: Social and Environmental Consequences of the Expanding Meat Industry* (Cambridge, MA: MIT Press, 2019); Alex Blanchette, *Porkopolis: American Animality, Standardized Life, and the Factory Farm* (Durham, NC: Duke University Press, 2020); Ted Genoways, *This Blessed Earth: A Year in the Life of an American Family Farm* (New York: W. W. Norton and Company, 2017); Rhoda Wilkie, *Livestock/Deadstock: Working with Farm Animals from Birth to Slaughter* (Philadelphia: Temple University Press, 2010).

6. Timothy Pachirat, *Every Twelve Seconds: Industrialized Slaughter and the Politics of Sight* (New Haven, CT: Yale University Press, 2011); Donald D. Stull and Michael J. Broadway, *Slaughterhouse Blues: The Meat and Poultry Industry in North America*, 2nd ed. (Belmont, CA: Wadworth, 2013).

7. For an elaboration on these dimensions, see Christopher Carter, *The Spirit of Soul Food: Race, Faith, and Food Justice* (Champaign: University of Illinois Press, 2021).

8. For a scholarly discussion of transnational animal law, see Charlotte E. Blattner, *Protecting Animals within and across Borders: Extraterritorial Jurisdiction and the Challenges of Globalization* (Oxford: Oxford University Press, 2019). For a pertinent analysis of the animal welfare science, see Marc Bekoff and Jessica Pierce, "Animal Welfare Cannot Adequately Protect Nonhuman Animals: The Need for a Science of Animal Well-being," *Animal Sentience* 1, no. 7 (2016).

9. See also Ted Genoways, *The Chain: Farm, Factory, and the Fate of Our Food* (New York: HarperCollins, 2014).

10. See also Leah Garcés, *Grilled: Turning Adversaries into Allies to Change the Chicken Industry* (New York: Bloomsbury, 2019).

11. Paul Shapiro, *Clean Meat: How Growing Meat without Animals Will Revolutionize Dinner and the World* (New York: Gallery Books, 2018); Chase Purdy, *Billion Dollar Burger: Inside Big Tech's Race for the Future of Food* (New York: Penguin, 2020).

12. "Mission and Values," Food Empowerment Project, accessed December 12, 2022, https://foodispower.org/mission-and-values/.

13. The capitalization of lauren Ornelas's name reflects her preferences.

14. See, for example, Jeffrey Moussaieff Masson, *The Pig Who Sang to the Moon: The Emotional World of Farm Animals* (New York: Ballantine Books, 2003); Barbara J. King, *Personalities on the Plate: The Lives and Minds of Animals We Eat* (Chicago: University of Chicago Press, 2017).

15. Jonathan Safran Foer, *Eating Animals* (New York: Hachette, 2010).

16. Dinesh Joseph Wadiwel, *The War against Animals* (Leiden, Netherlands: Brill, 2015).

17. Leslie Irvine and Colter Ellis, "Reproducing Dominion: Emotional Apprenticeship in the 4-H Youth Livestock Program," *Society and Animals* 18, no. 1 (2010): 21–39.

CONCLUSION

1. See, for example, Brinda Jegatheesan, Marie-Jose Enders-Slegers, Elizabeth Ormerod, and Paula Boyden, "Understanding the Link between Animal Cruelty and Family Violence: The Bioecological Systems Model," *International Journal of Environmental Research and Public Health* 17, no. 9 (2020): 3116–3138.

2. Carol J. Adams, *The Sexual Politics of Meat: A Feminist-Vegetarian Critical Theory*, 20th anniversary ed. (New York: Bloomsbury, 2010).

3. See, for example, Jennifer Stojkovic, *The Future of Food Is Female* (Los Angeles: VWS Press, 2022).

4. Jasmin Singer, ed., *Antiracism in Animal Advocacy: Igniting Cultural Transformation* (Brooklyn: Lantern Publishing and Media, 2021).

5. Audre Lorde, "Learning from the 60s" (speech, Harvard University, Cambridge, MA, February 1982).

6. See also Aysha Akhtar, *Our Symphony with Animals: On Health, Empathy, and Our Shared Destinies* (New York: Simon and Schuster, 2019); Barbara J. King, *Animals' Best Friends: Putting Compassion to Work for Animals in Captivity and in the Wild* (Chicago: University of Chicago Press, 2021); Anne Benvenuti, *Kindred Spirits: One Animal Family* (Atlanta: University of Georgia Press, 2021).

Index

Page numbers in italics indicate figures.

Abuse. *See also* Animal cruelty; Hoarding;
    Investigating/prosecuting violent crimes
    against animals
    abandonment, 25
    of animals and humans, link between (*see*
    Human-animal violence link)
    dogfighting, 23–24, 87–89, 109, 114
    horrific cases of, 25, 27
    male vs. female abusers, 22, 57, 66, 105–
    106, 109, 227
    psychology of abusers, 39, 52, 110–111
    public interest in, 3
    and reluctance to call police, 63–64
    trust relearned by animals, viii–ix
Acosta, Vanessa, 50–53
Adams, Carol J., 201–202, 227
Adams, Eric, 213
Ag-gag laws, 211
Agricultural Fairness Alliance, 209
Aguirre, Julio, 92, 98–101
Akashinga, 132–133
Akashinga: The Brave Ones (Wilhelm), 133
ALDF (Animal Legal Defense Fund), 53,
    103, 111, 188, 227–228
AlignCare program, 78
Allen, Greg, 52
Almy, Jessica, 214, 218

Alternative protein industry, 214–215,
    217–218
American Bird Conservancy, 145
American Humane, 57, 171
American Humane Education Society, 33
American Society for the Prevention of
    Cruelty to Animals. *See* ASPCA
American Veterinary Medical Association, 167
Amigo (horse), 187
Amphibians, 152–153
AniCare Approach, 109
Animal care and control services. *See also*
    Shelters for animals
    for collecting strays vs. investigating cruelty,
    11
    dispatchers for, 10–13
    as first responders, 9–10
    on Native reservations, 10
    officers of (*see* Investigators/officers)
    process for reporting cruelty, 10, 12
    scope of, 11
    as underfunded/understaffed, 11–12, 26
Animal cruelty. *See also* Crime; Investigating/
    prosecuting violent crimes against animals
    dedicated units, 34–36, 60–61
    as a gateway crime (*see* Human-animal
    violence link)

Animal cruelty (cont.)
  investigations of, animal nonprofits on,
    44
  laws against, 33–34, 38, 45–46 (*see also*
    Laws/law enforcement)
  against police/service dogs, 47
  socioeconomic determinants of, 38–39,
    105–106
  training for officers, 33–34, 37–38, 43,
    47–49
Animal Cruelty as a Gateway Crime program,
  55
Animal Cruelty Investigation Squad (NYPD),
  34–36
Animal Cruelty Investigations Unit (El Paso,
  Tex.), 52–53
Animal Cruelty Investigation Unit
  (Edmonton, Can.), 49–50
Animal Equality, 224–225
Animal harm spectrum, 28, 32
Animal Help Now, 142
Animal hotlines, 10, 61
Animal Justice, 112, 205
Animal Kill Clock, 205
Animal Legal Defense Fund. *See* ALDF
Animal liberation, 157, 211
Animal photojournalism, 223
Animal protection. *See also* Animal rescue;
    Conservation
  and biological reproduction, 197,
    242–243n12
  by businesspeople and chefs, 211–218
  cats kept indoors, 3
  collaborative (*see* Partnerships in animal
    protection)
  countries studied, 5, 233n1
  diversity of organizations involved in, 4–5,
    29
  of endangered species, 5
  funding for, 6, 11–12, 29–30, 44, 85, 131,
    141, 144–145, 157, 186, 208, 211, 226,
    228–229
  by government agencies, 29–32, 36, 45–49,
    50–53, 72–74, 98, 126, 186
  labor involved in, 3–4, 22–23, 26–28
  via laws (*see* Laws/law enforcement)
  vs. liberation, 157, 211
  meaning of, 4
  professionalization of, 225
  removing animals, 2–3
  and social harms (*see* Social harms and
    protections)
Animal Protection Act (Can.), 46, 82
Animal protection workers. *See also*
    Investigators/officers
  importance of, 227–228
  interaction with low-income animal
    caretakers, 73–74
  risks to, 1
  safety and working conditions of, 5, 21–23,
    25–28
  wildlife rehabilitators, 6
Animal rescue
  of captive animals, 159–164, 166–172
  of chickens, 199, 204, 219–221
  of farmed animals, 199, 219–221
  groups, 19–20, 84, 89–90 (*see also specific
    groups*)
  of horses, 188, 192, 195–197
  from labs, 175
  partnerships in, 51–53
  of wild animals, 117, 138, 141–149
Animals
  as family, viii, 71–72, 76
  in laboratories, 175–177
  pronouns for, 7
  sentience of, 98, 165–166, 189
  use of term, 233n3
  and work/labor, 182, 186
Animals & Society Institute, 109
Animal testing, 175–177
Animal Watch, 142
Animal welfare services. *See* Animal care and
    control services; Animal protection

Apache nation, 83–84
Apes, 159–160, 166. *See also* Chimpanzees;
    Gorillas; Orangutans
Arcand, Leah, 83
Argent, Gala, 242n8
ARK2000 (San Andreas, Calif.), 167–168
Arkow, Phil, 9, 57–58, 66
Arrington, Amanda, 70–71, 73, 75, 79, 85,
    224–225
Ascione, Frank, 57
Asilomar Accords, 18–19
ASPCA (American Society for the Prevention
    of Cruelty to Animals)
  on euthanization of shelter animals, 20
  fearful dogs rehabilitated by, 89–90
  founding of, 33, 180
  law enforcement by, 30, 33
  on registries for abusers, 104
ASPCA (NYC)
  attorneys' collaboration with, 35
  fieldwork by, 35
  forensics at, 94
  law enforcement by, 30
  NYPD's partnership with, 33–37, 50
  veterinarians' partnership with, 35
Association of Wetland Stewards for
    Clayoquot and Barkley Sounds (British
    Columbia), 152
Atwood, Margaret, 64
Avanzino, Rich, 18

BADRAP, 89
Baldwin, Shawna, 42–43
Baltazar Lugones, Tania ("Nena"), 161–162
BARK, 109
Barker, Bob, 19
Bauma, Andre, 129
Baur, Gene, 204
Beagle Freedom Project, 175
Beautiful Joe (Saunders), 33
Bébé (rabbit), 173
Belgium, 158–159, 165

Bergh, Henry, 180
Best Friends Animal Society, 89
Beyond Fences, 70–71
Bikaba, Dominique, 130
Birdie, Aryenish, 228
Birds, 145–147. *See also* Chickens
Birke, Lynda, 242n8
Black Beauty (Sewell), 33, 180
Black Mambas, 134–135
Boarini, Anna, 199
Bolivia, 161–162
Booker, Cory, 215
Bowman, Kerry, 129–131
Brandt, Keri, 242n8
British Union for the Abolition of Vivisection,
    175
Bronx Zoo (NYC), 167, 169
Brooke (nonprofit), 184–185
Bubbles (monkey), 164
Bush Babies, 135
Business ethics, 214
Business of animal protection, 212
Bwindi Impenetrable National Park
    (Uganda), 124

Cabrera Holtz, Elizabeth, 156–158
Calgary (Alberta), 40–44, 46, 50, 62
Calgary Humane Society (CHS; Alberta),
    41–42, 50
Canadian animal cruelty organizations,
    28–30. *See also* Calgary Humane Society;
    Edmonton Humane Society
Canadian Ape Alliance, 129–130
Canadian Centre for Alternatives to Animal
    Methods, 176–177
Canadian Centre for the Validation of
    Alternative Methods, 176–177
Captive animals, 155–177. *See also* Pets/
    companion animals
  and abolitionism, 166
  apes, 159–160
  in aquariums, 171–172

Captive animals (cont.)
in Belgium, 158–159
in Bolivia, 161–162
chimpanzees, 159–160, 162–163, 167
in circuses, 169
dolphins, 171–172
vs. domesticated animals, 155
elephants, 167, 169–170
ethics of keeping, 157–158, 176
for films and television shows, 171
gorillas, 162–163
habeas corpus orders for, 166–167,
188–189
hoarding of, 163
legal vs. illegal trade in, 156–157, 159
monkeys, 160–161, 163–164
motivations for keeping, 159
positive list of appropriate animals,
158–159
as property, 165
rabbits, 172–175
rewilding of, 160–161, 173
rights/legal status of, 165–167, 188–189
safety and health factors in keeping, 158
sanctuaries/rescue centers for, 159–164,
166–172
and sentience of animals, 165–166
tigers, 156, 169
turtles, 159
whales, 171–172
in zoos, 167, 169–171
Carter, Christopher, 207–208, 221
Cats, 3, 74–75
Cattle ranching, 201–203
Cecilia (chimpanzee), 167
Center for Alternatives to Animal Testing
(Johns Hopkins Bloomberg School of
Public Health), 177
Central Park carriage horses (NYC), 181–182
Centre for Justice & Reconciliation, 107
Chandrasekera, Charu, 176–177
Chavez, Veronica, 52

Chickens
abuse of, 204
caged, 206
catching/slaughter of, 200
feral, 220
laws protecting, 204
male chicks, slaughter of, 205
number killed for food, 204–205
personalities of, 218–219
and the poultry/egg industry, 199–202, 205
rescuers/rehabilitators of, 199, 204,
219–221
roosters, 87–89, 220–221
Chigumbura, Petronella, 133
Children's reactions to eating animals, 222
Chimpanzees, 6, 159–160, 162–163, 167,
223
Chimp Haven (La.), 160
Chimps of Fauna Sanctuary, The (Westoll), 160
Chitwan Declaration (2019), 126–127
Circuses, 169
City Wildlife (Washington, DC), 144–147
Clark R. Bavin National Fish and Wildlife
Forensics Laboratory (Ashland, Ore.), 94
Climate change, 152, 185, 207, 217, 225
Cobbe, Frances Power, 175
Cockfighting. *See* Rooster fighting
Coller, Jeremy, 216
Coller FAIRR Protein Producers Index, 216
Collicutt, Alanna, 82–83
Colombia, 98–101
Colombian Association of Legal Veterinary
Medicine and Forensic Sciences, 99
Columbia-Greene Humane Society/SPCA
(Hudson, NY), 31
Community Veterinary Outreach, 79
Comunidad Inti Wara Yassi (Bolivia),
161–162
Congo. *See* DRC
Conservation, 5, 117–135
in the Congo, 124, 126–127, 129–131
dangers of, 126–127

ecotourism, 126, 134
educational programs, 135
of elephants, 131
endangered species, 120–123, 173
environmental school, 131–132
of forests, 130–131
of gorillas, 123–126, 128–130
habitat protection/preserves/protected
   corridors, 118, 130
in Latin America, 149–151
laws to protect endangered animals,
   119
and the legal wildlife trade, 120
livelihood-centered, 122–123
of orangutans, 129–130
and poaching/wildlife trafficking, 119,
   121–122, 124–126, 132–134
and poverty, 121–122
by rangers, 126–127, 132–135, 226
and respect for nonhuman life, 131
as a science, 117–118
in South Africa, 134
species/ecosystem level, 117
and subsistence hunting by Indigenous
   peoples, 118–121
types of organizations, 118
by veterinarians, 128–129
at Virunga National Park, 124, 126–127,
   129
during war, 129–131
by women, 126–127, 132–135
Convention on Trade in Endangered Species
   of Wild Flora and Fauna, 119
Coons, Margaret, 213
Costa Rica, 150–151
Council of Europe, 176
Cowperthwaite, Gabriela, 172
Cows
   music enjoyed by, 218
   number killed for food, 204–205
   slaughter of, 205–206
   welfare vs. rights of, 210

Crime. *See also* Animal cruelty
   categories of, 59
   and policing (*see* Policing and incarceration)
   prosecuting (*see* Investigating/prosecuting
     violent crimes against animals)
   socioeconomic determinants of, 38–39,
     105–106
Cronin, Keri, 135
Crown Prosecution Service (England), 31
Cruelty free (term), 175
Cruelty Free International, 175
Cuffley, Alison, 82–83
Cunningham, Ilka, 45–47, 49–50, 53

Dashper, Kate, 242n8
David Suzuki Foundation's Butterflyway
   Project, 143
Deckha, Maneesha, 165
DeGeneres, Ellen, 125
De La Garza, Carolina, 53
Demers, Phil, 172
Democratic Republic of the Congo. *See* DRC
Denmark, 215
Derby, Pat, 168
De Rossi, Portia, 125
Derrida, Jacques, 221
Desmond's Law (2016), 112–113
Detroit Horse Power, 179
De Waal, Frans, 233n3
Dewey (monkey), 164
Dian Fossey Gorilla Fund, 124–125
Dioum, Baba, 132
Docs 4 Great Apes, 128–129
Dogfighting, 23–24, 87–89, 109, 114
Dogs
   bans on specific breeds of, 24
   courthouse, 48, 235n5 (chap. 3)
   fenced in vs. chained, 71
   legally mandated daily exercise for, 24
   living indoors vs. outdoors, 70–71
   in low-income neighborhoods, 72
   in native communities (rez dogs), 80–84

Dogs (cont.)
  origin of relationship with humans, 158
  rabies vaccinations for, 128
  rescued from labs, 175
Dolphins, 171–172
Domestic violence, 25, 56–57, 58–60, 62, 67
Domestic violence facilities, 64–66
Donald (chimpanzee), 163
Donkeys, 183–185
Donkey Sanctuary, 184
Doyle, Margaret, 42–43, 95–96
DRC (Democratic Republic of the Congo), 124, 126–127, 129–131
Ducks, 147, 205
Duffy, Amanda, 114–115
Dyck, Ted, 45–47, 49–50

Ebony Horse Club, 179–180
Edes, Craig, 83
Edmonton (Alberta), 40–41, 44–50, 53
Edmonton Humane Society (Alberta), 30, 44–45
Elephants, 5, 131, 167, 169–170
Ellen DeGeneres Campus of the Dian Fossey Gorilla Fund, 125
Elmhurst 1925, 212
El Paso (Tex.), 50, 52–53, 60
Encompass, 228
Equity, 78–79
Ermineskin Cree First Nation, 81–82
Esther the Wonder Pig, 219
European Link Coalition, 65
Euthanasia
  in animal shelters, 17–18, 20, 23
  of animals who can't be rehabilitated, 23
  and hoarding, 25
  of homeless animals, 17–18, 20
  for horses, 197
  mental toll on veterinary workers, 93–94
  vs. rehabilitation, 89, 91–92, 111
  of wild animals, 141
Exotic animals. See Captive animals

FAIRR (Farm Animal Investment Risk and Return), 216–218
Family violence. See Domestic violence; Human-animal violence link
Farm Forward, 207–208
Farming, 199–222. See also Chickens; Cows
  and animal slaughter, 205–206
  and animal welfare vs. rights, 209–210
  consumption of farmed animals, 207–208, 210–212, 222
  decline in, 204
  factory, 206–208, 212, 215–216, 221
  fur farms, 208–209
  sanctuaries for farmed animals, 199, 219–221
  subsidies for, 208–209, 211
  transitions to non-killing operations, 203, 212, 215, 217
Farm Sanctuary, 204
Farm System Reform Act, 215
Fauna Foundation (outside Montreal), 160, 223
FBI (Federal Bureau of Investigation), 59
Feeding Pets of the Homeless, 77
Felbab-Brown, Vanda, 119–120
Fernandez, Angela, 165
First Nations. See Native communities
Fitzgerald, Amy, 23
FLAP Canada, 145
Foer, Jonathan Safran, 221
Follow Your Heart, 212
Food Empowerment Project, 215–216
Forensic sciences, 92–93
Forensic Veterinary Investigations, 114
Fossey, Dian, 124–125, 128
  Gorillas in the Mist, 123–124
Foster networks/programs, 19–20, 64, 84
Four Paws, 156
Foxes, 208–209
Francione, Gary, 166
Fraser-Celin, Valli, 82–83
Friends of Animals Miami Foundation, 75

Frogs/toads, 152–153
Froh, Tia, 48

Gai, Jackie, 167–171
Gaillard, Sophie, 182–183
Galápagos Conservancy centers, 149
Galápagos Islands, 147, 149
Galdika, Biruté, 123
Garcés, Leah, 210, 212
Geiger, Martha, 183–185
Gentle Giants Draft Horse Rescue, 197
Geronimo Animal Rescue Team, 84
Gestation crates, 206, 217
Giant Tortoise Restoration Initiative, 149
Goodall, Jane, 123, 159–160
Good Food Institute, 214
Gorilla Doctors, 128
Gorillas, 5, 123–126, 128–130, 162–163
Gorillas in the Mist (Fossey), 123–124
Grandin, Temple, 210
Great Ape Project, 166–167
Greece, 104
Grupo Especial Contra el Maltrato Animal
    (Special Group for the Fight against
    Animal Abuse, Colombia), 100
Gucci, 120–121
Gypsy (elephant), 169

Hannah, Jan, 82
Happily Ever Esther Farm Sanctuary, 219
Happy (elephant), 167
Hartung, Thomas, 177
Hebiso, Sefiya, 184
Henry (horse), 190–191
Hercules (chimpanzee), 167
Hoarding, 1–2, 25, 109, 163
Hoffa, Jimmy, 181
Homeless Health Care Los Angeles, 76
Horses, 179–198
    access to hay/grass, 3, 187–188
    animal protection laws covering, 185–187
    awareness of welfare of, 180

carriage, 181–183
communication by, 190, 242n8
costs of care for abused, 188–189
cruelty to cart, 180
euthanasia for, 197
grief experienced by, 191–192
Indigenous communities' partnership with,
    180
in inner-city riding communities, 179–180
learned helplessness of, 190
male, castration/gelding of, 197,
    242–243n12
neglect of, 187
racehorses, 192–193, 197–198
rescuers/rehabilitators of, 188, 192,
    195–197
rights of, 188–189
slaughter of, 181, 193–195, 197
for transportation, 179–180
trimming whiskers of, 186
veterinarians for, 181–182
in violence link cases, 187
welfare standards/regulations for, 185–186,
    189–190
wild, 181
work-lives of, 180, 186
Horse Tale Rescue, 182
Hotlines for reporting abuse, 10, 12, 61
House sparrows, 146–147
Housing, 75, 77
Howell, Amanda, 188–189
Human-animal violence link, 55–67, 227
    action plans for prevention, 65–66
    Animal Cruelty as a Gateway Crime
        program, 55
    collaboration on prevention, 57–65
    education and awareness training on, 61–
        63, 66
    fleeing domestic violence with your pet,
        64–66
    horses in cases of, 187
    male abusers, 56, 59, 66, 227

Human-animal violence link (cont.)
  National Coalition on Violence against
    Animals, 60
  National Link Coalition, 9, 56–58, 64,
    103
  overview of, 55–56
  psychological and social factors in abuse,
    39–40, 66
  and reluctance to call police, 63–64
  reporting suspected abuse, 65
  simultaneous abuse, 56
  social work vs. policing, 65
  studies of, 56
  training officers on, 60–61, 67
Humane Canada, 64, 103
Humane future, 223–229
Humane jobs
  animal protection as, 26–27, 167,
    226–227
  in conservation, 122–123, 150, 153
  definition of, 6–7
  and farming/ranching, 203, 215
Humane societies, 69–70. *See also specific*
  organizations
Humane Society International, 70
Humane Society of the United States, 70, 73,
  83. *See also* Pets for Life
Huss, Rebecca, 111

Icahn, Carl, 217
Indigenous communities
  animal care and control services, 10, 81–82
  animal welfare leadership, 82–84
  assimilation of children from, 81
  forest conservation by, 130–131
  and horses, 180
  on humans in relation to other animals,
    165–166
  hunting/trapping by, 118–121, 139–140
  investigating/prosecuting violent crime
    against animals in, 107
  rez dogs, 80–84

Institut Congolais pour la Conservation de
  la Nature (Congolese Institute for the
  Protection of Nature), 126
International Animal Rescue, 117
International Anti-Poaching Federation
  (Zimbabwe), 227
International Anti-Poaching Foundation,
  132–133
International Fund for Animal Welfare, 81,
  121
International Institute for Environment and
  Development, 122
International Ranger Federation, 126
International Union for the Conservation of
  Nature, 122, 173
International Veterinary Forensic Science
  Association conference (St. Pete Beach,
  Fla., 2018), 90–92
International Wildlife Rehabilitation Council,
  146
In the Valley of Elah (film), 55
InvestEGGator turtle-egg decoys, 150
Investigating/prosecuting violent crimes
    against animals, 87–116
  animal fighting, 23–24, 87–90, 109, 111,
    114
  animal lawyers, 111–113
  Campeon (case study), 111
  Coco (case study), 110–111
  in Colombia, 98–101
  Desmond (case study), 112
  and educating lawyers, 102–103
  euthanasia vs. rehabilitation, 89, 91–92,
    111
  fines, 105
  forensic sciences, overview of, 92–93
  forensic veterinarians, 90–95, 99, 114
  in Greece, 104
  hoarding, 109
  and the human-animal violence link, 112
  incarceration and alternatives, 105–111
  in Indigenous communities, 107

individual vs. commercial abuse, 208
and law, 96–98
legislation, 112–113
male abusers, 87, 109
necropsies, 94, 113, 115
neglect, 107
no-contact orders and orders of protection,
104–105, 111
organized crime, 87–88
prohibition orders, 45, 101, 102, 106, 109
prosecution as a measure of success, 96
prosecutions, 101–103
punishing abusers, 101–102
Puppy Doe (case study), 90–92, 114–116
and race, 38, 65, 87, 102
reasons people harm animals, 105–106
registries, 104
reporting abuse, 95–96
and restorative justice, 107–108
and revenge, 108–109
role of public outrage, 105, 110, 112, 115
"tough-on-crime" approaches, 104–107
treatment and counseling, 105, 109, 112
violence link work, 95–96 (see also Human-
animal violence link)
wildlife policing units, 100
Investigators/officers
compassion of, 24
initial visit by, 12–16
investing in, 226
law enforcement by, 23–24
motivation of, 23
pay for, 22
problem-solving by, 28
psychological toll on, 22–23, 25–27
safety of, 16, 21–23, 27–28
Invisible Helpers (Brooke), 184
Irvine, Leslie, 78

Jenny (chimpanzee), 163
Jockeys, 198
Jonathan (Seychelles tortoise), 147

Jones, Erin, 150–151
Jones, Miriam, 199
jones, pattrice, 199–200, 219–221
Jory, Brian, 109
Jubilee 2000, 122
Justice (horse), 187–189
Justice facility dogs (courthouse dogs), 48,
235n5 (chap. 3)
Justice for Service Animals Act (Can.), 47

Kamins, Jake, 103
Karen C. Drayer Wildlife Health Center (UC
Davis Veterinary School), 128
Karisoke Research Center (Rwanda),
124–125
Kayne, Susan, 192–198
Kee, Vernan, 83
Khanna, Ro, 215
Kim, Christine, 76–77, 79
King, Barbara J., 191
King-Sonnen, Renee, 201–203, 221
Kinyua, Faith Wamalwa, 184
Kisamya, Aline Masika Kisamya, 126
Koko (gorilla), 162–163
Kozzie (horse), 191
Kumire, Vimbai, 132–135

Labchuk, Camille, 102, 208
Latin American Sea Turtles Organization, 150
Law N' Paws, 51–52
Laws/law enforcement, 9–20. See also Animal
care and control services; Investigators/
officers
animal cruelty, 33–34, 38, 45–46
first responders, 9–10, 33–37
labor rights for animals, 182, 186
limitations of enforcement, 16–17, 73–74,
156–157
prohibition orders, 45, 101, 102, 106, 109
as a public responsibility, 29
Lazenby, Rod, 16
Leaping Bunny certification, 174–175

Legal personhood, 165–167, 188
Lem, Michelle, 79
Leo (chimpanzee), 167
Lettini, Maria, 216–218
Lewis, Anne, 144–147
Light pollution, 145
Lights Out initiatives, 145
Lockwood, Randall, 39, 57–59, 106,
    108–109
Lonesome George (Pinta tortoise), 147–148
Lorde, Audre, 228
Los Angeles, 60
Lulu (elephant), 169–170
Lundgren, Charlotte, 242n8
Lyons, Sheila, 192–193

Mally's Third Chance Raccoon Rescue and
    Rehabilitation Sanctuary (Ontario), 138,
    141, 143
Mander, Damien, 132–134
Marceau, Justin, 106–107, 208
Marineland (Can.), 172
Marino, Lori, 172
Masson, Jeffrey Moussaieff, 191
McArthur, Jo-Anne, 135, 223–225
McDonald's, 217
McEwen, Beverly, 93
Meat and dairy created in labs, 214–215,
    217–218
Meat industry, 201–202
Meet the Chimps (TV show), 160
Mejdell, Cecilie M., 242n8
Mejía, Carolina, 182
Merck, Melinda, 62–63, 95, 99
Mercy for Animals, 210, 212
Merlot (justice facility dog), 48
Mexico, 175
Miami-Dade Animal Services, 74–75
Michael (gorilla), 162–163
Migrant workers, 215–216
Milks, plant-based, 212–213
Minks, 208–209

Miranda, Gabriela Queiroz, 149
Misogyny, 39–40, 66
Miyoko's Creamery, 212
Mkhabela, Leitah, 135
Mogahane, Felicia, 135
Monkeys, 160–161, 163–164
Monsma, Jim, 144
Montreal SPCA, 182–183
Mowat, Farley: Virunga, 123–124
Mules, 183
Munro, Helen, 93
Munro, Ranald, 93
Mustangs, 181
My Dog Is My Home, 76

National Alliance to End Homelessness, 76
National Audubon Society, 145
National Center for Prosecution of Animal
    Abuse (US), 103
National Centre for the Prosecution of
    Animal Abuse (Can.), 103
National Chicken Council, 200
National Coalition on Violence against
    Animals, 60
National Council of Juvenile and Family
    Court Judges, 103
National District Attorneys Association, 103
National Homelessness Law Center, 77
National Humane Education Society, 104
National Incident-Based Reporting System,
    59
National Institute of Cellular Agriculture, 215
National Link Coalition, 9, 56–58, 64, 103
National Museum of Animals and Society, 76
National Sheriffs' Association, 55
National Wildlife Federation, 152
National Wildlife Rehabilitators Association,
    146
Native American Humane Society, 82
Native communities. See Indigenous
    communities
Nature Conservancy, 173

Ndakasi (gorilla), 129
Ndezi (gorilla), 129
Ndume (gorilla), 162–163
Neglect. See also Hoarding
  vs. abuse, 28–29
  of horses, 187
  investigating/prosecuting, 107
Netherlands, 10, 19, 61, 159, 187
New England Anti-Vivisection Society, 175
New Iberia Research Center (UL Lafayette),
  167
New Jersey, 31
New York Police Department (NYPD),
  33–37
Nicholas (elephant), 169
Nichols, Brad, 27, 41–44
Nikki (monkey), 163–164
Nonhuman Rights Project, 165–167
Nonprofit organizations, 26, 30–31. See also
  Humane societies; SPCA
North American Primate Sanctuary Alliance,
  164
Northern Dogs project, 81
North Shore Animal League (NYC), 19–20
Norway, 61, 159
Nurse, Angus, 105–106
Nuts for Cheese, 213
NYPD (New York Police Department),
  33–37

Oatly, 213
Oliver, John, 159–160
Ontario Turtle Conservancy Centre, 148–149
Orangutans, 129–130
Ornelas, lauren, 216

Parsons, Rachel, 142–143, 145–146
Partnerships in animal protection, 32–53
  American Humane Education Society, 33
  animal rescue, 51–53
  in Canada (see Calgary; Edmonton)
  in El Paso, 50, 52–53, 60

leniency vs. legal intervention, 36
NYPD's partnership with ASPCA, 33–37
  (see also ASPCA)
Paso Pacífico, 149–150
PAWS (Performing Animal Wildlife Society),
  167–170, 172
Peeps Foundation, 197
People for the Ethical Treatment of Animals
  (PETA), 18–19, 104
People not Poaching, 121–122
Performing Animal Wildlife Society (PAWS),
  167–170, 172
PETA (People for the Ethical Treatment of
  Animals), 18–19, 104
PetFinder, 19
Pets/companion animals
  ethics of keeping, 157–158
  as family, 71–72, 76
  percentage of homes having, 3
  of Ukranian refugees, 75
Pets for Life, 70–73, 75, 83, 227
Pettit, Andrea, 242n8
Phoenix, Joaquin, 224–225
Physicians Committee for Responsible
  Medicine, 176
Piazza, Jared, 207
Pigs, 205–206, 217–218
Poaching/wildlife trafficking, 119, 121–122,
  124–126, 132–134
Policia Ambiental (Colombia), 100
Policing and incarceration
  animal-cruelty training for officers, 33–34,
  37–38, 43, 47–49
  NYPD's partnership with ASPCA, 33–37
  police as first responders, 9–10, 33–37
  racial politics of, 38, 65, 67, 87, 102, 105
Poultry/egg industry, 199–202, 205
Poverty
  addressing root causes of, 79–80
  and conservation, 121–122
  social beliefs about, 73, 77, 79
Pozna (chimpanzee), 163

Price Is Right, The (TV show), 19
Primate Rescue Center (Ky.), 160, 162–163
Prince (elephant), 169
Project Chimps, 167
Proops, Leanne, 242n8
Prosecuting violent crimes against animals.
   See Investigating/prosecuting violent
   crimes against animals
Puppy Doe (dog), 90–92, 114–116
Puppy mills, 89–90

Quanto (police dog), 47

Rabbits, 172–175
Raccoons, 137–139, *139*
Rancher Advocacy Program, 203
Ranching, 201–203. *See also* Cows; Horses
Rancho Compasión, 212
Randell, Mark, 87–89
Randour, Mary Lou, 109
Reconciliation in Animal Welfare
   Symposium, 82–83
Red Rover, 64
Reisman, Robert, 94
Remington University (Medellín, Colombia),
   99
Rescue/rehabilitation. *See* Animal rescue;
   ASPCA (American Society for the
   Prevention of Cruelty to Animals);
   Dogfighting; Horses
Reservations, animal care and control services
   on, 10
Restorative justice, 107–108
Rez Road Adventures, 83
Rooster fighting, 87–89
Rowdy Girl Sanctuary, 202–203
RSPCA (Royal Society for the Prevention of
   Cruelty to Animals; UK and Australia),
   28, 31
Rubin, Jessica, 112–113
Running Rabbit, Norm, 82
Russell, Regan, 138

Sanctuário de Sorocaba (Brazil), 167
Sankoff, Peter, 45–46
Santa Cruz County animal service, 73–74
Santo Domingo (DR), 182
Saunders, Margaret Marshall: *Beautiful Joe*, 33
Save Rez Dogs, 83
Schinner, Miyoko, 212
Schwartz, Henry, 212
Sea World, 172
Senkwekwe Center (Virunga National Park,
   DRC), 129
Sentience of animals, ix, 7, 98, 165–166,
   189, 227
Sewell, Anna: *Black Beauty*, 33, 180
Shapiro, Kenneth, 109
Sheep, 205, 210
Shelter Animals Count, 19
Shelters for animals
   adoptions at, 17, 19
   euthanasia in, 17–18, 20, 23
   foster networks used by, 19–20
   no-kill, 18–19
   and spaying/neutering strategies, 19
   veterinarians at, 114
Shelters for humans, 76–77
Siksika First Nation, 82
Sinclair, Anna, 49
Singer, Peter, 211
Sissi (horse), 182
Skid Rover, 76
Slaughterhouses, 194, 206–207, 210
Smith-Blackmore, Martha, 64, 90–92, 94–
   95, 109–111, 114–116
Smithson, Dennis, 43–44, 60
Social harms and protections, 69–86, *86*
   animals in native communities, 80–84
   Beyond Fences, 70–71
   changing how we think about, 84–86
   and compassion for people, 69–70
   homelessness, 69, 72, 76–79
   isolated seniors, 69
   low-income people, 71–75

mental health challenges, 69
one welfare/one health, 70, 214
persons with disabilities, 69
Pets for Life, 70–73, 75, 83, 227
racial inequities, 75
social beliefs about poverty, 73, 77, 79
veterinary social work, 78–79
Society for the Prevention of Cruelty to
    Animals. *See* SPCA
Society for the Prevention of Little
    Amphibian Tragedies, 152
Society for the Protection of Animals Abroad,
    184
Solidarity, ix, 73, 203, 219, 225–226, 229
Sonnen, Tommy, 201–203
Sound Equine Solutions, 188
Spanjol, Kimberly, 109
Spaying/neutering, 19, 74–75
SPCA (Society for the Prevention of Cruelty
    to Animals), 9, 19, 30–31
Stevens, Dorothea, 83–84
Stewart, Ed, 168
Stosuy, Todd, 73–74
Strong Roots, 130
Sudan (white rhino), 117
Sunny (dog), vii–ix
Sweden, 185–187, 206

Tatu (chimpanzee), 223
Teamsters, 181
Thompson, John, 59–60
Thompson, Kirrilly, 242n8
Thoroughbred Aftercare Alliance, 197
Thoroughbreds, 192–194, 197
Tigers, 6, 156, 169
Tofurky, 212
Toronto Wildlife Centre, 146
Tortoise Breeding and Rearing Center
    (Galápagos Islands), 147
Tortoises, 147–149. *See also* Turtles/tortoises/
    terrapins
Touroo, Rachel, 94

TRAFFIC, 121
Transfarmation Project, 212
Transfrontier Africa NPC, 134
Transport Workers Union, 181
Tri-State Bird Rescue & Research (Del.), 146
Truitt, April, 164
Tucker (dog), 45
Turkeys, 205
Turtle Hospital (Florida Keys), 148
Turtle Hospital (Ontario Turtle Conservancy
    Centre), 148–149
Turtles/tortoises/terrapins, 147–152, 159
Tutu, Desmond, 6
Twenty-eight-hour law, 209

Unbound Project, 135, 223
Unbridled Thoroughbred Foundation, 192–
    193, 196
Uncle Baby Billy (rabbit), 173
UNESCO World Heritage sites, 149
Union of Concerned Scientists, 200
United Nations, 207
Universal Ranger Support Alliance, 127
University of California, Davis, 78
University of Konstanz, 177
Urban, Diana, 112–113
Urban Equestrian Academy, 179–180
Urrutia, Carolina, 153

Vegetarianism and veganism, 207, 212–214
Velvet (horse), 195
Veterinary clinics and medicine
    access by low-income people, 71–72, 74–75
    mental health crisis at, 93–94
    social workers' collaboration with, 78–79
    spaying/neutering of stray cats, 74–75
    violence link training at, 62–63
Veterinary forensics, 90–95, 99, 114
Veterinary Forensics Science Center
    (Gainesville, Fla.), 94
Vick, Michael, 87, 89, 111
VINE Sanctuary, 199, 219–221

Violence, definition of, 202

Violence link cases. *See* Human-animal violence link

Virunga (book; Mowat), 123–124

Virunga (film), 124, 129

Virunga Alliance, 126

Virunga National Park (DRC), 124, 126–127, 129

Vivisection, 175

Volcanoes National Park (Rwanda), 124

Wadiwel, Dinesh: *The War against Animals*, 221

Wadsworth, Chantal, 83

War against Animals, The (Wadiwel), 221

Wathan, Jen, 242n8

We Animals Media, 135, 223

Webster, Diana, 82–83

Westoll, Andrew: *The Chimps of Fauna Sanctuary*, 160

Whales, 171–172

Whale Sanctuary Project, 172

Wild animals, 137–153. *See also* Conservation
amphibians, 152–153
and biodiversity, 146
bird–glass collisions, 145
captive (*see* Captive animals)
chimpanzees, 6, 159–160, 162–163, 167, 223
consuming parts of, 159
ducks, 147
ecosocial reproduction by, 240n6
elephants, 5, 120, 131–132, 167, 169–170
endangered, 147–148, 152
euthanasia of, 141
formula/milk powders for, 146
frogs/toads, 152–153
gorillas, 5, 123–126, 128–130, 162–163
and habitat preservation, 146
human-caused threats to, 140, 146
Indigenous peoples' hunting of, 139–140
invasive species, 146–147

knowledge exchanges on, 146
migration by, 151
and natural resource management and conservation agencies, 140–141
orangutans, 129–130
"overpopulation" of, 143
poaching of, 150–151
and public health and safety, 145
rabbits, 172–175
raccoons, 137–139, *139*
Regan (case study), 137–139, *139*
rescuers/rehabilitators of, 138, 141–149
rewilding of, 143–144
turtles/tortoises/terrapins, 147–152, 159
veterinarians for, 146

Wild Flora and Fauna Attention Center (Centro de Atencion y Valoracion de Flora y Fauna Silvestre; Colombia), 153

Wildlife Conservation Society, 120–121, 167

Wilhelm, Maria: *Akashinga: The Brave Ones*, 133

Williams-Guillén, Kim, 150

Williamson, Matt, 47–48

Winders, Delcianna, 204, 208, 225

WisCARES, 78

Wolves in Sheep's Clothing (New Jersey State Commission of Investigation), 31

World Animal Protection, 121, 156–157

World Horse Welfare, 184

World Small Animal Veterinary Association, 62

World Wide Fund for Nature, 121

World Wildlife Federation, 156

World Wildlife Fund, 121, 127

Yellow Bird, Michael, 80, 82

Yellowstone (TV show), 201

Zoos, 167, 169–171